Regional Environmental Policy

This work has been published with the financial support of the
Volkswagenwerk Foundation.

Regional Environmental Policy

The Economic Issues

Edited by

Horst Siebert
University of Mannheim

Ingo Walter
New York University

and

Klaus Zimmermann
International Institute for Environment and Society
Berlin

New York University Press • New York *and* London

Library of Congress Cataloging in Publication Data
Main entry under title:

Regional environmental policy.

Proceedings of a conference held in Berlin, Nov. 13–
14, 1978
Includes bibliographies and index.
1. Environmental policy–Addresses, essays, lectures.
2. Regional planning–Addresses, essays, lectures.
I. Siebert, Horst, 1938–   II. Walter, Ingo, 1940–
III. Zimmermann, Klaus, 1944–
HC79.E5R44   301.31   79-2058
ISBN 0-8147-7805-4

Preface

The idea for an international symposium on regional dimensions of environmental policy was developed during the winter of 1976. The subject raises a number of difficult conceptual and practical questions that lend themselves both to economic analysis and to exchanges of views on institutional and policy initiatives—both in a static and intertemporal context—and to what criteria of equity and efficiency may be appropriately applied. How can the quality of the regional environment in its many dimensions be measured, as a prerequisite for the design of policies that make sense? What about interregional transfers of pollution? And how, particularly in countries organized along federal lines, can institutions be designed that will provide for a rational allocation of environmental resources? What is the regional allocation of costs and benefits associated with industrial, energy, and resources policies? All of these questions have been raised before in a variety of contexts and from a number of disciplinary perspectives, but they had not been brought together in a coherent focus on the regional environmental problem.

In order to accomplish this objective, we organized a conference on the subject, held in Berlin, Germany, on November 13 and 14, 1978. We asked several leading economists from a number of countries to contribute thematic papers on the main topics that seemed to suggest themselves and requested a second group of equally distinguished economists to present their views as discussions or extensions of the thematic essays. The conference proved to be interesting and informative, although the discussion inevitably raised more questions than it answered. The proceedings are reproduced as faithfully as possible in this volume.

This project was made possible by a generous grant from the Volkswagenwerk Foundation, and we would like to express our sincere gratitude for this support. Additional financial and logistical support was received from the International Institute for Environment and Society of the Science Center

v

Berlin. Thanks are due Meinolf Dierkes, Director of the Institute, for his consistent support as we developed and carried out the plans for the symposium, and to Helmut G. Meier, Secretary General of the Science Center. We are indebted to Dr. Martin Uppenbrink, Director of the German Federal Environment Office, for opening the conference in a most effective manner. We are also indebted for the participation of Edwin von Böventer, who contributed valuable comments throughout the symposium, as well as to Dieter Becker-Platen and Ferdi Dudenhöffer. Conference arrangements were efficiently provided in Berlin by Ms. Christa Scholl and Ms. Barbara Stening. Marion Epps in New York capably saw the volume through production in her usual indispensable way.

Horst Siebert, Mannheim
Ingo Walter, New York
Klaus Zimmermann, Berlin

Contents

About the Contributors

Ralph C. d'Arge is Professor of Economics at the University of Wyoming in Laramie, USA

Jean Philippe Barde is an economist in the Environment and Industry Division, Environment Directorate, Organization for Economic Cooperation and Development, Paris, France

Gardner Brown, Jr., is Professor of Economics at the University of Washington in Seattle, USA

John H. Cumberland is Professor of Economics and Director, Bureau of Business and Economic Research, University of Maryland, College Park, USA

Franz-Josef Dreyhaupt is an official of the Ministry of Labor, Health and Social Affairs of North Rhine-Westphalia, Germany

Ronald Edwards is Lecturer in Economics at the University of Aberdeen, Scotland

Alan Evans is Lecturer in Urban and Regional Studies at the University of Reading, England

Dieter Ewringmann is senior economist, Institute for Financial Research, at the University of Cologne, Germany

Gideon Fishelson is Professor of Economics at Tel Aviv University, Israel

Finn R. Førsund is Professor of Economics at the University of Oslo, Norway

René L. Frey is Professor of Economics at the University of Basel, Switzerland

Karl-Heinrich Hansmeyer is Professor of Economics at the University of Cologne, Germany

Allen V. Kneese is a senior staff member at Resources for the Future, Inc., in Washington, D.C., USA

Peter Nijkamp is Professor of Economics at the Free University of Amsterdam, Holland

Mancur Olson is Professor of Economics at the University of Maryland, College Park, Maryland, USA

David W. Pearce is Professor of Political Economy at the University of Aberdeen, Scotland

Rüdiger Pethig is Professor of Economics at the University of Oldenburg, Germany

Michel Potier is Head of the Environment and Industry Division, Environment Directorate, Organization for Economic Cooperation and Development, Paris, France

Remy Prud'homme is Professor of Economics at the University of Paris, Val de Marne, France

Jerome Rothenberg is Professor of Economics, Massachusetts Institute of Technology, Cambridge, Mass., USA

Klaus W. Schatz is senior economist, Institut für Weltwirtschaft in Kiel, Germany

Anthony Scott is Professor of Economics at the University of British Columbia, Vancouver, Canada

Horst Siebert is Professor of Economics at the University of Mannheim, Germany

Manfred E. Streit is Professor of Economics at the University of Mannheim, Germany

Rainer Thoss is Professor of Economics at the University of Münster, Germany

Thomas H. Tietenberg is Associate Professor of Economics at Colby College in Waterville, Maine, USA

Ingo Walter is Professor of Economics and Finance, Graduate School of Business Administration, New York University, USA

Lawrence J. White is Professor of Economics, Graduate School of Business Administration, New York University, and senior economist at the Council of Economic Advisers, Washington, D.C., USA

Michael Williams is on the staff of the John Muir Institute for Environmental Studies, Inc., Santa Fe, New Mexico, USA

Klaus Zimmermann is senior economist, International Institute for Environment and Society, Science Center, Berlin, Germany

CHAPTER 1

The Regional Dimensions of Environmental Policy

HORST SIEBERT

Environmental systems always have a spatial dimension, since the environment is defined over space. Except for the case of global or transnational systems, such as the ozone layer or the river Rhine, most environmental systems have spatial dimensions smaller than the national state, or define areas that cut across national political boundaries. Examples are river systems, groundwater systems, and airsheds. Considering environmental regions that are spatial subsystems of a national state, quite a few impressive economic problems arise.

THE PROBLEM

The space of a national state can be considered to be covered by different nets of regions; for instance, they can be considered as economic areas and environmental regions, varying with environmental media. A region can be defined as a set of spatial points that are either homogeneous with respect to some criteria (criteria of homogeneity) or are more intensively interrelated among each other than with other spatial points (criterion of functional interdependence). We may construct economic regions with sociocultural or historical criteria; administrative delineations of the past; or economic variables such as industrial structure, rates of unemployment, per capita income, or intensity of economic exchange via commodity trade and factor mobility. Accordingly, environmental regions may be defined by environmental characteristics. Since economic and environmental criteria are not

1

identical, economic and environmental regions will not overlap. Consequently, a spatial point x may belong to the economic region A and the environmental region α. Also, since environmental regions are defined with respect to environmental media, environmental regions for different media will not be identical. A spatial point x belonging to the environmental region α (i.e., water) may also belong to the environmental region β. It is only realistic to assume that the nets of different types of regions are not of the same size and that they consequently overlap.

Regions are interrelated among each other. Environmental disruption in one area will have feedbacks on other areas. Similarly, environmental policy for one region will have an impact on other areas. We may distinguish the following mechanisms of interaction:

1. Environmental regions are interrelated in that pollution in one area will affect environmental quality of another region by the interregional diffusion of pollutants. Rivers, groundwater, or the wind may carry pollutants to the other areas (interregional spillovers).

2. Economic regions are interrelated through the mobility of commodities. For instance, a strict environmental policy in one economic region may lead to an increased specialization toward less pollution-intensive commodities, with the other area specializing on more pollution intensively produced commodities. The exchange of goods will affect regional environmental quality.

3. Similarly, factors of production may migrate between (economic) regions, leaving the areas where factor prices are reduced owing to environmental policy.

4. Residents may migrate between regions owing to differences in environmental quality. Note that residents are not necessarily identical to workers and that environmental quality and factor income both determine the mobility of labor (and capital). If residents have an influence in the political process, their mobility will affect the target values of environmental quality.

5. Administrative or planning regions may be interrelated in the sense that environmental quality in one area is an argument variable in the welfare function (of the inhabitants) of the regions—that is, amenities in one area are esteemed by the inhabitants of the other area, either because the other region (or its inhabitants) assigns a value per se to these public goods, or because they use them during holidays for recreational purposes (temporal mobility of residents). Also, demonstration effects may occur between regions, with environmental quality in one area influencing the achievement levels in the other region.

6. Administrative regions may be interrelated by institutional arrangements such as a grants-in-aid system between regions. Also, the assignment of different types of taxes and expenditures to regions may create an interdependence among regions—that is, if regions interact in the political process

of assigning taxes and expenditures to administrative levels. It may also relate to the (unlikely) fact that regions may have to interact in order to determine the volume of expenditures (i.e., for interregional public goods) or taxation (financing interregional public goods).

Environmental policy will be addressed to the quality of environmental regions. A variety of policy instruments is at the disposal of the policymaker. Owing to the interrelations discussed, we may expect impacts not only on regional environmental quality but also on spatial structure and regional planning and possibly on other fields of policy.

The following problems arise: (i) Should nationally uniform or regionally differentiated environmental policy instruments be applied? (ii) Should the target values of environmental quality be differentiated among regions? (iii) Are planning approaches or more flexible concepts of environmental policy more likely to be successful? (iv) Should environmental policy be assigned to national authorities or to independent regional agencies? (v) Can the different types of regions (economic regions, areas for different environmental media) be delineated consistently? (vi) How does a regionalized environmental policy affect other fields of policy, such as regional planning or industrial policy?

ALLOCATIVE EFFICIENCY

The criteria of economic efficiency— that is, maximizing a social welfare function for a system of regions with environmental quality being an argument variable—clearly dictate a regional differentiation of environmental policy instruments for the following reasons. (Cf. Tietenberg [1974] and Siebert [1975].) Environmental quality may be more scarce in one region relative to another area because: (i) the region has a smaller assimilative capacity; (ii) consumers value environmental quality more highly and can manifest their preference in the political process accordingly; (iii) the region is more densely populated and a given quantity of pollutants creates greater social damage; or (iv) there is a larger quantity of emissions because of industrial structure, production, and abatement technology. As a result of these factors, we also can expect that the target values of environmental quality will differ among regions, assuming that the political process does not create a bias in revealing the preferences and that migration will not react instantaneously to differences in environmental quality.

Efficiency also dictates that spillover costs should be internalized by the decision units of the polluting region. This means that in setting the emission tax one should take into consideration not only environmental quality in the region of the polluter but also the regions affected by the interregional diffusion of the pollutants. Environmental policy instruments should not give incentives to a "high-stack policy"—that is, build higher stacks in order to diffuse pollutants to other areas. If the interregional diffusion of pollutants is of some magnitude to be of practical relevance, the polluter pays principle has to be interpreted regionally: the polluting area must cover the social costs that are caused by that area. Two possibilities arise: either the environmental policy instruments must be adjusted to take into account interregional pollution, or environmental regions must be delineated in such a way that interregional externalities are minimized (regional internalization of externalities).

Efficiency may also be interpreted over time. Then we have to explicitly introduce interdependencies in some of the variables over time such as the accumulation of pollutants and of purification capital. Other variables with temporal rigidities and time-consuming adaptations such as spatial structure and mechanisms of interrelation between regions may be introduced; but at the moment we are not yet able to solve such complex systems and interpret them meaningfully.

Assuming perfect foresight on the part of the planner, it is his task to determine an optimal path over time. In practice, the planner will not have perfect foresight and may not find the optimal path, thus causing a severe misallocation over time from an *ex post* point of view.

A more practical analogy to the problem of optimal intertemporal allocation of the environment is whether environmental policy should have a short-run or a long-run orientation. In the very long run, some of the mechanisms of interregional interaction will have a tendency to equalize environmental quality (and environmental quality targets) and, consequently, environmental policy instruments.

Assume, for instance, that region A is more polluted than region B. Introducing a higher emission tax in region A will lead to factor migration, since factor demand of the pollution intensively producing sectors in region A is reduced. The magnitude of a factor leaving the polluted area varies with the factor intensity of the pollution intensively producing sectors. If factors are immobile, the emission tax in region A will lead to a greater specialization toward less pollution-intensively produced commodities. The mobility of factors and the exchange of commodities will improve environmental quality in region A and increase pollution in region B. *Ceteris paribus*, in the long run, environmental quality and the emission charge will be identical.

This long-run equalization of emission charges presupposes identical production and abatement technologies for sector i in each region. The migration of residents will, however, work against the equalization of environmental quality, since people will leave the polluted area and migrate to the nonpolluted environment, increasing the demand for environmental quality there. The migration of residents will increase the tax in the nonpolluted area and will lower the emission tax in the polluted area. Consequently, emission taxes will tend to equalize, assuming identical political processes in both regions for revealing individual preferences.

Assume we have a *ceteris paribus* world—that is, we have identical production and abatement technologies for sector i in both regions. Then the theoretical problem arises whether the shadow prices can be used to stimulate the relevant adaptation processes. In this context, it should be remembered that the optimal quantities and optimal prices of a nonlinear program relate to the optimal solution. If all mechanisms of interaction—that is, mobility of factors and trade—are included in the model, and if they do not require time, the optimal shadow prices are relevant for environmental policy. In terms of practical policy, however, one must also consider that the mobility processes are very time-consuming or may even not occur in reality, owing to mobility obstacles. Consequently, it seems realistic not to rely on the long-run equalization of emission taxes and to differentiate environmental policy instruments regionally.

ENVIRONMENTAL EQUITY AMONG REGIONS?

In some federal states equity considerations may impose an additional restriction on environmental policy and the allocation of resources. The demand for similar living conditions among regions is an example. Equity considerations may act as a strong restraint on transformation space and may truncate an important part of that space or shift it inward. It should be noted that the equity restraint is not formulated with respect to economic welfare, since welfare cannot be measured. It is broken down into different restraints on determinants of welfare, such as social overhead capital, environmental quality, and income per capita. By partitioning, the restraint becomes more restrictive, since identical welfare among regions could be achieved by means of different combinations of social overhead capital, environmental quality, and income. In practice, restraints are not implemented rigorously and have a more indicative character. Since these equity considerations may be considered as a spatial implication of a welfare approach, a state of this type can be classified as a welfare state with a federal structure.

Besides this German-type welfare state with a federal structure, Frey distinguishes the classical federal state and the central state (see chapter 4). In the classical federal state (such as Switzerland the the United States), "regional authorities have the right to solve conflicts of goals according to preferences of their own population." The target of interregional equity, in terms of environmental quality, is normally not superimposed as a restraint on economic policy. In centralized nations such as France equity restraints do not seem to appear explicitly.

An alternative approach to equity restrictions on environmental quality is a "black-spot policy" (see chapter 8) where pollution intensively producing activities are concentrated in certain areas (Sweden). This approach of spatial separation attempts to bring about a specialization of national territory and relies heavily on land-use planning as an instrument of environmental quality management. This approach allows for better protection of less polluted areas, which may be partially motivated by using designated recreation areas as an argument variable in the welfare function of polluted areas. At the same time, it concentrates the "public bad" in some areas. Also, there is a strong incentive to locate the black spots near the border so that the burden is shifted to the neighbor (such as in the case of Sweden where black spots are located near Norway).

ALTERNATIVE APPROACHES

Two different approaches seem to prevail with respect to environmental policy in a regional setting. One approach relies mainly on a planning process— land-use planning and direct regulation; the other approach attempts to use some type of price mechanism as an incentive for environmental improvement.

Both approaches have as a common element informational requirements and an analysis of target setting in the political sphere. Chapters 2 and 3 of this volume demonstrate the informational requirements of environmental policy, especially on costs of abatements; monitoring possibilities with respect to environmental quality and measuring emissions; the identification and evaluation of damages, diffusion processes, and so on. Regional environmental information systems may be used to introduce alternative policy targets and restrictions and to simulate the implications of these restrictions with respect to trade-offs. Information about these trade-offs may produce feedback to the target-setting process. From a theoretical point of view, these informational systems represent allocation models similar to the general equilibrium type of model. They point out, however, different features, such as multiple objectives and normative restraints.

Whereas regional information systems and planning models also yield a set of shadow prices, they rely more on interventionist types of policy instruments, such as land-use planning or direct regulation of emissions in individual firms. A practical example of this approach seems to be the air quality management in some federal states of Germany, where governmental agencies determine permissible levels for the individual firm or even individual equipment, according to the state of the art. We may call this the "individual-stack approach." The government agency concerned negotiates with firms regarding the acceptable quantity of emissions, the production technologies to be permitted, the abatement technologies to be used, or the new firms to be located in the area. For instance, government officials must demonstrate to industry that more environmentally friendly production and abatement technologies exist than are actually used. The burden of proof is on the government, and there is no incentive for improved technology except for bureaucratic pressure.

The alternative position to the planning approach questions whether all the information needed for these models is available—for instance, whether the response functions of polluters are known. It is felt that the problem is much too complex to be handled by a planning procedure and that complex problems need simple solutions. At the same time, the idea is to introduce more flexibility into the system. For instance, if economic incentives can be found to reduce emissions, the land-use restraint will be scaled down in importance. The "Navajo fee" may serve as an example (see chapter 7). If we rely only on land-use planning, the building of additional energy plants on the Navajo reservation has to be forgone. If the "Navajo fee" is strong enough incentive, the construction of additional plants on the reservation may be feasible. Emission taxes, markets for pollution rights, and other measures may be considered in this context. The idea is to institutionalize some general rules and to let these rules provide sufficient incentives to solve environmental problems.

THE INSTITUTIONAL SETTING

If environmental policy is to be regionalized, the question arises whether environmental policy should be undertaken by autonomous regional authorities or by the national government (see chapter 6). This assignment problem may differ according to the organizational scheme prevailing, that is, whether the question applies to central states or to federal states. One basic problem is interregional spillovers. Either the administrative area must be large enough to internalize all externalities, so that there will be no interregional spillovers, or a mechanism must be found to monitor interregional diffusion, implement an interregional diffusion norm, or place an appropriate shadow price on the pollutants crossing regional borders. The assignment problem must be solved in such a way that a high-stack policy is not undertaken. If interregional spillover is a relevant problem, handling the spillover is a precondition for the regionalization of environmental authorities.

Regional authorities do have the advantage of being able to identify regional preferences, through referenda or party voting, for example. This implies that to some extent people can determine their way of living and are not controlled by decisions of the central government or even international agencies (such as the European Economic Community). Observing fiscal equivalence for different types of public goods (e.g., schools, theaters, land-use planning, transportation systems, river systems, airsheds) may, however, create a net of multiple organizational units. Organization for different types of public goods will be characterized by overlapping spatial areas and may present a system of differing spatial grids. The organizational structure will be even more complex if the organizations not only provide public goods but also have taxing rights.

Solutions to the assignment problem vary according to the environmental media considered and the instruments used.

Noise is a regional problem and may therefore be controlled partly by regional authorities. Since product norms, however, will play an important role and since product norms should not be differentiated regionally, an anti-noise policy must be nationalized.

Water quality management can be handed over to regional authorities if interregional diffusion norms can be controlled and if they can be easily changed in the future. Observe that in the case of water, interregional diffusion norms are identical to ambient standards at a given spot of a river and that they can be considered as the target variable of environmental quality. If water management relies on emission taxes only and does not use interregional diffusion norms and if these emission taxes are set by regional authorities, the taxes should be set in such a way to take into account downstream damages. Bargaining may be necessary to set the tax. Such a procedure seems very impractical. Alternatively, one could conceive of a surcharge levied by some national or interregional agency, that would take into account downstream damages. Again, this seems impractical. In the case of water management, the use of regional authorities operating within the restraints of interregional diffusion norms, seems to offer a practical solution. Only if the problem of interregional diffusion is negligible can a national emission tax be used.

In the case of *air quality* management, the solution varies again with the preferred policy instruments and with the magnitude of interregional pollution. If such pollution is negligible, regional authorities can be used. Otherwise air quality management must be undertaken nationally, since bargaining among regions seems unrealistic. A national emission charge can be combined with a regional surcharge that is levied by regional authorities. Note that a regional surcharge can account for regional differences in tastes and environmental endowments. If interregional diffusion is of significant magnitude, however, the surcharge, must account for damages in the polluted area. Consequently the surcharge cannot be set by the polluting region. Here again, interregional diffusion complicates the picture and requires the imposition of a surcharge by a national agency or by a common interregional agency.

Toxic wastes should be controlled nationally, and toxic materials in products should be controlled nationally according to liability rules or product norms.

From a theoretical point of view, a bargaining solution between autonomous regional authorities may be considered. Such a procedure represents an application of the Coase theorem, with regions bargaining on the quantity of pollutants being diffused interregionally. Though the problem is very interesting from a theoretical point of view—and game theory is a powerful theoretical tool with which to approach this problem—a bargaining solution may not be very practical. Looking at the problem of transnational pollution, which is similar to the interregional diffusion question, and at the difficulties arising with proposed solutions, one can only be skeptical about the effectiveness of such an approach.

CONSISTENCY OF POLICIES AND GOAL CONFLICTS

Consistency relates to the following problems: (i) If there is only one policy target, do the policy instruments used all work in the same direction? (ii) Do the policy instruments used over time contradict each other? (iii) Do the policymakers at different levels all work toward attaining the target? (iv) If there are different targets of policy, to what extent is there a goal conflict, and are these goal conflicts treated in a rational way?

Since environmental policy relates to different environmental media, environmental policy areas will overlap. A high emission tax for airborne residuals in the air quality region may introduce an incentive to emit these pollutants into the region's river system. We cannot object to individual firms or households that substitute processes at politically set prices. The problem is whether policy can react adequately and whether policy can anticipate the reactions of individuals. If the decision-making process of environmental policy is rather slow and emission taxes are rigid, inconsistencies in environmental policies can arise. The requirement is that policy instruments used for different media should be coordinated: emission taxes should set the correct relative prices among pollutants for different media or, if one favors direct controls, the correct structure of emission norms.

Regional planning (or land-use planning) can be regarded as instrumental to environmental policy, especially by preventing pollution intensively producing firms from siting in agglomerations. On the other hand, environmental policy may be an instrument of regional policy. Environmental policy can be considered as an attempt to attribute social costs to economic activities. In this interpretation, environmental policy helps to express regional comparative advantage correctly—that is, a region with a large endowment of assimilative capacity may experience an increase in its comparative advantage owing to environmental policy. On the other hand, a heavily industrialized area may have experienced an artificial comparative advantage before environmental policy has been implemented. Its agglomeration economies may have been overestimated. If both regional planning and environmental policy are efficiency oriented, one should not expect goal conflicts. If, however, other targets such as environmental equity are introduced, one can expect goal conflicts.

Sector policy (industrial policy) may become a new area of economic policy in European countries. If sector policy, in terms of resource allocation among sectors, is based on an efficiency criterion, we can expect that it will be consistent with environmental policy. This will also hold if sector policy concentrates on easing necessary adaptation processes for the economy. However, if sector policy is based on other factors, such as employment targets or keeping up given sectoral (and employment) structures, it may very well conflict with environmental policy.

Environmental policy defines the frame of reference for private decisions. It attempts to do away with artificial distortions among pollution-intensive and environmentally benign sectors. Consequently it can be expected that environmental policy may have repercussions on industrial organization, or what in Europe is called competition policy. Consider, for instance, the case of air quality management and different policy instruments. Land-use restraints in a given region prevent the growth of existing firms as well as closing it to newcomers. Land-use restraints represent a policy-caused barrier to market entry. The individual-stack policy, which is based on the state of art, starts from a static concept of an economy, does not introduce sectoral changes, and does not incorporate newcomers. Once the standards for pollutants ambient in the environment are fixed, the existing firms receive artificial protection against newcomers. The auctioning of permits (pollution licenses) may explicitly let newcomers bid for the right to release a specific quantity of emissions. However, very often the location of new firms is not explicitly considered in this context. Also, the firms in a region (and the potential newcomers) compete in the regional labor market. Assume, for instance, that a large firm in an area buys up more pollution permits than it plans to use. If the individual-stack policy is maintained, environmental policy introduces an artificial barrier to market entry. It seems that the use of emission taxes prevents these unwanted side effects on the competitive structure. Also, letting newcomers bargain on pollution rights with existing firms introduces some flexibility into the system.

OPEN QUESTIONS

Solutions for environmental quality management in a regional setting will be affected by the specific assignment of taxation and expenditure as well as by grant-in-aid schemes between different levels of government. If the national government has a large amount of funds at its disposal, it may be able to induce regional authorities to behave more along the lines desired by the national government. Also, a given institutional taxation-expenditure scheme may be "extrapolated" and applied to environmental problems even if other solutions are available.

How individual preferences are aggregated institutionally strongly influences the choice of solutions of our problem. Through which mechanisms of social choice (referenda, voting) are individual preferences revealed, and by which rules are they aggregated? We observe that the benefits of environmental quality may devolve upon a different area than that which bears the costs. How are these interregional spillovers of benefits and costs to be taken into account in the mechanisms of social choice? For instance, interregional diffusion norms have to be set by mechanisms of social choice. Can the regional inhabitants state their preferences only on a regional level within the limits of an interregional diffusion norm set by a national government? Besides regional discrepancies in the benefit area and the cost area of a public good, we have the well-known free-rider problem. Moreover, social mechanisms of choice also include a political web of parties, interest groups, and bureaucracies.

The regionalization of environmental policy is here mainly motivated by efficiency considerations. The environment is considered as a scarce resource, and institutional arrangements should be found that allocate the environment in an optimal way among its competing uses as public consumption good, receptor of wastes, and supplier of natural resources. In contrast to these allocation benefits, regionalization of environmental policy will also produce costs. These costs relate to the building of regional institutions, the administration of taxes, the implementation of emission norms or permit systems for new firms according to the state of the art, and so on. Though most of the papers in this book come down on the side of regionalization, we have no quantitative indication of what the costs are of the regionalization of environmental policy.

REFERENCES

Coase, R. H. "The Problem of Social Cost." *Journal of Law and Economics* 3 (1960): 1–44.

OECD. *The Mutual Compensation Principle. An Economic Instrument for Solving Certain Transfrontier Pollution Problems.* Paris, 1973.

Pethig, R. "Pollution, Welfare and Environmental Policy in the Theory of Comparative Advantage." *Journal of Environmental Economics and Management* 2 (1976): 160–169.

Richardson, H. W. *Regional and Urban Economics.* Harmondsworth, 1978.

Siebert, H. "Regional Aspects of Environmental Allocation." *Zeitschrift für die Gesamte Staatswissenschaft* 131 (1975): 446–513.
———. *Ökonomische Theorie der Umwelt.* Tubingen 1978.
Tietenberg, T. H. "On Taxation and the Control of Externalities." *American Economic Review* 64 (1974): 462–466.
Walter, I. *International Economics of Pollution.* London, 1975.

CHAPTER 2

Regional Environmental Information Systems

RAINER THOSS

This chapter consists of two parts. In the first part, I shall try to answer some of the questions put forward by the editors of this volume. Those questions are mainly concerned with the relations between different information devices and their relevance for regional and environmental policy. They refer to the choice of appropriate indicators, to the role of materials balances and input-output analysis, and to mathematical programming models. Another series of questions concerns the relations between the information to be provided for regional policy and for environmental policy. In the second part, I shall illustrate some of these points by making reference to a specific regional environmental model of the Frankfurt Metropolitan Area.

ASSESSMENT AND MANAGEMENT OF REGIONAL ENVIRONMENTAL QUALITY

An account of the different information devices available in the literature can best be organized by reference to the different problems that have to be solved by any policymaker who wants to improve regional environmental conditions, which in turn form but one part of the living conditions of the population of a region. Just as such a policymaker would organize the preparation of his decisions in a stepwise procedure, different methods and models can be considered as consecutive steps to obtain the necessary information for the planning of regional and environmental policy, namely: (a) measuring environmental quality; (b) describing the causes of environmental impacts; (c) describing the possible effects of policy instruments; and (d) choosing appropriate targets.

13

Measuring environmental quality by appropriate indicators. The first step to take in tackling this problem would be to define an appropriate set of environmental quality indicators and to measure their values at different points of time and at different locations. Such a system of indicators should include at least the most important variables that describe the environmental status of a region, such as the quality of water and air, the amount of solid waste, the amount of noise pollution, and the erosion of amenities.

Conceptually, such a monitoring system for regional environmental quality is not different from other indicators of regional socioeconomic performance. Therefore, in Germany, the Council of Advisors on Regional Policy has treated regional environmental quality indicators as an integral part of a monitoring system for regional policy (*Beirat für Raumordnung* [1976, pp. 29-60]).

The data collected for this purpose include, in addition to environmental indicators, income and employment levels, infrastructure conditions, social structure, and the intraregional spatial structure. With respect to environmental quality, the following indicators are proposed: (a) for air quality, sulfur dioxide and dust concentrations; (b) for surface water quality, biological situation and temperature; (c) for groundwater, quantity and quality; (d) for noise, noise-polluted areas and population; and (e) for amenities, land use.

The erosion of amenities clearly is the most difficult issue to take into account in any quantitative monitoring system. To a certain extent, however, changes in land use may serve as a proxy. The proposed set of indicators contains a large list of land-use indicators, including such variables as woodland, conservation areas, recreational areas, groundwater protection areas, and, on the other hand, built-up areas and transport areas. Of course, there are many deteriorations of amenities that do not lead to a change of land use, and these are not depicted by such indicators. But a large part of the erosion of amenities can be registered in this way. In general, it can be said that the total set of indicators provides at least a crude picture of the environmental status of a region.

Linking the environmental quality indicators to the sources of pollution. The next step in the preparation of information for regional environmental policy would be to establish the relations between observed levels of regional socioeconomic activities and the indicators of environmental quality. In the simplest case, such an account of socioeconomic-environmental linkages can take the form of a verbal environmental impact statement. A more formal model would try to describe the impacts of human action on environmental quality by a system of balance equations (one for each pollutant) and technical (behavioral) hypotheses. All such descriptions of interdependencies between the ecological and economic variables are based on the "materials balance approach" developed by Allen Kneese (Kneese et al. [1970]). By way of definition, any balance equation describes the amount of pollution that is observed at the end of a period as the difference between the amount existing at the beginning of the period, the pollutants generated within the period, and the reduction of pollutants by the natural environment and by human protective action, plus imports minus exports.

Application of input-output coefficients has proved to be a powerful tool for explaining the generation of pollutants (to be inserted in the materials balances) as by-products of socioeconomic activities. This holds true as well for the more detailed, firm-oriented approach put forward by Kneese and his former associates at Resources for the Future, as for the more sector-oriented approach developed by Cumberland (1966, 1974, esp. pp. 25-34), Isard (1972), and Leontief (1970). Both approaches have their relative advantages and disadvantages, which derive from the necessary degree of aggregation. Such coefficients describe the technological behavior of polluters, and it is assumed that the quantity of inputs as well as polluting by-products is a function of outputs (or other activity levels). This assumption enables us to estimate the total quantity of each pollutant emitted for varying levels and compositions of socioeconomic activities. The model thus simulates the ecological consequences of alternative technologies of production and patterns of consumption. For abatement processes, the coefficients show the efficiency of alternative technologies.

Figure 2-1 shows the types of relations that should be taken into account if one attempts to describe the impacts of alternative economic actions on environmental quality within a given region. It indicates that industries and households influence the environment by discharging residuals and extracting raw materials and that—in addition—they compete with the ecosystem for the scarce factor, land.

If the system can be approximated by a system of linear equations or inequalities, the interrelations can be described by an impact matrix, the columns of which indicate the effects of an activity on the different balance equations, whereas each line sums up the effects of different activities.

Thus, materials balances and environmental input-output models are nothing but accounting systems for externalities of production and consumption, from which the damages of environmental impacts may be calculated.

It should be noted that not only the levels of environmental quality indicators but also all the above-mentioned other indicators of the quality of regional living conditions (employment, income, infrastructure) depend on the same levels of economic activities, so that a separation of regional and environmental policy does not seem feasible.

Linking the levels of polluting activities to the levels of policy instruments. A further step toward extending the scope of the regional environmental information system would be to add behavioral equations to describe

Figure 2–1: RELATIONSHIP BETWEEN HUMAN SOCIETY AND THE ENVIRONMENT

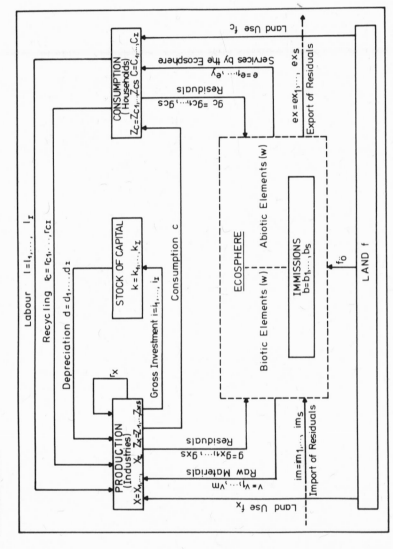

the expected (average) reaction of polluters to alternative instruments of environmental policy, such as effluent standards, subsidies, Pigouvian taxes, or other charges (see Kneese [1974]). Such regional response functions may be derived from interviews with potential polluters or estimated by regression analysis. So far, however—and again in analogy to the situation with regional policy instruments—very little practical experience exists in this field, so that a substantial amount of research effort is warranted.

The importance of this feature of an information system would lie in the fact that, for instance, the effects of alternative control methods or of different levels of charges could be tested before they are actually applied. Such testing undoubtedly would greatly enhance the efficiency of environmental and regional policy. Even without such response functions, an environmental information system provides valuable information not only for environmental but also for regional policy, because it permits us to simulate the consequences of hypothetical exogenous impacts. It can clarify, for instance, the environmental impacts of alternative scenarios of industrial development or alternative abatement technologies or alternative spatial distributions of industries and population. All of this information is just as valuable for environmental as well as for regional policy.

It should also be clear that this information is just as valuable for a market economy as for a planned economy. In both cases, the policymaker depends on estimates of what levels of instruments are necessary to reach a given desired environmental quality. The only difference lies in the type of instruments at his disposal. In one case, an economy may rely more on incentives; in the other, more on effluent standards. As to the questions on the normative content of such a system, it should be seen that any system contains an implicit normative element with respect to its specification: which indicators and equations are deemed "relevant" and which are not depends on a value judgment.

Introducing environmental and socioeconomic targets. In addition to such implicit value judgments, normative considerations are explicitly introduced by the fourth step of expanding the information system: the introduction of target values for the above-mentioned social and environmental indicators. Instead of simulating the effects of exogenous impacts, the information system now simulates the consequences of alternative targets.

More specifically, it may be used to: (a) check the consistency of environmental and socioeconomic targets; (b) calculate "costs" of one target in terms of another target, which may lead to revisions of initial intentions in view of their social opportunity cost; (c) show the consequences of targets for the state variables of the system; and (d) estimate the appropriate levels of instruments (if the relevant response functions are included).

Targets may take the form of a substitutive objective function, where each indicator has to be weighted by its marginal rate of substitution (U.S. EPA [1973, pp. I-63-I-83]). Such a function may be maximized or minimized, subject to the constraints given by the rest of the system (Russell [1973, esp. p. 19] and Spofford et al. [1976, esp. p. 21]). Or the targets may be introduced into the system as additional inequalities or equations, which are added to the original impact model described in the preceding paragraphs. The already mentioned Council of Advisors on Regional Policy in our country has opted for the latter. They proposed to take each indicator separately and to specify a certain maximum or minimum level that should be reached in all regions in order to provide equal minimum living conditions in all parts of the country (*Beirat für Raumordnung* [1976, pp. 39–43]). The council, therefore, clearly followed the path proposed by Cumberland (chapter 9) of specifying national minimum conditions for all regions but permitting regional authorities to strive for even better environmental quality.

Such targets of environmental policy—together with information on the carrying capacity of the environmental media of the region—could be used for a market solution of environmental protection, because they determine the amount of "pollution rights" that may be created in a given region. They can also be added to the information system and be tested for their consequences. The tests may then indicate the necessity of a revision in view of the high opportunity costs involved, or a regional differentiation of targets. This revision, however, will affect interregional equity, in terms of either environmental quality or economic conditions. At any rate, after simulating the costs of alternative targets, the policymaker can be brought in and can choose a definite set of targets in view of their "prices" in terms of other targets.

Again, if such a system may be approximated by linear relations, its interrelations may be represented by an impact matrix. Such a structure is shown in Figure 2-2, which also answers the question about the relations between normative considerations of decision makers and the design of information systems, because it shows that normative ideas about what would be a desirable state of environmental (and other) affairs in the region can be made an *integral part* of the model.

It should be emphasized that any model of this type that includes an objective function is a special variant of cost-benefit analysis, where units of the objective function are used as a measuring rod for benefits and all costs are calculated as opportunity costs in terms of benefits forgone.

AN EXAMPLE

Turning now to the question of practical experience, I would like to illustrate some of the previously discussed features by referring to a model for the

Figure 2–2: SOCIO-ECONOMIC-ECOLOGICAL INTERRELATIONS—A DECISION PROBLEM

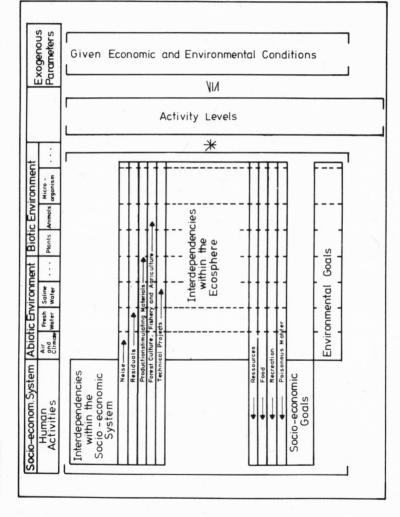

larger Frankfurt area. In order to analyze the interrelations between environmental and regional development policies, we have subdivided the Frankfurt planning region, which consists of several cities and surrounding counties, into a regional grid of twenty-one subregions. In so doing we have taken care to approximate as well as possible the existing environmental subregions and watersheds by community (not county) borders. The result is shown in Figure 2-3.

On the basis of this grid we try to derive information on whether and how further economic development of the region could be distributed in the different subregions.

The model we have constructed for this purpose contains the following relations. A first set of balance equations and behavioral functions describes the sectoral and regional production of, and the demand for, goods and services. These balances are derived from an input-output model for fifty-six sectors, which was published by the Deutsches Institut für Wirtschaftsforschung, Berlin, describing the inter- and intrasectoral interdependencies of the economy. According to the purpose of the model, this matrix was extended in two directions. First, waste and sewage plants (residual treatment activities) have been introduced into the input-output framework in order to calculate treatment costs in terms of intermediate and primary inputs. Second, a choice between alternative processes of production is made possible by the introduction of several productive processes for some sectors relevant to recycling.

Accordingly, the direct and indirect effects of alternative environmental and economic targets on the structure and levels of production can be investigated. Economic targets, for example, consist of constraints with respect to income and labor as well as to the composition of final demand.

A second set of equations describes the sectoral and regional generation and treatment of industrial sewage. Combined with transformation equations, they describe the impact of sewage discharge on the river water quality at critical points. Ambient standards (targets) insure that the desired quality is obtained (Thoss and Wiik [1974]).

The most important rivers of the research area and their catchment areas are investigated simultaneously. A further division of the rivers into homogeneous sections makes it possible to take the widely differing carrying capacity of each river section as well as the actual loading explicitly into account. The Naturwissenschaftliches Forschungsinstitut Senckenberg in Frankfurt has collected and analyzed the data necessary for the simulation of the self-purification processes and oxygen balances of the rivers at 134 sampling points since 1975. The amounts of sewage to be treated and the additional plants requested for primary, secondary, and tertiary treatment are determined by the model, taking into account the public and private treatment capacities already installed in the different regions.

Figure 2–3:   REGIONAL CLASSIFICATION OF THE INVESTIGATION AREA

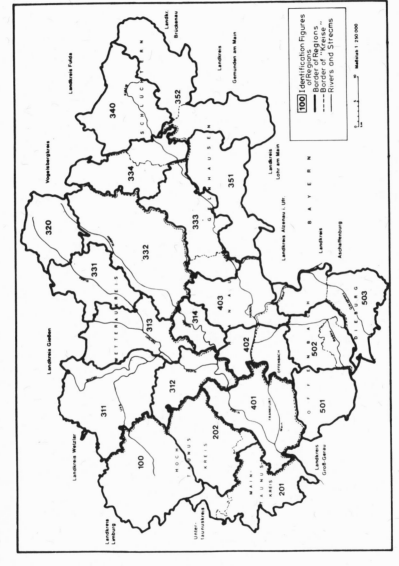

A third set of equations describes the generation, recovery, and disposal of waste materials. Thus, the model demonstrates the importance of the spatial allocation of production, the choice of technology [Thoss [1976]), and sectoral recycling. Recycling is explicitly introduced in three sectors: nonferrous metals, glass, and energy.

A fourth set of equations is concerned with the different types of land use. Multiple use of space is considered, where appropriate. Restrictions on socioeconomic and ecologic land-use demands form the feasible space for optimization.

Furthermore, two independent submodels for energy and transportation, as well as the resulting emissions, have been developed. *Submodel 1* consists of energy and emission balances as well as energy and air pollution standards. Considered are thirty-four energy commodities (types of energy)—some of which can be substituted for each other—and eight noxious residuals (Thoss and Döllekes [1974]). Problems of the optimal allocation of energy as well as the effects of the introduction of new cleaning techniques and energy-saving production technologies are investigated. *Submodel 2* contains transport balances for seven different modes of transportation. Five pollutants are considered. This model provides the possibility of investigating the effects of substitution among different modes of transportation—considering the demand for transportation services as well as available capacity and pollutant restrictions—on the economic and environmental system.

Figures 2-4 to 2-9 show some of the results. First, I would like to demonstrate the kind of information that can be derived for the state variables of the system. The first two graphs, Figures 2-4 and 2-5, are concerned with population and employment in the twenty-one subregions. The first column always shows the actual situation in 1972; the second column indicates how the spatial distribution should be changed in order to improve overall environmental quality and economic performance. Regional policy measures should be directed toward achieving a more even spatial distribution, since this would permit reaching the environmental targets with the least opportunity costs.

Next, I have selected graphs concerned with the spatial distribution of industry. Figures 2-6 and 2-7 show the actual and optimal distribution of two sectors (chemicals and electrical machinery, respectively) across regions. Figure 2-8 demonstrates the effects on sectoral structure within one of the subregions. Detailed maps in Figures 2-9 and 2-10 refer to forest areas, total open space, recreational area, and agricultural land, respectively, and show the percentage changes that should be considered by land-use policy.

Finally, I would like to draw attention to Figure 2-11, which shows one of the results of a sensitivity analysis and may be relevant to our later discussion of regional spillovers of environmental policy. The curves show the consequences of raising water quality standards (targets) in one of the subregions,

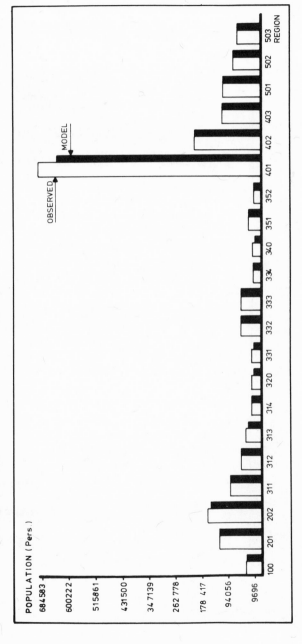

Figure 2—4: POPULATION IN 1972 COMPARED WITH THE OPTIMAL
POPULATION CALCULATED BY THE MODEL

Figure 2–5:   STRUCTURE OF LABOR IN 1972 COMPARED WITH THE OPTIMAL
STRUCTURE CALCULATED BY THE MODEL

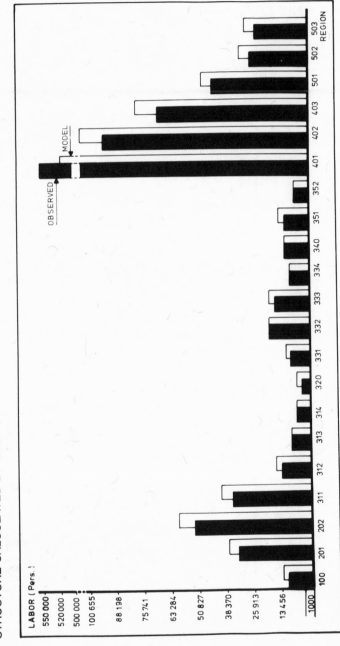

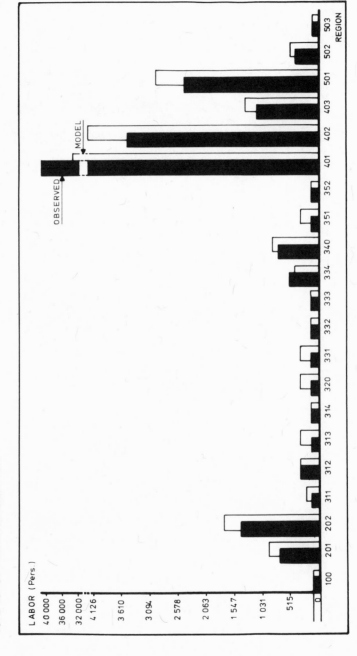

Figure 2–6: REGIONAL DISTRIBUTION OF LABOR IN THE CHEMICAL INDUSTRY
1972 vs. OPTIMAL ALLOCATION

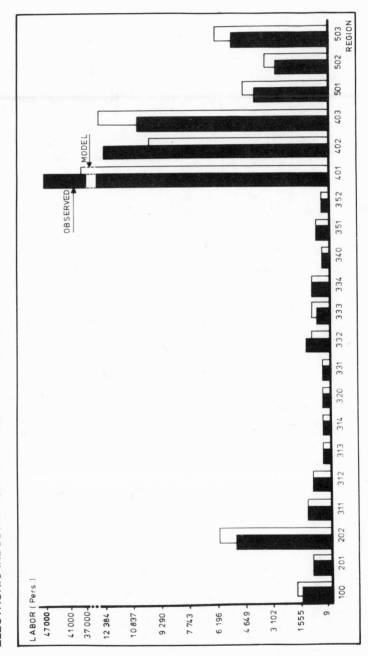

Figure 2–7: REGIONAL DISTRIBUTION OF LABOR IN THE ELECTRICAL AND ELECTRONIC INDUSTRY 1972 vs. OPTIMAL ALLOCATION

Figure 2–8: SECTORAL DISTRIBUTION OF LABOR IN 1972 COMPARED WITH
OPTIMAL STRUCTURE IN REGION 312

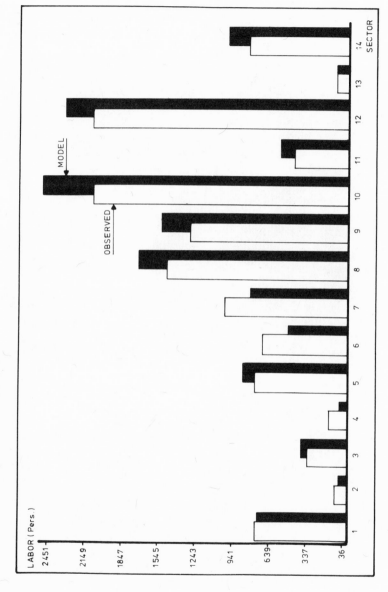

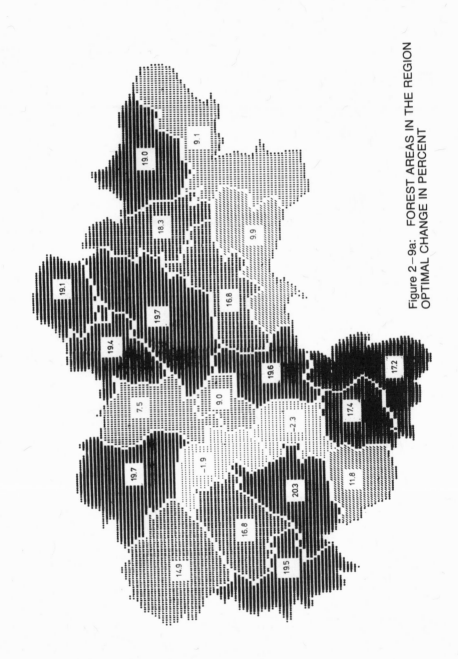

Figure 2−9a: FOREST AREAS IN THE REGION
OPTIMAL CHANGE IN PERCENT

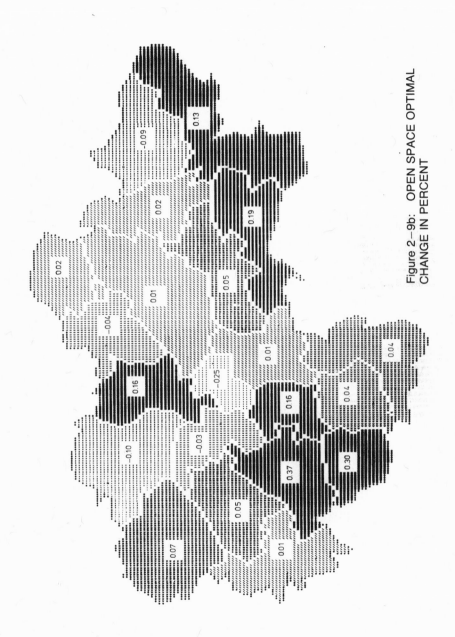

Figure 2–9b: OPEN SPACE OPTIMAL CHANGE IN PERCENT

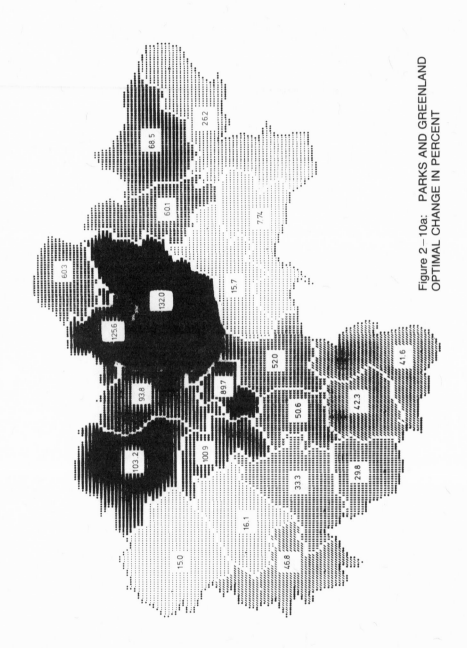

Figure 2–10a: PARKS AND GREENLAND
OPTIMAL CHANGE IN PERCENT

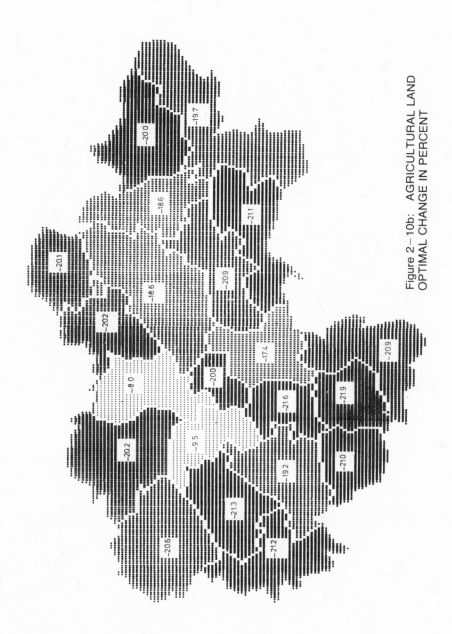

Figure 2–10b: AGRICULTURAL LAND
OPTIMAL CHANGE IN PERCENT

Figure 2–11:   CONSEQUENCES OF RAISING WATER QUALITY-
STANDARDS IN REGION 331—EFFECTS ON
PRODUCTION IN REGIONS 331 AND 312

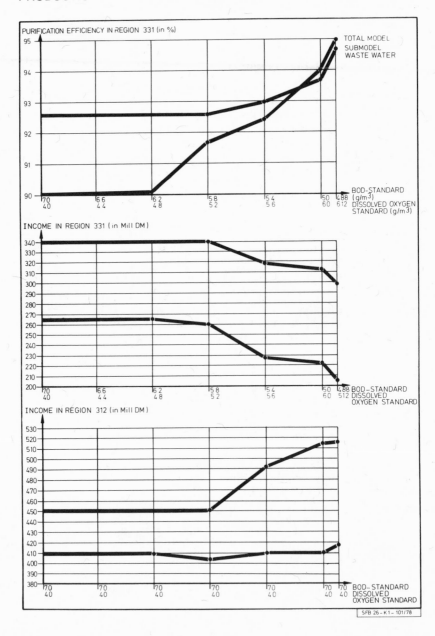

area 331. The curves in the upper part show how treatment activities must be improved within the region in order to comply with the rising pollution requirements, that is, permitting less BOD (biological oxygen demand) and requiring more dissolved oxygen per m^3. The curves in the center section demonstrate the consequences for national income that can be produced within the region: up to a certain level, income consequences can be avoided by simply changing the sectoral composition of production. After all possibilities of interregional reallocation have been exhausted, however, any further tightening of BOD targets has to be paid for by giving up some regional income.

Note that—as is shown by the curves in the bottom third of this figure—the opposite is true for region 312, which is situated downstream from region 331. Inhabitants of that region can continue to enjoy their original water quality of 7 mg BOD per m^3; but because of the reduction of pollution in the upstream region they can now expand their production and increase their income. I think that this example highlights the value of such information for regional as well as environmental policy.

REFERENCES

Beirat für Raumordnung. "Gesellschaftliche Indikatoren für die Raumordnung." *Empfehlungen vom 16 Juni 1976.* Bonn, 1976, pp. 27–95.

Cumberland, J. H. "A Regional Interindustry Model for Analysis of Development Objectives." In *Papers of the Regional Science Association* 17 (1966): 65–95.

———. "Energy, Environment and Social Science Research Priorities." In OECD, *Energy and Environment.* Paris, 1974. Pp. 1–50.

Isard, W. *Economic-Ecologic Analysis for Regional Development.* New York, 1972.

Kneese, A. V. "The Application of Economic Analysis to the Management of Water Quality: Some Case Studies." In J. Rothenberg and I. G. Heggie, eds., *The Management of Water Quality and the Environment.* London, 1974. Pp. 73–103.

———, R. V. Ayres, and R. C. d'Arge. *Economics and Environment: A Materials Balance Approach.* Baltimore, 1970.

Leontief, W. "Environmental Repercussions and the Economic Structure: An Input-Output Approach." *Review of Economics and Statistics* 52 (1970): 262–271.

Russell, C. S. *Residuals Management in Industry: A Case Study for Petroleum Refining.* Baltimore, 1973.

Spofford, Jr., W. O., C. S. Russell, and R. A. Kelly. *Environmental Quality Management/An Application to the Lower Delaware Valley.* Washington, D.C., 1976.

Thoss, R. "A Generalized Input-Output Model for Residuals Management."
     In K. R. Polenske and J. Skolka, eds., *Advances in Input-Output Analy-
     sis*. Cambridge, Mass., 1976. Pp. 411–432.
—— and H. P. Döllekes. "Energy and Environmental Planning." In OECD,
     Energy and Environment. Pp. 77–106.
—— and K. Wiik. "A Linear Decision Model for the Management of Water
     Quality in the Ruhr." In J. Rothenberg and I. G. Heggie, eds., *The
     Management of Water Quality*. Pp. 104–133.

DISCUSSION

Clean Air Plans in Air Quality Control Regions as an Instrument of Environmental Policy

FRANZ J. DREYHAUPT

I intend to present a general view of a new instrument of the German
Federal Immissions Control Act of 1974, which is called the Clean Air Plan.
This is not a hypothetical but a real instrument. It is a new strategy for air
pollution control, which is consistently used in North Rhine-Westphalia. The
strategy contains a number of single elements, all of which are included in the
Clean Air Plan. These elements are: (a) emissions inventory, (b) immissions
inventory, (c) effects inventory, (d) causal analysis, (e) prognosis of air pollution, and (f) measures plan.

In Germany, we differentiate the technical terms "emission" and "immission." Emission is the ejection of flue gas and the like into the atmosphere.
Immission means air pollution components found in man's living space, which
affect human beings, animals, plants, or materials; it is, in short, termed "air
quality."

The strategy is applied only in so-called Air Quality Control Regions. These
are highly polluted areas of a minimum surface of 50 square kilometers.

Highly polluted means that the air quality standard for *one* air pollution component is exceeded, *or* that the air quality standards for *two* components are approached (90 percent), *or* that the sum of the quotients of concentration and respective standard for three or four components exceeds the limiting value of two. An area has also to be defined as an Air Quality Control Region if there are established harmful effects on man, animals, vegetation, or materials owing to air pollution.

The Air Quality Control Regions are determined by regulations of the state government. In North Rhine-Westphalia, there is an Air Quality Control Region that follows the Rhine from Cologne to Duisburg and the Ruhr from Duisburg to Dortmund. This region has a total surface of about 3,000 square kilometers. We have divided this region, for practical reasons, into five subregions, which are characterized by the name of the respective biggest town— Cologne, Düsseldorf, Duisburg, Essen, and Dortmund. The whole Air Quality Control Region has a population of six million to seven million and is the industrial core of the Federal Republic of Germany, representing 70 percent of the iron and steel industry, 90 percent of the coal mines, 30 percent of the chemical industry, and 30 percent of the oil refineries.

It is evident that in such highly industrialized conurbations conflicts between the interests of industry and population are unavoidable. The Clean Air Plan's aim is to improve air quality on the one hand and to guarantee industrial activity as the basis of an industrial nation on the other.

For two of the subregions, Cologne and Duisburg, we finished the Clean Air Plans in 1976 and 1977, respectively. We are preparing the Clean Air Plans for the subregions Dortmund and Essen, to be finished by December 1978 and 1979, respectively. The last Clean Air Plan, for Düsseldorf, will follow in December 1980. And then—in 1981—we begin again with the subregion Cologne, issue the second Clean Air Plan for this region, and so on.

Before presenting a general view of the two finished Clean Air Plans for the subregions Cologne and Duisburg, I should like to describe the elements of a Clean Air Plan very concisely.

EMISSIONS INVENTORY

Emissions inventories are records of all man-made air pollution sources in a given area, in the present case, the Air Quality Control Region. These sources are classified according to their appearances as *point*, *line*, and *area* sources, indicated by the coordinates of their geographic positions.

Furthermore, the sources are classified according to the conditions affecting their emissions, namely: (a) geometric dimensions of the source; (b) quantity and temperature of waste gases; (c) nature and quantity of the emitted air pollution components; and (d) frequency and duration of emissions.

The data are obtained in different ways for the various main groups of air pollutant emitters: (1) Heavily emitting industries are obliged by law to make emissions declarations every year. (2) Small-scale industries are investigated by competent supervisory authorities, such as factory inspectorates. (3) For domestic heating, we get reports from the chimneysweeps, which make it possible to calculate the masses of the various fuels consumed per year and unit area. From these data, the emissions of the different air pollution components—for instance, carbon monoxide, hydrocarbons, sulfur dioxide, and dust—are calculated with the help of specific factors. (4) For road traffic, we use traffic counts, in which emissions are similarly calculated with the aid of the appropriate specific emission factors.

IMMISSIONS INVENTORY

Immissions inventories are records of the immission concentrations of the relevant air pollutants. These data are obtained mainly by immissions measurements, but are also obtained by transforming data from the emissions inventory. The emissions inventory is organized in such a way that it is possible to get for every subarea of the Air Quality Control Region that set of source data—"source configuration"—which is necessary to transform emissions data into immissions data. For this transformation, a diffusion model that describes the emission-transmission-immission linkage is used. Needed meteorological data are obtained from airport meteorological stations and from special stations that were set up in the Air Quality Control Region for both meteorological and immissions measurements. The immissions inventory serves as a basis for comparison with immissions standards or air quality standards, which are the same.

EFFECTS INVENTORY

Effects inventories are records of all detected noxious, dangerous, or undesirable environmental effects caused by air pollution, inclusive of immissions standards violations. All results of effects studies on man, animals, vegetation, and materials in the Air Quality Control Region are recorded if such results are available. Effects studies are carried out systematically for vegetation and corroding materials by evaluating biological indicators—for instance, the die-off rate of lichen—and by measuring the corrosion loss of small iron plates, respectively.

In determining effects on man, we make medical investigations in representative groups of children and older males. Furthermore, we establish inventories of unpleasant odors for specific areas.

CAUSAL ANALYSIS

As a step toward actual status determination, the causes of detected effects —which also includes immissions standards violations—are to be analyzed. This may be achieved along various lines, for example, by calculations with reversed emission-transmission-immission connections, through conclusions by analogy, or by plausibility considerations. Such causal analysis is a precondition for the most important part of the Clean Air Plan, namely, the Measures Plan.

PROGNOSIS OF AIR POLLUTION

Emissions and immissions prognoses are necessary because the implementation of a Clean Air Plan from start to finish will normally take five years. The structures of the Air Quality Control Region change over the years, and so do the emissions and immissions. There are, for example, newly built residential areas with new sources of domestic emissions, new streets and roads with traffic emissions, and new industrial plants with their specific emissions. On the other hand, existing residential areas and road systems are altered; and industrial units are converted, extended, dislocated, shut down, technically improved with respect to emissions, or are subjected to other measures affecting emissions. It is possible to predict such regional or local developments within the given time schedule by seeking information from local governments, communities, firms, and other institutions. But unfortunately information gathered from these sources is not very reliable. Of more importance are investigations into development lines that are of supraregional influence on air pollution. Examples are: (a) new ordinances for improvement of automobile exhausts; and (b) new ordinances limiting the content of air-polluting components in fuel, such as the gasoline-lead law or the ordinance limiting the sulfur content in diesel oil and light fuel oil, which are operative in all states of the Federal Republic of Germany.

Another example of supraregional development is an expected change in the practice of home heating, in particular the decreasing use of hard coal as against the increasing use of gas or the shift from individual home heating to district heating.

The prognostication of supraregional, regional, or local development lines leads to a corresponding prognosis of the development of emissions, which can be transformed into a general immissions prognosis.

The heart of the Clean Air Plan is a "measures-and-actions plan" based on the evaluation of the data of the various inventories and other elements previously described. In these measures, certain industrial polluters may become involved as well as authorities responsible for urban planning. It is important to note that all measures specified in the Clean Air Plan can be taken only if reference to pertinent legislative enactments is possible, because the Clean Air Plan does not constitute a legal act; it is an action plan for the various appropriate authorities.

FIRST RESULTS OF TWO CLEAN AIR PLANS

The Clean Air Plan for the Cologne subregion was promulgated by the minister of labor, health, and social affairs of the state of North Rhine-Westphalia in December 1976. This Clean Air Plan was the first one put into effect not only in North Rhine-Westphalia but in the Federal Republic of Germany as a whole. The second Clean Air Plan was issued by the same minister for the western Ruhr area (the Duisburg region) in December 1977. Note the general demographic data shown in the accompanying table.

Surface: Cologne   649 square kilometers
   Duisburg   771 square kilometers
Population: Cologne   1.4   million
    Duisburg   1.26 million
Population density: Cologne   2,160 inhabitants per square kilometer
      Duisburg   1,780 inhabitants per square kilometer
Number of automobiles per 1,000 inhabitants: Cologne   303
             Duisburg 302
Heat consumption for home heating per 1,000 habitants:
  Cologne   42 terajoule units
  Duisburg   43 terajoule units

These data show no significant differences between the two subregions. But with respect to air pollution, there is an essential difference, namely, the structure of industry. The Cologne subregion is not as highly industrialized as is the Duisburg subregion. Above all, there is no heavy industry in the Cologne region, that is, there is no iron and steel industry; and there are no coal mines with their linked industries, such as coke-making plants. Such heavy industry is predominant in the Duisburg region. On the other hand, in the Cologne region the relevant pollution is due to crude oil refineries, the chemical and petrochemical industry, the metal-processing industry, and the automobile industry.

Another general point is of importance: owing to the fact that the Duisburg region is a coal-mining district, we find hard coal used predominantly in domestic heating fuel as against the predominance of light fuel oil in the Cologne region.

Emissions inventory. In both subregions about one thousand air pollution components were found and classified according to the following three main categories of pollutants: anorganic gases, organic gases and vapors, and suspended particulate matter.

Table 2-1 shows the masses per year of emissions of the three main categories of pollutants and the percentage of the three main groups of air pollutant emitters: industry, domestic heating and small-scale industry, and automobile traffic. This table allows the following conclusions: The total masses of emissions per year are much higher in the Duisburg subregion than in the Cologne subregion. The masses of emissions per year in the Duisburg subregion in comparison to the Cologne subregion are about four times as much for anorganic gases, about twice as much for organic gases, and about seven times as much for dust. The percentage of industry's contribution to the total emissions is extremely high—between 85 and 95 percent.

The emissions inventory allows us to subdivide the total figures of this table into the figures for single components. I did this, for example, for the industrial anorganic emissions in the Duisburg subregion in Table 2-2.

In Table 2-2 we see the very important and astonishing percent of carbon monoxide, namely 82.5 percent of the total anorganic gases. An we see too sulfur dioxide, with 11.6 percent. These facts give rise to two questions: (1) What is the reason for the high carbon monoxide emissions? (2) Do we find correspondingly high immissions of carbon monoxide and sulfur dioxide?

There is a high level of carbon monoxide emission in the Duisburg subregion because of the concentration of the iron and steel industry there. The specific sources of carbon monoxide are the ore-sintering plants, the blast furnaces, and the top-blowing converters. We did not know about this phenomenon until we had drawn up the emissions inventory in 1973. After these findings, of course, we were concerned about correspondingly high immissions in the region. Fortunately, our measurements showed no significant values, that is, carbon monoxide concentrations were below 1 mg/m^3 as a yearly average as against an air quality standard of 10 mg/m^3.

For the so-called ubiquitous air pollution components—sulfur dioxide, carbon monoxide, nitrogen oxides, dust, and organic gases—we make so-called emission grid charts as shown in Figure 2-12. This figure shows the sulfur dioxide emission grid for the Duisburg subregion. In each unit area of a surface of 1 square kilometer one will find the mass of emitted sulfur dioxide per year and unit area. The percentage of the three main groups of air pollutant emitters—industry, domestic heating, and automobiles—is shown by the different shades. So one can check in a very simple way where the focal points are for industrial emissions, domestic heating, or automobile traffic. In this chart, the specialist will easily recognize that the focal points of sulfur dioxide emissions are congruent, to a large extent, with the industrial areas of the region.

Table 2-1. Total masses of emissions per year in the subregions Cologne and Duisburg.

Emissions Component	Industry		Domestic Heating and Small-scale Industry		Automobile Traffic	
	Cologne	Duisburg	Cologne	Duisburg	Cologne	Duisburg
Anorganic gases	297,687 t/a 55.2%	1,674,312 t/a 85.9%	107,012 t/a 19.9%	163,929 t/a 8.4%	134,407 t/a 24.9%	110,907 t/a 5.4%
Organic gases and vapors	84,117 t/a 88.4%	150,607 t/a 87.5%	6,323 t/a 6.6%	12,367 t/a 7.2%	4,751 t/a 5.0%	9,054 t/a 5.1%
Dust	25,201 t/a 82.3%	192,872 t/a 95.4%	4,967 t/a 16.2%	9,062 t/a 4.5%	470 t/a 1.5%	286 t/a 0.1%

Table 2-2. Industrial anorganic emissions in the Duisburg subregion.

Emissions Component	(t/a)	(%)
Anorganic gases of which are:	1,670,506	100.0
CO	1,378,197	82.5
SO_2	193,370	11.6
NO_2	75,144	4.5
N_2O	16,049	0.95
HCl	4,165	0.24
NH_3	1,002	0.06
Cl^-	995	0.06
HF	709	0.04
H_2S	388	0.02
F^-	306	0.02
Noble gases	127	0.008
Cl_2	21	0.001
HCN	16	0.001
Other anorganic compounds	10	0.0006

Immissions inventory. As we do in the case of emissions inventory, we thus prepare immission grid charts for the ubiquitous air pollutant components, mainly as results of systematic measurements. Furthermore, we prepare such charts for ten to fifteen other components, which we found to be relevant in a preliminary investigation. In these cases the data are obtained preferably by use of a diffusion model, but partially also by measurements. Figures 2-13 and 2-14 present, as an example, the sulfur dioxide immissions situation in the Duisburg subregion.

Figure 2-13 shows the yearly average of sulfur dioxide concentration for each unit area. The yearly average concentration corresponds to the so-called long-term air quality standard. The concentration values are obtained from the measurement results on the four corner points of each unit area as arithmetic mean values. The red areas indicate areas that exceed the air quality standard.

Because for some components we have *two* air quality standards in Germany, we have also a sulfur dioxide immissions chart, which corresponds to the so-called short-term air quality standard, which means a 95 percent value. Figure 2-14 shows the short-term sulfur dioxide load in the Duisburg subregion. Here, too, the batched areas indicate areas that exceed the air quality standard. One can see that the number of batched areas in this case is higher than in the case of the long-term values; the short-term air quality standard is more stringent.

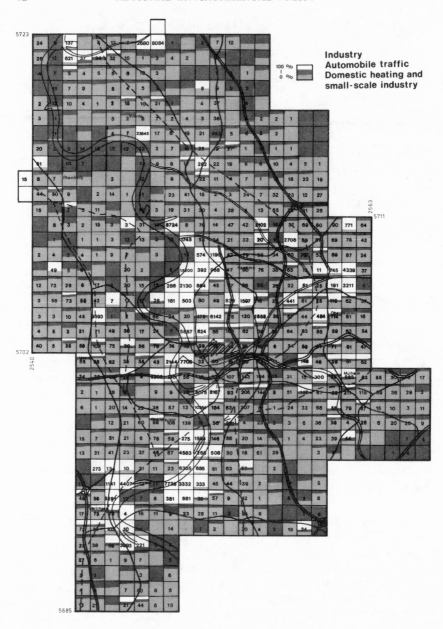

Figure 2-12

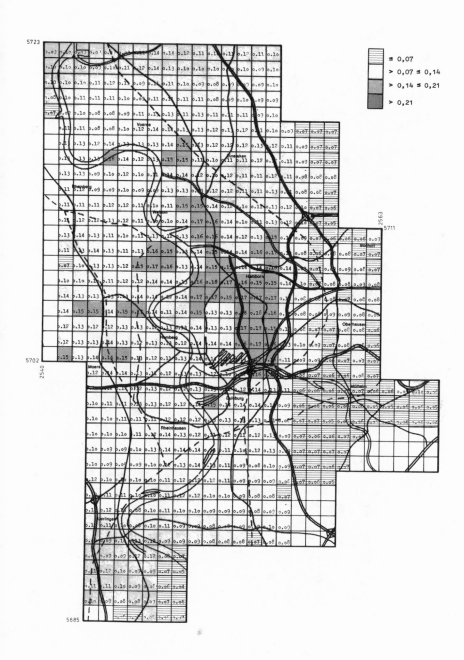

Figure 2-13

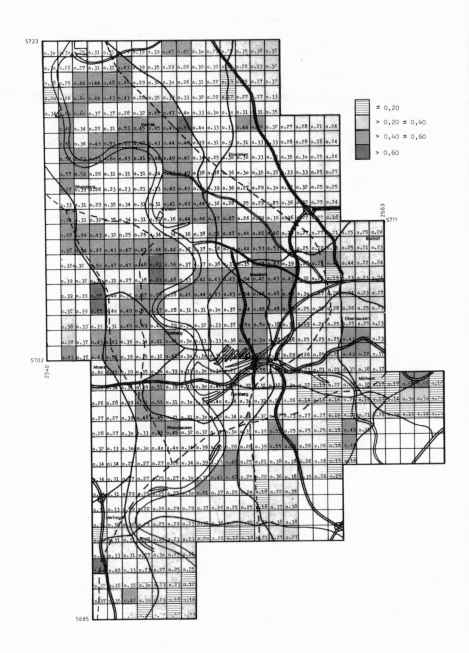

Figure 2-14

The total results of the immissions inventories for the Cologne and Duisburg subregions are shown in Table 2-3. A comparison of the Cologne and the Duisburg subregions leads to the following conclusions: (a) the situation in the Duisburg subregion is more critical than in the Cologne region because the number of areas exceeding the air quality standard is much higher; (b) the most important air pollution components in the Cologne region are organic gases and dust precipitation; (c) the most important air pollution components in the Duisburg region are sulfur dioxide, dust precipitation, and hydrogen sulfide.

Effects inventory. While the emissions and the immissions inventories are rather precise, the results of the effects inventories are less satisfying; since the systematics and the methods for effects investigations are not yet standardized. For the Cologne subregion, we were able to draw the following conclusions: (a) despite of higher frequency of chronic bronchitis and higher carboxyhemoglobin values compared with clean air regions, a significant correlation with specific air pollution components was not established; (b) immissions by malodors were attributed to specific industrial plants; (c) vegetation damage due to air pollution was established in one case; and (d) the sulfur dioxide immissions led to erosion damage to the Cologne cathedral, but the extent of the damage depends to a high degree on the kind of stone material used.

For the Duisburg subregion, the conclusions referring to the effects inventory are—corresponding to the higher immissions load—a little alarming: (a) the carboxyhemoglobin value is significantly higher in the investigated male group than in the comparable clean air region; (b) 22.7 percent of the investigated males have symptoms of chronic bronchitis as against 10.7 percent in the clean air region; (c) cases of sinusitis occurred with a higher frequency than in the clean air region; (d) ten of twenty-six investigated areas are highly loaded by malodor; (e) vegetation damage in form of leaf necroses up to 35 percent of the whole leaf surface occurred in gladiolus and similar sensitive plants; and (e) severe damage to trees and bushes was established within a certain limited area.

Causal analysis. It turned out that causal analysis with ubiquitous air pollution components is very difficult, whereas the assignment of individual immissions components to distinct sources proved to be possible. In drawing up the Measures Plan, less emphasis was laid on the immissions-emissions relations than on violations of emissions standards and of the state of the art in air pollution control technology. However, in the Duisburg subregion with the aid of the diffusion model we found a number of industrial chimneys that have a significant influence on the sulfur dioxide concentration.

Prognosis of air pollution. In both the Cologne and Duisburg subregions it was not possible to get conclusive prognoses of industrial development.

Table 2-3. Number of unit areas exceeding the air quality standards.

Air Pollution Component	Cologne Region		Duisburg Region	
	Yearly Average Value	95% Value	Yearly Average Value	95% Value
SO_2	–	–	56	154
HF	–	–	–	42
Organic gases	X	7	X	18
Dust precipitation	16	9	131	139
Dust concentration	–	–	–	–
Pb	–	X	1	X
Zn	–	X	–	X
Cd	–	X	–	X
NO_2	–	2	–	–
CO	–	–	–	–
Ammonia	1	7	–	–
H_2S	1	7	4	23
HCl	1	1	–	–
Ethylene	1	3	–	–
VC	X	3	X	–
Benzene	X	3	X	1
Phenol	–	–	–	–
Dimethylformamide	–	–	X	X
Formaldehyde	X	X	X	–

46

But the structural prognoses referring to domestic heating and automobile traffic lead to the conclusion that the emissions in both cases will decrease between now and 1985, for reasons mentioned in the introduction; for instance, the ordinance concerning the sulfur content in diesel fuel and light fuel oil. This conclusion also indicates a tendency to a decrease in immissions in these sectors.

MEASURES-AND-ACTIONS PLAN

Measures in the sectors of domestic heating and road traffic beyond the generally prognosticated improvements seem not to be possible. For the Duisburg subregion, we have emphasized that the possibilities of an accelerated change from individual home heating—above all, from the use of coal ovens—to district heating should be checked by the community.

The main attention of the Measures Plan is directed at the industrial sector. The "saving goals" in the Cologne subregion, involving about four hundred single measures—referring to the total industrial emissions masses at the beginning of our investigations up to the end of 1981—are for anorganic gases, 20 percent; for organic gases, 65 percent; and for dust, 35 percent. For the Duisburg subregion the saving goals involving about three hundred single measures up to the end of 1982 are for sulfur dioxide, 14 percent; for organic gases, 17 percent; and for dust, 30 percent.

DISCUSSION

Limitations on Effective Environmental Information Systems at the Regional Level

RONALD EDWARDS

The papers by Professor Thoss and Mr. Dreyhaupt constitute an essentially complementary pair. On the one hand, Professor Thoss is concerned to detail the kind of framework that can link the gathering of information on environmental matters to final policy measures; on the other, Mr. Dreyhaupt's paper contains examples of some of the practical difficulties this can run up against.

The main concern of this comment will be to outline some of the main limitations to the formalization of information systems as proposed by Professor Thoss, while drawing on some of the practical experience of the German Clean Air Plan for the best Ruhr district, as detailed by Mr. Dreyhaupt.

THE MEASUREMENT OF POLLUTION AND DAMAGES

One of the first problems to which Professor Thoss refers is the monitoring of the regional environmental qualities. His view is that there is no *conceptual* difference between the measurement of environmental quality indicators and other socioeconomic variables.

On one level I can agree with this suggestion, in that some of the same problems exist in attempting to proxy regional welfare by, say, regional income as affect the translation of measured amounts of pollution into welfare loss. However, the latter is subject to many difficulties the former type of relation does not meet, and this particular aspect leaves a very large gap in the type of information system proposed.

Leaving aside for a moment the tremendous difficulties involved in the association between pollution damage and subjective welfare, there is a whole range of pitfalls involved in "merely" linking measured amounts of pollution to pollution damage, which, presumably, is the actual concern of policymakers.

For instance, Professor Tietenberg eloquently points out that many environmental policy decisions should be devolved to a regional level, since not only abatement costs but also *damage functions* may differ between regions, owing to differences in assimilative capacity, spatial distribution, and so on (see chapter 3).

This point is neatly reflected in Mr. Dreyhaupt's paper in his reference to the lack of precision of the "effects inventory" of the monitoring of the Clean Air Plan (owing mainly to the lack of standardization of the investigative techniques), and indeed by Professor Thoss himself when he refers to the difficulty of assessing the erosion of amenities.

The basic question here (and indeed throughout this discussion) is about the role of the decision maker or policymaker, and about the sort of information he can expect to get from the type of model used by Professor Thoss. Obviously, in the absence of a set of damage functions, the amount of information (or judgment) the policymaker must supply *himself* increases. However, given the state of the art in respect to estimating pollution damages, the *explicit* recognition of the role of value judgment in this context is, perhaps, a very good thing.

PRODUCTION, CONSUMPTION, AND POLLUTION

The next main question considered by Professor Thoss is really the heart of the information system and should be perhaps one of the most positive aspects of it. It is the modeling of the interrelationships between the various regional socioeconomic activities and the amounts of pollution generated.

The approach favored by Professor Thoss is of the input-output, or the more general activity analysis (or programming) sort. The overwhelming advantage of such an approach is that is enables the precise tracking of any change in the level of any economic activity through its backward linkages into its final effects on pollution levels. This raises the extremely important point that economic and environmental policies are inextricably linked at the regional level.

As Professor Thoss argues, this type of linear analysis has proved very powerful in the assessment of short- and medium-term impacts in other areas of interest, though there are perhaps a couple of relatively minor and essentially practical questions that should be raised about its applicability in this context.

First, input-output tables, or technology coefficients, are difficult and consequently expensive to estimate with any degree of accuracy, particularly when they are required to include pollution information. Although it is possible to approximate regional tables by "borrowing" the relevant sectoral information from their national counterparts, it is doubtful whether this procedure can adequately capture all of the particular technological characteristics of a region. This brings into question the viability of the general use of these sorts of models for all regions, though exceptionally problematic areas may still warrant such treatment.

The second point concerns the relevant scale of analysis for this kind of system. The main advantage of the technique at the national level is that it facilitates an examination of all the *intranational* linkages. This advantage is considerably weakened at the regional level, where *intraregional* linkages tend to play a relatively minor role. Interregional trade flows become more important as the size of the area considered decreases, and these must be treated as exogenous to this type of model. Once again, the advantages and viability of Professor Thoss's suggestion seem to accrue at the *national* rather than at the regional level.

This point also gives rise to doubts about the capacity of this framework to deal with the not insignificant phenomenon of interregional spillovers of pollution. The basic problem is that if pollution emissions cannot be linked to activities *within* the region they remain essentially "unexplained" and must be handled by a supplementary information system. Similarly, if activities in the region give rise to pollution in a different geographical area, how is this to be treated? This point reappears in the discussion of the objective function.

Though subject to many difficulties of this nature, some such *ex ante* determination of pollution levels is highly desirable. The alternative is discussed by Mr. Dreyhaupt in his sections on "causal analysis," whereby it seems that pollution emissions are to be empirically linked to their sources after the fact by some reverse dispersion models. This procedure has two main difficulties, which the adoption of Professor Thoss's scheme could mitigate. First, it is often virtually impossible to attribute monitored pollution to specific sources. As Mr. Dreyhaupt points out, the causal analysis applied to the Cologne and Duisburg areas had difficulty in determining the sources of ubiquitous air pollution components, such as SO_2. The problems with this *ex post* procedure appear to lie not in determining the emission sources but in apportioning the total monitored pollution between specific individuals.

Second, with no consideration of *how* (rather than where) the pollution arises in the first place, there can be no account taken of the impacts of what Mr. Dreyhaupt calls the Measures Plan, that is, pollution control. Professor Thoss quite rightly draws attention to these impacts on the various "nonenvironmental" socioeconomic aspects of the region and gives them appropriate priority in the information system.

Mr. Dreyhaupt does, however, raise a question that is far from adequately treated by Professor Thoss, which has to do with the spatial distribution of regional pollution. If the pollution-production relations are determined at the sectoral or industry level, rather than firm by firm, or emission source by emission source, it is difficult to see how specific local problems can be handled in Professor Thoss's system. It is perfectly possible that the call to abate noise in one subarea could result in the reduction of noise emission from a source many miles away rather than in the relevant location, if pollutants are treated at sectoral, rather than at local level.

This sort of difficulty can be overcome in three ways. First, the "region" (for environmental policy purposes) could be defined as an area in which discrepancies in the spatial distribution of pollutants is insignificant. Unfortunately, for some types of pollution (e.g., static noise emission), this would limit the analysis to very small areas indeed, and in view of the arguments about the relevant size of region for this type of system, this is not really viable.

Second, the production-pollution relations could be formalized to take space into account, by defining separate relations for some specific individual emissions sources. Constraints (or terms in the objective function) could be added for each of these, so that *local* (rather than regional total) standards (or preferences) could play an explicit role. This kind of disaggregation would, however, significantly increase the cost of building the information system and render it a much more complicated tool to work with. Also, since the regional socioeconomic structure is less likely to be stable at this level (given industrial relocations, population movements, etc.) than at the more aggregate sectoral level, this would limit the time span over which any particular model could be regarded as either accurate or applicable.

The third alternative is again for the policymaker to add such informal information he deems necessary to solve this problem. That is, once regional totals are determined by the formal information system, the spatial distribution can be apportioned by a more judgmental approach, taking into account the sort of stochastic, or local considerations which would be so difficult to handle within Professor Thoss's framework.

RESPONSE TO POLICY MEASURES

Professor Thoss proceeds to discuss the extension of the information system to include reaction functions to various policy instruments. This is an extremely important aspect of any information system. Once the socio-economic feasibility (and desirability) has been established through the production-pollution relationships described above, it is of paramount importance to determine how the targets can be achieved, or indeed whether they *can* be achieved through the available instruments.

There are, however, serious difficulties in trying to model responses to instruments, particularly for interfacing with the production model, as Professor Thoss points out. The simplest response in the context is the effect on output of pollution-generating activities. Output effects are very easy to handle within the confines of Professor Thoss's system, since these do not necessarily affect the production coefficients.

Much more problematic are induced changes in technology, which do alter the production relations of the information system. Although it is possible to handle this phenomenon to a certain extent through the use of activity analysis (i.e., allowing for a number of alternative processes for producing any commodity), use of this method is limited to cases where the alternative techniques are known and can be specified in terms of their coefficients. It may be impossible to allow for such phenomena as endogenously induced technical progress in an *ex ante* sense, except in the most general way (e.g., by assuming some sort of directional change in the magnitudes of the various input-output coefficients). This problem is not specific to linear production models but occurs to virtually the same extent (in a practical sense) with any production function.

Two types of technical change, which will change the production-pollution relations, should be considered. First, we may expect direct abatement measures will be taken in the form of "add-on" technology (e.g., soundproofing, smoke scrubbers, etc). Although affecting the direct relationship between activity levels and pollution emission, these should have relatively little effect on the actual production processes themselves and may be amenable to modeling as responses to environmental policy in the short term and even the medium term. Second, there may be technical change of a more basic nature that actually affects the production processes themselves as well as the production-pollution links. Since this type of phenomenon (although perhaps endogenously induced by the policy instruments) tends to be largely exogenously determined in nature, it is doubtful whether it can be modeled to the same extent, particularly in a quantitative sense. It is to be expected that this will occur as a medium- to long-term response to environmental policy, again casting doubt on the viability of the type of formalized information system envisaged by Professor Thoss in the field of long-term environmental planning.

This is not of course to argue that response functions have no role to play. It is merely suggested that the *timing* of these responses should be considered, along with their quantitative impacts, in an effort to determine final effects on the regional economy.

The point is echoed to some extent by Mr. Dreyhaupt in his references to future pollution levels and the goals of the Measures Plan. Here, it seems, the *intent* of the policy is to induce fairly dramatic changes in technology (e.g., from coal-fired domestic heating to community central heating) in what is essentially the medium term. It is doubtful whether functions involving this type of response could be combined with a production model relying on an essentially fixed technology to give meaningful impact statements.

THE POLICY TARGETS

The final step in Professor Thoss's information chain is to convert the so far "positive" conclusions into more normative statements about what should be done. This involves combining the impact model with some form of objective function, or formal declaration of goals.

As Professor Thoss mentions, there are essentially two ways in which this combination can be implicitly or explicitly effected. First, the environmental attributes of the region can be given "prices," or valuations (relative to all other socioeconomic targets), and incorporated into a good objective function. This function can then be optimized, subject to the constraints of the production-pollution system. Second, rather than giving them an explicit price, an objective function *excluding* environmental considerations can be optimized, subject to a set of constraints including environmental standards (maximum permissible emission level, etc). The latter, it is argued, has the advantage that interregional equity considerations can be taken directly into account by insuring that the same minimum quality constraints apply everywhere.

In fact, however, there is no formal difference between the two approaches, since one is really the *dual* of the other. In the first case, given a set of valuations we can solve for the optimum pollution and output levels; in the other, the dual solution gives us the implicit valuations, or shadow prices, of the pollutants for a given set of standards or levels.

It is surely against the spirit of his own analysis for Professor Thoss to argue for identical standards among regions on equity grounds, even if valuations of the environment were identical between regions. In a sense, equity considerations are served if these valuations are explicitly entered into the objective formation.

The resulting optimal levels of pollution may then differ between regions, owing either to differences in production-pollution relationships or to differences in the valuations placed on other socioeconomic indicators. Any interregional equity problem must be looked for, not directly in terms of differences in recommended environmental standards, but in the initial interregional distribution of production structures, that is, in the *general* economic infrastructures. In view of this, it may be totally inequitable to maintain identical standards across regions (even if the same damage and benefit functions pertained everywhere).

This whole point highlights the biggest gap in the information structure proposed and emphasizes the role of the policymaker. The fact is that there is no "objective" mechanism whereby either regional valuations of the environment can be obtained or standards can be set. It is very significant that Mr. Dreyhaupt states the goals (or standards) of his Clean Air Plan without referring to *how* they were set. It is at this point that value judgment must again explicitly enter the system (as Professor Thoss points out).

In fact, however, its role even here is very often disguised. It could be argued that the approach of setting standards rather than "dreaming up" valuations is more often adopted, since there are at least some objective criteria to which we can refer (e.g., health requirements), even though the two are essentially the same. A major contribution of Professor Thoss's paper is that it *emphasizes* the role of value judgment as a necessary and "*integral part* of the model."

CHAPTER 3

Conceptual Foundations of Regional Environmental Policy

PETER NIJKAMP

I. INTRODUCTION

The last decade has been marked by a rising tide of scientific concern with environmental problems, both at a *global and worldwide scale* and at the *microscale of the daily quality of life*. Economics has tried to keep pace with this development by attempting to offer a framework *for analyzing the environmental economic relationships* and for clarifying *the choice mechanism underlying* the *economic growth-environmental protection dilemma*.

The efforts of economists involved in environmental analysis have resulted into a wide variety of theories and methods focusing on a more appropriate study of environmental problems. In the field of welfare economics the notion of *external effects* developed many decades ago by Alfred Marshall and Arthur Pigou, among others, has shown a revival during the last decade. In spite of its theoretical elegance, the externalities concept has not offered an operational framework for environmental analysis and environmental management, mainly because this concept is relevant only in a free-market system (which does not exist in its pure form). Even applied welfare-theoretic methods such as a social cost-benefit analysis are not able to overcome the frictions inherent in heroic assumptions on atomistic utility-maximizing behavior, flexible tax schemes, perfect information, marginal social costs, fictitious shadow prices, and absence of interest conflicts. Therefore, it may be meaningful to develop a complementary approach that fits better into real-world problems and that may overcome the glaring failures of traditional welfare analyses.

54

The aim of the present paper is to provide a conceptual foundation and a methodology for analyzing choice problems regarding a broad spectrum of social options incorporating *inter alia* growth targets, environmental preservation, energy saving, distributional efficiency, spatial allocation, and so forth. Thus, the paper is addressed to an *integrated choice framework* of socioeconomic, spatial, and environmental phenomena. Furthermore, the spatial aspects of these choice problems will further be taken into account by assuming an integrated interregional model with spatial spillover effects. It will be shown that *multiobjective optimization theory* provides a fruitful frame of reference for an integrated economic-environmental decision analysis. Especially the notion of *displaced ideals* in combination with *interactive* information and learning procedures can be regarded as an operational contribution to environmental economics. This notion will be illustrated for a linear multiregional-environmental-economic model. Some recent advances in nonlinear multiobjective optimization theory will be discussed as well. The paper concludes with an outline of future research.

2. SPATIAL-ENVIRONMENTAL POLICY ANALYSIS: METHODOLOGY

A spatial-environmental policy analysis may place emphasis on a variety of different aspects; for instance, on the availability of relevant policy information, the spatial interaction patterns of policy decisions, the feasibility of spatial-environmental instruments, and so forth. In order to provide a logical framework of analysis and a conceptual basis for integrated policymaking, it may be worthwhile to formulate in advance a set of criteria which have to be fulfilled by an *adequate spatial-environmental policy analysis*. In my opinion, a large set of criteria that constitute an ideal frame of reference are relevant. Clearly, the ideal frame will never be reached precisely by any theory, but it may be extremely worthwhile to keep a certain achievement level in mind. The following criteria may be mentioned *inter alia*: (a) a definition of categories and concepts that is relevant from the viewpoint of economic analysis and environmental management; (b) objectifiable information (including qualitative and ordinal data) that provides a platform for a broader scientific discussion; (c) integration of incommensurable and intangible elements of environmental-economic phenomena (and not only as pollution management items); (d) integration of all broader aspects of environmental choice problems (e.g., allocative efficiency and distributional equity of environmental commodities, interest conflicts among environmental groupings, impacts of uncompensated social costs, etc.); (e) a justification of the scale and scope of the analysis concerned (e.g., a micro-, meso-, or macrolevel), in which also potential differences in scale between environmental and economic analysis are explained; (f) an assessment of the degree of uncertainty and reliability of influences (via stochastic analyses, fuzzy set methods, simulations, risk analyses, etc.); and (g) a description of the relevant planning and policy levels and of all actors involved, as well as a description of all conflicting priorities (e.g., jurisdictional conflicts on nonpriced commodities).

Several of these criteria are also relevant for many other social theories and methods of analysis. It is clear that the above-mentioned criteria need a methodological framework that goes far beyond the traditional neoclassical (Pigouvian) approach to spatial-environmental problems. The absence of the measuring rod of money forces the economist to broaden his view toward a cross-disciplinary approach in which all relevant aspects of spatial and environmental problems are taken into account. It seems to us that there is a wide variety of disciplines that may provide some guiding principles or foundations for a more integrated and comprehensive environmental-economic analysis. The following ingredients for such a broader view may be mentioned briefly:

Physical principles accruing from a static or dynamic materials-balance model (cf. Kneese et al. [1970]). Especially the first law of thermodynamics (the law of loss of low entropy) are extremely useful to indicate that the minimization of throughput (rather than the maximization of throughput) is a meaningful economic paradigm for a society that is reaching its ecological and physical limits to growth.

Ecological principles emerging from an (eco-) systems approach. In this respect, the notions of *energy-food* chains in ecosystems and of *equilibrating forces* in dynamic ecological systems deserve much attention. These notions provide the tools to study the stability of ecosystems. In this respect, the "new paradigm" approach, reflected among others in studies on the "steady-state economy" (cf. Daly [1973]) and on the "fundamental scarcity of low entropy" (cf. Georgescu-Roegen [1971]), rests essentially on ecological principles. Catastrophe theory and bioeconomic theory may also constitute a cornerstone for the analysis of the stability of ecosystems.

Juridical principles associated with the property of goods. Here the notion of common and nonappropriable goods is important to analyze the economic and distributive impacts of environmental policy principles such as the *polluter pays* and the *pollutee pays* principle. Such juridical principles determine to a great extent also the contents of systems of compensation payments and changes (cf. Mishan [1968]).

Sociopsychological principles arising from social choice theory. The modern psychometric perception and preference analyses offer a great perspective to gauge the human need of nonpriced commodities. Especially the recently developed multidimensional scaling techniques are useful instruments to study choices in the field of nonmarket commodities (e.g., physical planning and environmental management; see Nijkamp and Voogd [1978] and Nijkamp [1978c]). Maslow's hypothesis about a *hierarchical ranking of human needs* may also be an important element for environmental analysis in a nonmarket setting.

Social principles related to the social carrying capacity of our society. The notion of "social limits to growth" in a dynamic economy seems to be equally important as the ecological and physical limits to growth (see Hirsch [1976]), because mental health and general well-being do not necessarily run parallel to economic growth (see also Scitovsky [1976]).

Operations research principles resulting from mathematical decision theory. A wide variety of (mainly unpriced) *choice attributes* can be studied in a systematic and comprehensive way by means of modern *multiobjective optimization* methods and multicriteria analyses. By taking into consideration a whole set of relevant decision criteria, a more balanced decision structure may be created in which environmental phenomena may play an essential role (see Delft and Nijkamp [1977] and Nijkamp [1977]).

Spatial-geographical principles resulting from the presence of physical space. Space is a medium through which actions and externalities can be transferred. On the other hand, the limited area of available space may constrain economic activities or intensify environmental decay.

Information-theoretic principles related especially to the collection and storage of relevant data. In addition to the criterion that environmental data should have a greater accessibility and accuracy as they are being used more frequently (the *frequency-probability criterion*), the *intensity criterion* (e.g., the range of an ecological catastrophe) may be used to warrant environmental data collection and storage for a long time series on phenomena with a low probability of occurrence but with an enormous impact.

The foregoing list of different principles and guidelines demonstrates the cross-disciplinary character of problems of an adequate allocation of the "new scarcity" in a spatial-environmental framework. The subsequent sections of this paper will be devoted to constructing an operational spatial-environmental framework that is capable of integrating, in principle, all various and heterogeneous aspects (both priced and nonpriced) of social decision-making in the environmental field, although it has to be admitted that in the short run not all methodological requirements can be met.

3. MULTIREGIONAL AND MULTIDIMENSIONAL WELFARE PROFILES

It has been emphasized by many authors that welfare is not a unidimensional variable but includes a *wide variety of indicators that ultimately make up the economic health of a nation or region.* The *"social indicator move-*

ment" and the *"environmental impact movement"* reflect the fact that welfare is a multidimensional phenomenon that has to be characterized by a large set of underlying variables. Consequently, instead of a scalar welfare indicator a welfare *vector* has to be used. This vector, which will be called a *welfare profile* in the present paper, incorporates *inter alia* socioeconomic and environmental variables. Thus, a welfare profile may be divided into a series of subprofiles such as the (socio-) economic profile (average income, skewness of income, employment, investments, etc.) and the environmental profile (level of pollution, congestion, availability of natural aers, etc.). It is clear that a meaningful description of the level of welfare should be related to an adequate spatial scale (cf. the notion of externality field). Therefore, an appropriate representation of multidimensional welfare in a spatial system requires a matrix **W** (see Hafkamp and Nijkamp [1978]), which gives a quantitative description of the actual state of the welfare elements of the regional economics:

$$\mathbf{W} = \begin{matrix} & \overbrace{1 \ldots R} \\ 1 \\ \vdots \\ N \end{matrix} \begin{bmatrix} & \\ & w_{nr} \\ & \end{bmatrix} \tag{3.1}$$

where w_{nr} represents the level of variable $n\,(n = 1, \ldots, N)$ in region $r\,(r = 1, \ldots, R)$. Clearly, all N variables n are measured in different dimensions.

It should be noted that the elements of **W** are not completely independent: they are simultaneously determined by the evolution of the whole spatial system. Therefore, a proper analysis of the interdependencies in such a system requires the construction of an *interregional model* that links all variables together and that can be used to predict in a comprehensive manner the development of a set of spatial profiles:

$$\mathbf{W} = F(W, E), \tag{3.2}$$

where E stands for a matrix including exogenous variables and instrumental variables.

If such a model is to be used as a *policy model*, one may add to it a set of *side conditions* in order to control the spatial system within predetermined levels $\mathbf{W}^{\min}$ and $\mathbf{W}^{\max}$:

$$\mathbf{W}^{\min} \leqslant \mathbf{W} \leqslant \mathbf{W}^{\max} \tag{3.3}$$

Furthermore, one has to introduce a *criterion function* (an objective function or social preference function) on the basis of which a policymaker may judge the feasibility and desirability of a certain state of welfare:

$$\max \omega = \omega(\mathbf{W}) \tag{3.4}$$

Sometimes it may be more appropriate to use a *multidimensional* criterion function in order to take account of the variety of preferences in political decision-making (see for an extensive exposition Delft and Nijkamp [1977]).

Another question which has to be considered is: How are discrepancies between spatial profiles to be measured?

First of all, one should be able to rank the outcomes w_{nr} by means of an (implicit) rank criterion. For example, up to a certain limit more employment is better than less employment; more pollution is worse than less pollution; and so on.

Next, one may carry out a *standardization* of the elements of the welfare profile in order to obtain comparable units of measurement (see also Paelinck and Nijkamp [1976]). The following standardization, which proved to be rather appropriate, will be used here (see also Nijkamp and Rietveld [1978]).

$$z_{nr} = \frac{w_{nr} - w_n^{min}}{w_n^{max} - w_n^{min}} \qquad \text{if } n \text{ is a benefit criterion} \qquad (3.5)$$

and:

$$z_{nr} = \frac{w_n^{max} - w_n}{w_n^{max} - w_n^{min}} \qquad \text{if } n \text{ is a cost criterion,} \qquad (3.6)$$

where w_n^{min} and w_n^{max} are defined as:

$$w_n^{min} = \min_r w_{nr} \qquad (3.7)$$

and:

$$w_n^{max} = \max_r w_{nr} \qquad (3.8)$$

Now, it is easily seen that $0 \leqslant z_{nr} \leqslant 1$. Moreover, it is clear that the most desirable state of a profile variable implies $z_{nr} = 1$, and the less desirable state $z_{nr} = 0$. Especially for the computational stage of a model such a standardization is rather efficient.

Then the *dicrepancy* $d_{rr'}$ between the spatial profiles of any pair of regions r and r' can be measured as:

$$d_{rr'} = \sum_{n=1}^{N} |z_{nr} - z_{nr'}| \qquad (3.9)$$

or as a more general Minkowski matrix:

$$d_{rr'} = \left\{ \sum_{n=1}^{N} |z_{nr} - z_{nr'}|^\lambda \right\}^{1/\lambda}, \qquad \lambda \geqslant 0 \qquad (3.10)$$

Clearly, the elements of the discrepancy index can also be *weighed*, provided information is available on the trade-offs between these elements (see for a broader discussion on this subject Blommestein et al. [1978]). It should be noted that the absolute level of a discrepancy index has no meaning; only its relative value with respect to other states of the economy is relevant.

Now, the next section will be devoted to the way in which the elements of a spatial welfare profile can be linked together in an environmental policy model.

4. INTERACTIVE MULTIDIMENSIONAL COMPROMISE POLICY MODELS

In the preceding section a systematic framework for representing welfare profiles was presented. So far, however, no attention has been paid to political priorities, welfare choices, or optimizing behavior.

It is generally accepted that policymakers and planners have to base their decisions on a multiplicity of criteria (efficiency criteria, equity criteria, social criteria, ecological criteria, etc.). Hence, in addition to a careful examination of the set of feasible solutions, decision makers have to evaluate the various alternative solutions. The existence of multiple decision criteria, the limited availability of information, the uncertainty about the set of feasible alternatives, and the gradually developing institutional procedures of decision and planning strategies usually preclude a straightforward application of traditional optimality principles.

In the present section this problem will be attacked by introducing the following elements in a political evaluation procedure:

(a) The presence of multiple objective functions. For each element of the welfare profile described in section 3 a corresponding objective function will be assumed. For example, one may assume maximization of production *and* minimization of pollution. A further analysis of these problems requires the application of some principles from multiobjective decision theory (see Delft and Nijkamp [1977] and Nijkamp [1978b]).

(b) The presence of an interactive choice strategy. Owing to uncertainty and limited information, the choice-making process is a *learning* procedure. This implies that information about the set of feasible alternatives is provided in a stepwise way to the decision maker so that he may formulate certain priorities regarding the outcome of the decision procedure. The latter information is used to truncate the set of feasible solutions and to specify some trial solutions that may again be judged by the decision maker. This procedure can be repeated until finally a (convergent) compromise solution can be identified.

In the context of decision models, a multidimensional view of welfare leads to a plea for multiobjective optimization models, in which multiple (conflicting) objective functions are to be optimized simultaneously. The reasons for the existence of multiple objective functions may be: The presence of noncommensurable objectives, the presence of different interest groupings, or the presence of spillover effects.

In general formal terms, a multiobjective optimization model may be represented as:

$$\begin{cases} \max \boldsymbol{\omega}(x) \\ x \in K \end{cases} \tag{4.1}$$

where $\boldsymbol{\omega}(x)$ is a vector of objective functions, x a vector of decision variables, and K a feasible area.

There is a large set of methods to analyze and solve these types of decision models (an extensive survey of the literature in this field is contained in Delft and Nijkamp [1977] and Nijkamp [1977]). A central role in multiobjective optimization theory is played by the concept of a Pareto solution[1] (or noninferior, efficient, or nondominated solution). A Pareto solution reflects the common feature of multiobjective optimization models that the value of the one objective function cannot be improved without affecting the values of the remaining objective functions. Such a solution shows the conflicting nature of these models: any feasible point that is not dominated by other points can be regarded as a Pareto solution.

In formal terms, a Pareto solution can be defined as follows: a Pareto solution is a vector x^* for which no other feasible solution vector x does exist such that:

$$\begin{cases} \omega(x) \geqslant \omega(x^*) \\ \text{and} \\ \omega_j(x) \neq \omega_j(x^*), \qquad \text{for at least one } j \end{cases} \tag{4.2}$$

It has been proved, among others, by Geoffrion [1968] and Kuhn and Tucker [1968], that a feasible solution is a Pareto solution x^*, if and only if a vector of weights $\boldsymbol{\lambda}$ does exist (with $\iota'\boldsymbol{\lambda} = 1$ and $\boldsymbol{\lambda} \geqslant 0$), such that x^* is the optimal solution of the following unidimensional program:

$$\begin{cases} \max \pi = \boldsymbol{\lambda}'\{\boldsymbol{\omega}(x)\} \\ x \in K \end{cases} \tag{4.3}$$

---

1. It should be noted that the concept of a Pareto solution in multiobjective theory has nothing to do with the Pareto solution from social welfare theory (apart from a vague similarity). The Pareto solutions discussed here are technical solutions: given a certain model and a set of objective functions, the Pareto frontier can always be identified (at least in principle).

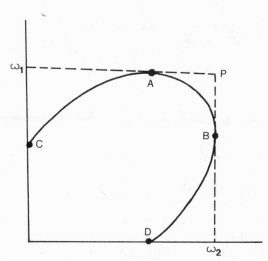

Figure 3-1. A functional space with the efficiency frontier of two objectives.

By means of a parametrization of λ the whole set of Parento solutions can, in principle, be determined, although in practice the algorithms for determining this set appear to be rather time-consuming. Since the vector λ is a set of weights associated with each Pareto solution, it plays an important role in determining an ultimate equilibrium or compromise solution of a multiobjective model, particularly because any good solution of a multiobjective decision model should, by definition, be a Pareto solution.

A figurative representation of the set of Pareto solutions (the efficiency frontier) is contained in Figure 3-1, based on two objective functions.

A closer examination of Figure 3-1 leads to the conclusion that only the points on the edge between A and B are relevant Pareto points, because: (1) all interior points are dominated by the points on the edge; (2) all points on the edges CA and DB are dominated by point A and B, respectively; and (3) no point on the edge AB dominates any other point on this edge.

Point P of Figure 3-1 can be regarded as the *ideal point*, which is used as a reference point for evaluating the points on the efficiency frontier. One may assume that the ultimate equilibrium (compromise) solution is that point which has a minimum discrepancy with respect to P.[2] This minimum discrepancy can be measured by means of a Minkowski metric ψ. This gives rise

---

2. This assumption is based on the plausible notion that rational decision-making attempts to minimize the distance between the reality (the range of feasible alternatives) and the ideal (but normally unfeasible) situation.

to the following compromise model (cf. also [3.10]):

$$
\begin{cases}
\min \psi = \left\{ \sum_{j=1}^{J} (1 - \hat{\omega}_j)^\nu \right\}^{1/\nu} \\
\hat{\omega}_j = \dfrac{\omega_j(x) - \omega_j^{\min}}{\omega_j^{\max} - \omega_j^{\min}} \quad , \\
x \in K
\end{cases}
\tag{4.4}
$$

where $\hat{\omega}_j$ is the standardized value of objective function ω_j.

The solution of this compromise model can be calculated by applying nonlinear programming techniques. When $\nu = 1$ or $\nu = 2$, (4.4) can be directly solved by means of linear and quadratic programming algorithms, respectively.

In many decision procedures, however, the first compromise is not regarded as the final equilibrium solution, so that a certain *interactive* learning procedure has to be developed in order to reach such a final solution in a series of steps. Thus, the provisional solution has to be presented to the decision maker as a trial solution that has to be judged by him. The decision maker has to indicate which objective functions are to be improved and which give already satisfactory results.

Let us denote now the set of objective functions that are to be increased in value by S, so that the decision maker's preferences can be taken into account by specifying the following constraint:

$$
\omega_j(x) \geqslant \overline{\omega}_j(x) \qquad \forall\, j \in S
\tag{4.5}
$$

In consequence, the following model has to be solved:

$$
\begin{cases}
\max \boldsymbol{\omega}(x) \\
x \in K \\
\omega_j(x) \geqslant \overline{\omega}_j(x) \qquad \forall\, j \in S
\end{cases}
\tag{4.6}
$$

Given the latter new multiobjective programming model, a new ideal point P_1 can be calculated in a way analogous to the first phase. Clearly, this displacement of the ideal point is due to condition (4.5). After the calculation of the new ideal point, a new compromise solution can be determined by means of (4.4), and so on, until finally a satisfying compromise is attained. The various successive steps are briefly represented in Figure 3-2. It has to be emphasized that the minimum distance procedure is an unweighted procedure; during a set of iterative steps a compromise is attained. Therefore, the interactive learning character of this procedure is essential in order to

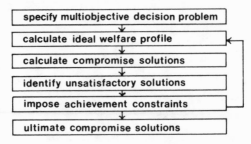

Figure 3-2. Representation of the steps of an interactive multiobjective decision model.

prevent a policymaker from taking biased decisions on the basis of a single-step choice algorithm.

Clearly, a consistent decision maker would reach the same compromise on the basis of alternative methods (such as game methods).

This method of *displaced ideals* originally developed by Zeleny (1976) can be regarded as one of the most practical interactive multiobjective decision techniques. This procedure implies that instead of the optimizer concept a "satisficer" concept is used, so that the ultimate compromise result complies with certain achievement levels specified by the decision maker (cf. also Simon [1957]). Such compromise policy models are extremely important for environmental policy problems in which usually a certain compromise between diverging options (e.g., maximum production, minimum pollution, and minimum energy use) has to be found. These interactive multiobjective programming models provide a conceptual and operational basis for compromise principles in integrated environmental-economic decision-making.[3]

5. SPATIAL ASPECTS OF ENVIRONMENTAL POLICY

As exposed above, the elements of a spatial multidimensional welfare profile are not independent with respect to each other. Both at the *intra*regional and the *inter*regional level there is a high degree of mutual interaction owing to sectoral linkages, technical relationships, behavioral conditions, spatial spillovers, and diffusion of pollutants. Consequently, any decision in the one region will affect the welfare profile in other regions. For example, a rise in production in region A or a shift from natural gas to oil in electricity plants in region A will lead to a change in the spatial pollution pattern, so that the welfare pattern of a surrounding region B is affected by production

---

3. It is clear that, once a certain compromise solution has been found, the corresponding trade-offs can be identified as well.

and technology changes in region A. This can be formalized as follows:

$$\mathbf{w}_r = \mathbf{f}(\mathbf{w}_1, \ldots, \mathbf{w}_r, \ldots, \mathbf{w}_R), \tag{5.1}$$

where $\mathbf{w}_r$ represents the $(N \times 1)$ welfare profile of region r $(r = 1, \ldots, R)$. Assuming a linear intraregional and interregional impact system (e.g., an input-output model, linear emission and diffusion models, etc.), one may write (5.1) in an integrated way as:

$$\mathbf{w} = A\mathbf{w} + \mathbf{c}, \tag{5.2}$$

where $\mathbf{w}$ is a long-stretched vector of order $RN \times 1$ and where $\mathbf{c}$ is an exogenous vector. Clearly, in this case the following multiplier system is obtained:

$$\mathbf{w} = (I - A)^{-1}\mathbf{c}, \tag{5.3}$$

provided the matrix with impact coefficients A is nonsingular.

Since the elements of the welfare profile are the constituents of the vector of regional objective functions, there is essentially a double conflict in case of a simultaneous maximization of all regional objective functions within the spatial system at hand: (1) there is a direct conflict between objectives *within* one region (e.g., production versus environmental quality); and (2) there is an indirect conflict between objectives belonging to different regions (e.g., environmental quality of region A versus abatement efforts in region B). This double conflict is represented schematically in Figure 3-3.

Environmental quality in a polluted region clearly affects environmental quality in an adjacent clean region. This implies that the achievement values of the regional welfare variables show a high degree of interdependence. This "keeping-up-with-the-Joneses" phenomenon introduces a dynamic element in the method of displaced ideals described earlier. It is plausible to assume that the ideal value of objective n in region f in period t is a fraction of the difference between the value of objective n in period $t - 1$ and the maximum value of this objective over all regions in period $t - 1$, that is,

$$\Delta\omega_{nr,t} = \alpha_{nr} \,|\omega_{nr,t-1} - \omega_{n,t-1}^{max}| \tag{5.4}$$

Model (5.4) constitutes the cornerstone for the regional assessment of trial-and-error solutions presented during the interactive decision procedure. It is clear that this situation incorporates many dynamic elements, because the reference pattern for judging provisional solutions may change over time owing to the dynamics of an interregional system in which growing and lagging regions may change positions. This also leads to a situation of *displaced ideals* in a dynamic sense.

This situation is sketched in Figure 3-4, in which for a simple two-region case a hypothetical dynamic impact pattern of the first objective over both regions is presented (see also Figure 3-3).

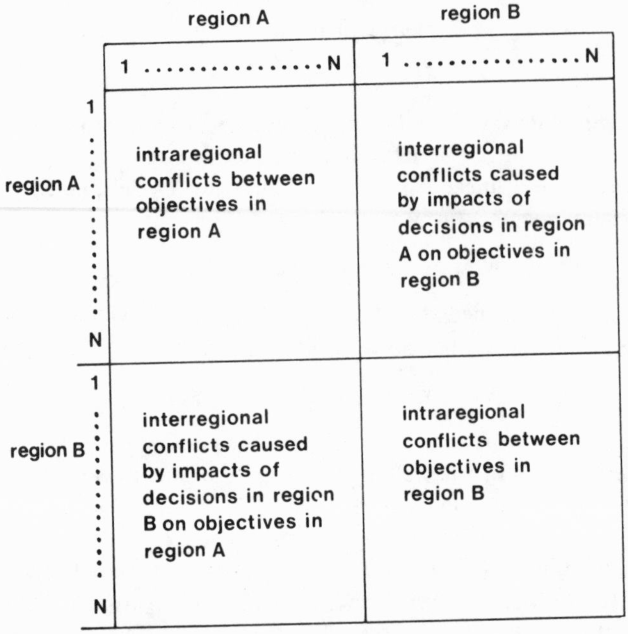

	region A	region B
	1 ....N	1 ....N
region A 1 ⋮ N	intraregional conflicts between objectives in region A	interregional conflicts caused by impacts of decisions in region A on objectives in region B
region B 1 ⋮ N	interregional conflicts caused by impacts of decisions in region B on objectives in region A	intraregional conflicts between objectives in region B

Figure 3-3. A conflict scheme between and within regions A and B.

The foregoing analysis once more shows that an *optimal* allocation of resources, production, and pollution over a set of regions is almost a metaphysical question. Instead of traditional allocative efficiency, it is more reasonable to use the notions of compromises and displaced ideals to arrive

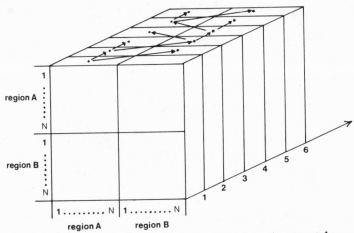

Figure 3-4. Displaced ideals in an interregional environmental-economic setting.

at an operational and plausible description and analysis of spatial environ-mental-economic policies.

So far, no attention has been paid to specific policy instruments to control the interregional developments. The foregoing analysis also indicated that a regional differentiation of these instruments is necessary in order to arrive at compromise solutions that are satisfactory for all regions of the spatial sys-tem. This holds true both for a system of charges (e.g., emission taxes) and for a system of standards (e.g., emission norms). It is clear that the choice for the use of these instruments may be based on both effectiveness and effi-ciency criteria (see Nijkamp [1977]), but this problem is essentially also a multiobjective policy problem that has to be solved in relation to, and simul-taneously with, the above-mentioned multiobjective decision models. The notion of compromise principles applies here as well, as can also be observed from the mixed standard-charge systems for environmental management in many countries.

6. AN EMPIRICAL ILLUSTRATION

The notions of compromise solutions and displaced ideals associated with interactive multiobjective optimization will now be illustrated on the basis of an interregional multisectoral model developed for the Rhine delta region near Rotterdam (see ESSOR [1977]; Hafkamp and Nijkamp [1978]; Werf [1977]). This model contains *inter alia* input-output relationships, labor and investment relationships, and emission relationships. The structure of the model is kept rather simple in order to comply with the need of an opera-tional approach to a multiobjective decision problem placed in the framework of interactive choice strategies. The input-output model is a full information input-output model (incorporating all interregional flows); it was constructed for two regions, namely, the Rhine delta area (R) and the remaining part of the Netherlands (N), and included twenty-seven sectors. A full description of the model can be found in the above-mentioned references; in this chapter, only the schematic structure of the model will be presented (see Figure 3-5) in order to serve the illustrative purposes of this section. Clearly, the spatial scale of this model is still fairly aggregate, and the integration of ecological and land-use variables is still missing here; but this model may be satisfactory to demonstrate the use of welfare profiles and multidimensional optimization in environmental analyses.

The dashed lines represent *inter*regional linkages, namely input-output relationships and pollution relationships. This model can easily be extended with final demand relationship, price and tax relationships, capacity con-straints, labor market conditions, pollution standards, and the like. The lat-ter problem of imposing political constraints on the working of the model will now be further discussed in relation to a multiobjective policy approach.

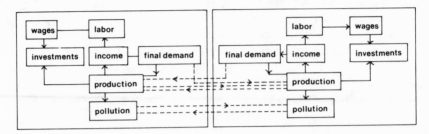

Figure 3-5. Schematic representation of a two-region environmental-economic model.

The assumption will be made that there are two conflicting policy objectives: maximization of production (q) *and* minimization of pollution (p). Clearly, a simultaneous optimization of these objective functions will lead to contradictory results. Therefore, it may be worthwhile to apply the concept of a compromise solution discussed in section 4 and next to employ an interactive procedure in order to find a satisficing solution after a series of displaced ideals. According to the exposition of multiobjective decision models presented in section 4, the first step of the analysis is to calculate the outcomes of a separate optimization of the objective functions for both regions R and N. The results, taken from a more extensive study of Hafkamp and Nijkamp (1978), are included in Table 3-1. These results demonstrate that the minimization of pollution leads to a significantly lower level of production, than a maximization of production, and vice versa.[4]

On the basis of Table 3-1 the ideal solutions can be identified directly: the first columns of regions R and N represent the ideal production profile, while the last columns of regions R and N represent the ideal pollution profile. Given these ideal solutions, a first compromise solution can be calculated (see Table 3-2). These results show that the compromise solution is equal to the solution of the minimum pollution program (see Table 3-1). This is due to the fact that the model has a linear structure with constant production coefficients, so that a minimization of pollution implies also a minimization of production. Consequently, the scores on the distance function for the compromise procedure are equal, so that a minimization of this function corresponds to a minimum pollution level. It is clear that in a medium- and

---

4. Pollution is measured here as the unweighted aggregate pollution (10^3 tons per year) over four types of pollutants. Production is measured in 10^3 man-years. Clearly, the aggregation of pollutants is not necessary, but this aggregation facilitates the interpretation of the illustrative results given in Tables 3-1—3-3.

Table 3-1. Results of a separate optimization of objective functions.

| | Region R | | | | | Region N | | | |
| | max q | | min p | | | max q | | min p | |
Sectors	q_R	p_R	q_R	p_R	Sectors	q_N	p_N	q_N	p_N
1	0.386	2.404	0.316	1.996	1	14.213	88.409	11.629	72.332
2	0.000	0.000	0.000	0.000	2	0.448	1.970	0.367	1.611
3	0.015	0.392	0.012	0.320	3	0.345	9.207	0.282	7.524
4	0.379	1.162	0.310	0.952	4	10.057	30.877	8.229	25.263
5	1.760	8.995	1.440	7.358	5	12.979	66.324	10.619	54.263
6	0.668	2.029	0.546	1.660	6	3.014	9.162	2.466	7.497
7	0.060	0.175	0.049	0.144	7	4.778	14.047	3.909	11.492
8	0.059	0.189	0.049	0.156	8	2.211	7.054	1.809	5.771
9	0.006	0.018	0.005	0.016	9	0.744	2.374	0.609	1.943
10	0.128	1.030	0.105	0.844	10	2.528	20.322	2.068	16.771
11	0.124	0.999	0.102	0.820	11	2.379	19.124	1.946	15.646
12	0.358	2.876	0.293	2.356	12	4.248	34.152	3.476	27.947
13	8.767	24.461	7.173	20.013	13	11.538	32.190	9.439	26.335
14	0.174	3.069	0.142	2.508	14	3.019	53.308	2.470	43.620
15	1.389	2.972	1.136	2.431	15	18.289	39.139	14.964	32.023
16	1.651	41.636	1.351	34.072	16	13.386	337.760	10.952	276.209
17	0.473	24.934	0.387	12.678	17	4.684	247.107	3.832	125.536
18	2.018	20.340	1.651	16.642	18	18.191	183.363	14.883	150.021
19	3.498	21.265	2.862	17.401	19	25.856	157.204	21.154	128.616
20	4.972	22.272	4.068	18.225	20	104.606	468.633	8.559	38.344
21	0.826	2.461	0.676	2.014	21	30.459	90.768	2.492	7.426
22	0.822	2.449	0.672	2.003	22	74.020	220.579	6.056	18.047
23	0.433	1.290	0.354	1.005	23	51.229	152.663	4.191	12.488
24	0.074	0.221	0.061	0.182	24	9.893	29.482	0.809	2.411
25	0.318	0.000	0.260	0.000	25	37.393	0.000	3.059	0.000
26	0.014	0.000	0.115	0.000	26	10.903	0.000	0.892	0.000
27	0.000	0.000	0.000	0.000	27	0.000	0.000	0.000	0.000

long-term decision model the assumption of fixed technical parameters may be relaxed. This problem is dealt with in section 7.

So far, no political priority has been taken into account (except coefficients, so that a minimization of pollution implies also a minimization of the choice of the relevant set of objective functions).

Next, one may turn to the second stage of the interactive multiobjective programming model. Assume that the nation as a whole wants to increase the employment levels such that the sectoral unemployment rates in both regions do not exceed 5 percent. This side condition can be incorporated as a constraint in model (4.6.), so that a new run of the model can be carried out. Clearly, the employment objective leads again to the same results as in Table 3-1, but the pollution objective leads to a higher level of pollution

Table 3-2. A first compromise solution.

Sectors	Region R		Region N	
	q_R	p_R	q_N	p_N
1	0.316	1.966	11.629	72.322
2	0.000	0.000	0.367	1.611
3	0.012	0.320	0.282	7.524
4	0.310	0.952	8.229	25.263
5	1.440	7.358	10.619	54.263
6	0.546	1.660	2.466	7.497
7	0.049	0.144	3.909	11.492
8	0.049	0.156	1.809	5.771
9	0.005	0.016	0.609	1.943
10	0.105	0.844	2.068	16.771
11	0.102	0.820	1.946	15.646
12	0.293	2.356	3.476	27.947
13	7.173	20.013	9.439	26.335
14	0.142	2.508	2.470	43.620
15	1.136	2.431	14.964	32.023
16	1.351	34.072	10.952	276.209
17	0.387	12.678	3.832	125.536
18	1.651	16.642	14.883	150.021
19	2.862	17.401	21.154	128.616
20	4.068	18.225	8.559	38.344
21	0.676	2.014	2.492	7.426
22	0.672	2.003	6.056	18.047
23	0.354	1.005	4.191	12.489
24	0.061	0.182	0.809	2.411
25	0.260	0.000	3.059	0.000
26	0.115	0.000	0.892	0.000
27	0.000	0.000	0.000	0.000

(owing to the higher employment constraints). Given these results, a new compromise solution can be calculated, and so forth. In this way, a final converging solution can be derived. Clearly, several alternative experiments and scenarios can be constructed to generate satisficing compromise solutions (cf. the Dutch selective investment laws).

Multiobjective policy models are also extremely useful to analyze hierarchical decision problems for a spatial system composed of a nation, a set of regions, and a set of local communities. The coordination problems of an

Table 3-3. Results of an employment option in the second stage of interactive procedure in case of a separate minimization of pollution.*

Sectors	Region R		Region N	
	q_R	p_R	q_N	p_N
1	0.334	2.076	12.275	76.354
2	0.000	0.000	0.388	1.702
3	0.013	0.347	0.298	7.940
4	0.329	1.010	8.686	26.667
5	1.520	7.769	11.218	57.282
6	0.577	1.753	2.603	7.913
7	0.052	0.152	4.127	12.132
8	0.051	0.164	1.910	6.091
9	0.005	0.016	0.643	2.051
10	0.111	0.892	2.183	17.555
11	0.107	0.863	2.187	17.582
12	0.309	2.485	3.669	29.495
13	7.572	21.126	9.964	27.800
14	0.150	2.651	2.322	41.003
15	1.199	2.566	15.795	33.802
16	1.426	35.959	11.561	291.561
17	0.427	22.529	4.049	213.546
18	1.743	17.568	15.864	159.904
19	3.020	18.363	22.330	135.769
20	4.294	19.235	9.034	40.472
21	0.714	2.126	2.631	7.839
22	0.710	2.115	6.393	19.050
23	0.382	1.137	4.424	13.185
24	0.064	0.192	0.854	2.546
25	0.275	0.000	3.230	0.000
26	0.121	0.000	0.945	0.000
27	0.000	0.000	0.000	0.000

*It is clear that the ideal production profiles are here again equal to those included in Table 3-1, while the new ideal pollution profiles are made up by the second and fourth column of Table 3-3.

integrated policy framework at different levels (with conflicting priorities) can also be analyzed and solved via interactive multiobjective learning models. In schematic form, this may be represented as shown in Figure 3-6. These types of models can also be used in a simulation framework.

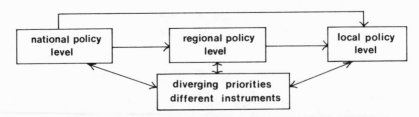

Figure 3-6. An integrated control system for hierarchical environmental decision-making.

It is clear that the priorities and policy instruments for environmental management are codetermined by data about the state of the economy. In this respect, it is worthwhile to create a series of scenarios about expected developments (e.g., a further decrease of world trade, a sharp rise in energy prices, a continuation of economic growth, etc.). Each of these scenarios gives rise to a certain ultimate outcome of the multiobjective policy model. Even when these types of models would not lead to a direct political choice in favor of a certain solution, these multiobjective methods are extremely useful in demonstrating the impacts of alternative policies so that they may rationalize the decision process.

7. EXTENSION TOWARD NONLINEAR ENVIRONMENTAL-ECONOMIC MODELS

The major part of environmental-economic models have a linear structure. Although this is conceivable from a practical point of view, it may sometimes be worthwhile to include nonlinearities (e.g., in production technology, in abatement technology, and in pollution diffusion). The present section will show that in this case the application of geometric programming theory may be helpful to solve nonlinear models (expositions on geometric programming can be found, among others, in Duffin et al. [1967] and Nijkamp [1972, 1978a]).

In order to facilitate the exposition on the use of geometric programming, a simple model will be presented based again on two conflicting objectives: maximization of production and minimization of pollution.

The supporters of economic growth want to maximize production q, that is,

$$\max \phi_1 = q \qquad (7.1)$$

The production is assumed to be related to productive investments i by means of a nonlinear technological function incorporating scale advantages, that is,

$$q = \alpha i^{\beta}, \qquad \beta > 1 \qquad (7.2)$$

The environmentalists aim at maximizing environmental quality e, that is,

$$\max \phi_2 = e \qquad (7.3)$$

This objective function can be operationalized by assuming that environmental quality can be improved by spending a large part of available resources to the preservation of environmental commodities (such as abatement investments) and to the creation of natural areas. By denoting these environmental investments by z, the second objective function may now be written as:

$$\max \phi_2 = \theta z^\mu, \qquad (7.4)$$

where the assumption is made that environmental quality is related in the following way to environmental investments:

$$e = \theta z^\mu, \qquad \mu \leqslant 1 \qquad (7.5)$$

The latter relationships indicates that every decrease in environmental quality (caused by an increase in production or consumption) may be compensated by environmental investments. The meaning of this assumption can be illustrated by assuming the existence of a certain pollution emission relationship (see Nijkamp [1977]). The pollution is assumed to be related to the production by means of a nonlinear emission function:

$$p = \gamma q^\delta, \qquad \delta \leqslant 1 \qquad (7.6)$$

Next, the assumption is made that the emission coefficient γ can be influenced by implementing abatement investments z, that is,

$$\gamma = \eta z^{-\epsilon} \qquad (7.7)$$

Substitution of (4.6.) into (4.5.) yields the result:

$$p = \eta z^{-\epsilon} q^\delta, \qquad (7.8)$$

so that any increase in emission of pollution can be reduced by implementing more abatement investments.

Clearly, the maximum of (7.1.) would be infinite if there would be no constraints on the investments. Similarly, the maximum of ϕ_2 would be infinite if there were no constraints on the available resources. Therefore, it is plausible to assume an upper limit t for the total investment budget that may be allocated between productive investments and environmental investments, that is,

$$i + z \leqslant t \qquad (7.9)$$

The variables i and z may be regarded as the decision variables that determine the value of the arguments of the urban (or regional) welfare profile, namely, q and e. The decision space is represented in Figure 3-7. It is clear

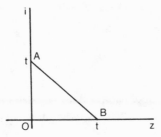

Figure 3-7. Decision space of productive and abatement investments.

that a maximization of (7.1.) subject to (7.9.) will give A as the optimal solution. The maximization of (7.3.) subject to (7.9.) obviously leads to B as the optimal solution; the compromise may be located somewhere on AB.

A compromise solution between maximum growth and maximum environmental quality can be formally found by using the idea of a multiobjective programming analysis set out in section 4.

By applying the idea of a *geometric* parameterization of the objective functions (see [4.3]), the following geometric programming model associated with the above-mentioned model can be specified:

$$\begin{cases} \max \phi = \phi_1^{\lambda_1} \phi_2^{\lambda_2} \\ \text{s.t. (7.9.)} \end{cases} \tag{7.10}$$

where λ_1 and λ_2 are the parametric weights (elasticities). The latter objective model can be rewritten in a standard geometric programming format as:

$$\begin{aligned} \min \dot{\phi} = \phi^{-1} &= \phi_1^{-\lambda_1} \phi_2^{-\lambda_2} \\ &= \alpha^{-\lambda_1} i^{-\beta\lambda_1} \theta^{-\lambda_2} z^{-\mu\lambda_2} \\ &= \alpha^* i^{-\beta\lambda_1} z^{-\kappa\lambda_2} \end{aligned} \tag{7.11}$$

where:

$$\alpha^* = \alpha^{-\lambda_1} \theta^{-\lambda_2} \tag{7.12}$$

Obviously, a high value of i and z will lead to a low value of $\dot{\phi}$. Finally, the following model can be obtained.

$$\begin{cases} \min \dot{\phi} = \alpha^* i^{-\beta\lambda_1} z^{-\kappa\lambda_2} \\ \text{s.t.} \\ t^{-1} i + t^{-1} z \leqslant 1 \end{cases} \tag{7.13}$$

which corresponds to a standard geometric programming model. According to geometric programming theory, the dual constraints of this model can be written as:

$$
\begin{bmatrix}
1 & 0 & 0 \\
-\beta\lambda_1 & 1 & 0 \\
-\kappa\lambda_2 & 0 & 1
\end{bmatrix}
\begin{bmatrix}
v_1^0 \\
v_1^1 \\
v_2^1
\end{bmatrix}
=
\begin{bmatrix}
1 \\
0 \\
0
\end{bmatrix}
\tag{7.14}
$$

The number of degrees of freedom of these dual constraints appears to be equal to 0, so that the dual variables can be directly solved from (7.14.) by means of a simple matrix inversion. This leads to the following result:

$$
\begin{bmatrix}
v_1^0 \\
v_1^1 \\
v_2^1
\end{bmatrix}
=
\begin{bmatrix}
1 & 0 & 0 \\
-\beta\lambda_1 & 1 & 0 \\
-\kappa\lambda_2 & 0 & 1
\end{bmatrix}^{-1}
\begin{bmatrix}
1 \\
0 \\
0
\end{bmatrix}
=
\begin{bmatrix}
1 \\
\beta\lambda_1 \\
\kappa\lambda_2
\end{bmatrix}
\tag{7.15}
$$

According to the primal-dual geometric relationships, the following optimal solutions of the variables i and z can be derived:

$$
i^0 = \frac{\beta\lambda_1}{\beta\lambda_1 + \kappa\lambda_2} \, t
\tag{7.16}
$$

and

$$
z^0 = \frac{\kappa\lambda_2}{\beta\lambda_1 + \kappa\lambda_2} \, t
\tag{7.17}
$$

By means of a parametrization of (7.10.), the efficiency frontier of the objective functions ϕ_1 and ϕ_2 can, in principle, be determined (see Figure 3-7). This figure demonstrates that by means of new multiobjective programming techniques, in principle, an ultimate compromise solution can be identified.

Our conclusion is thus that nonlinear optimization models describing conflicts between diverging objectives can be attacked by means of generalized multiobjective polynomial models.

The ideal point P of Figure 3-8 (with coordinates q^* and e^*) can now be

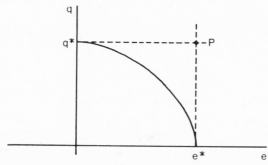

Figure 3-8. The efficiency frontier of q and e.

used as a frame of reference for an interactive approach based on a successive series of displaced ideals. This implies that a trial solution has to be identified that is calculated by means of a Minkowski metric for a minimum discrepancy between the ideal point and the efficiency frontier. Therefore, the following program has to be solved (see also [4.4.]):

$$\begin{cases} \min \psi = \{(1 - \pi_q)^\nu + (1 - \pi_e)^\nu\}^{1/\nu} \\[2mm] \text{s.t.} \\[2mm] \pi_q = \dfrac{\phi_1 - \phi_1^{\min}}{\phi_1^{\max} - \phi_1^{\min}} \\[4mm] \pi_e = \dfrac{\phi_2 - \phi_2^{\min}}{\phi_2^{\max} - \phi_2^{\min}} \\[4mm] \phi_1 = \alpha i^\beta \\[2mm] \phi_2 = \theta z^\kappa \\[2mm] i + z \leqslant t \end{cases} \qquad (7.18)$$

where $\phi_1^{\min}$ and $\phi_2^{\min}$ are the minimum feasible values of ϕ_1 and ϕ_2, respectively, and $\phi_1^{\max}$ $(= q^*)$ and $\phi_2^{\max}$ $(= e^*)$ the maximum feasible values of ϕ_1 and ϕ_2, respectively.

The latter program is again a *geometric* program, as can easily be seen by rewriting (7.18.) as:

$$\begin{cases} \min \psi = r^{1/\nu} \\[2mm] r^{-1} r_q^\nu + r^{-1} r_e^\nu = 1 \\[2mm] r_q + \pi_q = 1 \\[2mm] r_e + \pi_e = 1 \\[2mm] (\phi_1^{\max} - \phi_1^{\min}) \pi_q \phi_1^{-1} + \phi_1^{\min} \phi_1^{-1} = 1 \\[2mm] (\phi_2^{\max} - \phi_2^{\min}) \pi_e \phi_2^{-1} + \phi_2^{\min} \phi_2^{-1} = 1 \\[2mm] t^{-1} i + t^{-1} z \leqslant 1 \\[2mm] \phi_1 = \alpha i^\beta \\[2mm] \phi_2 = \theta z^\mu \end{cases} \qquad (7.19)$$

The latter program can be solved by means of standard geometric (polynomial) programming techniques. The solution of this program is a point somewhere on the efficiency frontier of Figure 3-7 and will be denoted by $\hat{q}_1$ and $\hat{e}_1$. This trial solution may be used as a tool in an interactive environmental decision-making process: the only information needed concerns the question of which value of the trial solutions is not satisfactory. This gives rise to a new constraint that may be added to (7.13.) (see also section 4). Consequently, a (horizontal or vertical) *displacement* of the ideal solution P toward the axis of the satisfactory solution takes place. Then the procedure may be repeated again and again, until finally a converging compromise solution is attained.

Our conclusion is that geometric programming models may be useful tools for interactive decision models based on the method of displaced ideals.

8. CONCLUSION

The foregoing sections aimed at providing a logical and operational framework for environmental decision-making. The aim of the paper has not been to demonstrate the failure of the traditional Pigouvian approach to externalities but to show the relevance and operationality of a broader integrated approach based on a cross-disciplinary multicriteria analysis. I am convinced that this approach, which has demonstrated its operational character in several environmental studies in the United States, France, and the Netherlands, offers a new perspective for environmental economics. This approach is especially useful to treat complicated economic-environmental systems in a logical and systematic manner and to reduce them to reasonable and manageable dimensions. Progress in future environmental policy research may be expected when at least the following conditions are fulfilled: (a) there is a close orientation of environmental policy models toward the institutional aspects of environmental-economic planning (e.g., via flexible interactive learning models and scenario analyses for conflicting options); (b) there is a sufficient amount of relevant information, so that also detailed spatial elements and nonlinearities can be dealt with in empirical models; (c) there is a more adequate construction of dynamic models that are capable of taking into account perturbations and disequilibrium situations; (d) there is a better integration of risk aspects, especially for events with a wide range and a low probability; and (e) traditional economic paradigms should not necessarily be the pivot of environmental economics; satisficing principles (e.g., related to steady-state conditions) and compromise principles (related to a reconciliation of diverging options) may be a meaningful alternative and at least a complementary paradigm.

REFERENCES

Blommestein, H., P. Nijkamp, and P. Rietveld. "A Multivariate Analysis of Spatial Inequalities." Research Memorandum no. 1978-10. Department of Economics, Free University. Amsterdam, 1978.

Daly, H. E. ed. *Toward a Steady-State Economy*. San Francisco: Freeman, 1973.

Delft, A. van, and P. Nijkamp. *Multicriteria Analysis and Regional Decision-Making.* The Hague: Martinus Nijhoff, 1977.

Duffin, R. J., E. L. Peterson, and C. M. Zener. *Geometric Programming.* New York: Wiley, 1967.

ESSOR. *Een Prognose van Economische Ontwikkelingen in het Rijnmond-gebied tot 1980.* Rotterdam: Openbaar Lichaam Rijnmond, 1977.

Geoffrion, A. M. "Proper Efficiency and the Theory of Vector Maximization." *Journal of Mathematical Analysis and Application* 22 (1968): 618–630.

Georgescu-Roegen, N. *The Entropy Law and the Economic Process.* Cambridge, Mass.: Harvard University Press, 1971.

Hafkamp, W., and P. Nijkamp. A Comprehensive Interregional Model for Environmental Policy." Research Memorandum no. 7809. Department of Economics, University of Amsterdam. Amsterdam, 1978.

Hirsch, F. *Social Limits to Growth.* Cambridge, Mass.: Harvard University Press, 1976.

Kneese, A. V., R. U. Ayres, and R. C. d'Arge. *Economics and the Environment.* Baltimore: The Johns Hopkins University Press, 1970.

Kuhn, H. W., and A. W. Tucker. "Nonlinear Programming." In P. Newman, ed., *Readings in Mathematical Economics.* Baltimore: The Johns Hopkins University Press, 1968. Pp. 3–14.

Mishan, E. J. *The Costs of Economic Growth.* London: Stoples Press, 1968.

Nijkamp, P. *Planning of Industrial Complexes by Means of Geometric Programming.* Rotterdam: Rotterdam University Press, 1972.

———. *Theory and Application of Environmental Economics.* Amsterdam: North-Holland, 1977.

———. "A Theory of Displaced Ideals." Research Memorandum no. 1978-6. Department of Economics, Free University. Amsterdam, 1978a.

———. "Competition among Regions and Environmental Quality." In W. Buhr and P. Friedrich, eds., *Competition among Small Regions.* Baden-Baden: Nomos, 1978b. Pp. 153–170.

———. "Conflict Patterns and Compromise Solutions in Fuzzy Choice Theory." Research Memorandum no. 1978-7. Department of Economics, Free University. Amsterdam, 1978c.

——— and P. Rietveld. "Conflicting Social Priorities and Compromise Social Decisions." In I. Cullen, ed., *London Studies in Regional Science.* London: Pion, 1978.

——— and J. H. Voogd. "The Use of Multidimensional Scaling Methods for Evaluation." Research Centre for Physical Planning PSC-TNO. Delft, 1978.

Paelinck, J. H. P., and P. Nijkamp. *Operational Theory and Method of Regional Economics.* Farnborough: Saxon House; and Lexington, Mass: D. C. Heath, 1976.

Scitovsky, T. *The Joyless Economy.* Oxford: Oxford University Press, 1976.

Simon, H. A. *Models of Man.* New York: Wiley, 1957.

Werf, P. van der. "Developing the Rijnmond Model." In J. S. Cramer,

A. Heertje, and P. E. Venekamp, eds., *Relevance and Precision*. Amsterdam: North-Holland, 1977. Pp. 159–204.

Zeleny, M. "The Theory of Displaced Ideal." In M. Zeleny, ed., *Multiple Criteria Decision Making*. Berlin: Springer, 1976. Pp. 153–206.

DISCUSSION

On the Efficient Spatial Allocation of Air Pollution Control Responsibility

THOMAS H. TIETENBERG

"As with war, the momentum of trends underlying population growth–pollution, resource depletion–also suggests the presence of forces that are not subject to control by independent action, however enlightened, on the part of national governments. Only new organization forms with a planetary scope that corresponds to the planetary dimension of the situation can offer any prospect of a timely, corrective, and adequate response."

—Richard Falk (1971, p. 97)

1. INTRODUCTION

As illustrated by the above quotation a number of analysts have concluded that environmental problems in general and pollution problems in particular are global in nature. (See also Mesarovic and Pestel [1976].) Furthermore, they suggest that the solution to these problems must come from world governments. Some have suggested the absence of such planetwide governing bodies is one of the major constraints on our ability to allocate our environmental resources in a collectively rational way. The most prominent foundation for these conclusions is the premise that environmental problems are interdependent, both in terms of synergistic effects and in terms of their geographic dimension. This interdependence, it is argued, creates a need for a holistic approach that can be implemented only by a world government.

In this paper I would like to examine one aspect of this question by applying the efficiency criterion to the problem of air pollution control. No attempt will be made to derive the proofs that lie behind these results, since they are already published elsewhere.[1] Rather, I will attempt to convey the results, their implications, and the assumptions that lie behind them.

To introduce the kind of model specification that underlies my conclusions, I will present a simple, static formal general equilibrium model that embodies pollution in a spatial context. I will then use the optimum conditions from this model as a point of reference for discussing whether or not the efficient level of pollution varies spatially or is uniform for the world as a whole. Then the discussion turns to the issue of whether or not the policy instruments should be spatially differentiated and, if so, how they should be designed. Finally, in the least formal and most speculative section of the paper, I will draw out some of the implications of this analysis for the general problem of whether the efficiency criterion suggests a positive role for national, regional, state, and/or local governments.

2. A SIMPLE, STATIC GENERAL EQUILIBRIUM MODEL

At the simplest level, the problem of efficient pollution control is one of finding the appropriate level of commitment of resources to the production of pollution abatement and the production of other desired commodities. This efficient allocation will depend on a variety of factors. A simple one-pollutant general equilibrium model serves to define these factors and to illustrate their interrelationships.

Let the country of interest be divided into M regions. Suppose there are I consumers who have utility functions of the form:

$$U_i = U_i(\mathbf{R}, \mathbf{X_i}) \qquad i = 1, \ldots, I \qquad (2.1)$$

where $\mathbf{R}$ is an M-dimensional vector representing the concentrations in M separate regions of the world of our single, nonreactive pollutant and $\mathbf{X_i}$ is the K-dimensional vector of K commodities consumed by the ith consumer.[2]

Any particular element of the R vector, $\mathbf{R_m}$, can be defined as:

$$\mathbf{R_m} \equiv \sum_{\ell=1}^{M} a^{\ell m} \left[\sum_{k=1}^{K} f_k^{\ell}(Y_k^{\ell}, Z_{kj}^{\ell}) \right] \qquad (2.2)$$

---

1. The relevant articles are listed in the references section at the end of the paper.

2. To keep the notation from becoming cluttered, consumers are not identified with regions and the transportation costs associated with commodities are ignored.

where $a^{\ell m}$ is the linear diffusion coefficient that translates emissions in the ℓth region into a pollutant concentration in the mth region, and f_k^{ℓ} is the emission rate of the kth firm in the ℓth region, which is a function of the output level of that firm (Y_k^{ℓ}) and the resources committed to pollution abatement (Z_{kj}^{ℓ}).[3] The output level is determined by a production function:

$$Y_k^{\ell} = g_k^{\ell}(W_k^{\ell}) \qquad (2.3)$$

where W_k^{ℓ} is the amount of the factor of production committed to the production of consumption commodities. The supply must be equal to the demand in the product market:

$$\sum_{\ell=1}^{M} g_k^{\ell}(W_k^{\ell}) = \sum_{i=1}^{I} X_{ik} \qquad k = 1, \ldots, K \qquad (2.4)$$

Finally, the factor market must also be in equilibrium:

$$\sum_{k=1}^{K} [W_{kj}^m + Z_{kj}^m] = \bar{Z}_j^m \qquad j = 1, \ldots, J; \; m = 1, \ldots, M \qquad (2.5)$$

where $\bar{Z}_j^m$ is the fixed endowment of the jth factor in the mth region.

Any efficient allocation can be expressed as an allocation $\{W, X, Z\}$ that maximizes:

$$\theta = \sum_{i=1}^{I} \alpha_i U_i(X, \mathbf{R}) \qquad (2.6)$$

subject to the constraints (2.2), (2.3), (2.4), and (2.5).

After substituting for $\mathbf{R_m}$ and Y_k^{ℓ} using equations (2.2) and (2.3) the equations that characterize the efficient allocation are:

$$\frac{\partial \theta}{\partial X_{ik}} = \alpha_i \frac{\partial U_i}{\partial X_{ik}} - P_k = 0 \qquad i = 1, \ldots, I; \quad k = 1, \ldots, K \qquad (2.7)$$

$$\frac{\partial \theta}{\partial Z_{kj}^m} = \sum_{i=1}^{I} \alpha_i \sum_{\ell=1}^{m} \frac{\partial U_i}{\partial R_{\ell}} \cdot \left[a^{m\ell} \cdot \frac{\partial f_k^m}{\partial Z_{kj}^m} \right] - \gamma_j^m = 0$$

$$j = 1, \ldots, J; \quad m = 1, \ldots, M; \quad k = 1, \ldots, K \qquad (2.8)$$

$$\frac{\partial \theta}{\partial W_{kj}^m} = \frac{\partial g_k^m}{\partial W_{kj}^m} \cdot P_k - \gamma_j^m + \sum_{i=1}^{I} \alpha_i \left[\sum_{\ell=1}^{M} \frac{\partial U_i}{\partial R_{\ell}} \cdot a^{m\ell} \cdot \frac{\partial f_k^m}{\partial g_k^m} \cdot \frac{\partial g_k^m}{\partial W_{kj}^m} \right] = 0$$

$$j = 1, \ldots, J; \quad m = 1, \ldots, M; \quad k = 1, \ldots, K \qquad (2.9)$$

---

3. The linear relationship between concentrations at a receptor location and emissions at the source is accurate for steady-state or average relationships (see Martin and Tikvart [1968]).

where P_k and γ_j^m are, respectively, the shadow prices associated with constraints (2.4) and (2.5). Equation systems (2.8) and (2.9) can then be combined to yield:

$$\sum_{i=1}^{I} \alpha_i \left[\sum_{\ell=1}^{M} \frac{\partial U_i}{\partial R_\ell} \cdot a^{m\ell} \cdot \left[\frac{\partial f_k^m}{\partial Z_{kj}^m} - \frac{\partial f_k^m}{\partial g_k^m} \cdot \frac{\partial g_k^m}{\partial W_{kj}^m} \right] \right] = \frac{\partial g_k}{\partial W_{kj}} \cdot P_k$$

$$j = 1, \ldots, J; \quad k = 1, \ldots, K; \quad m = 1, \ldots, M \qquad (2.10)$$

This equation formalizes the intuitive notion that factors should be allocated so as to equate the marginal damage cost with the marginal opportunity cost of control. The advantage of the formalization is that it makes the components of the damage function quite clear, and this information can be used to draw conclusions about the vector of efficient pollutant concentrations.

3. EFFICIENT AMBIENT STANDARDS (OR INMISSION NORMS)

The targets of pollution control policy are the levels of concentration of the pollutant in the ambient environment. The question of interest is whether the efficient levels of these concentrations are the same for each region or whether they differ by region. (Formally, the question is whether in an efficient allocation the elements of the M-dimensional vector **R** are identical and can therefore be represented by a scalar.)

In answering this question for air pollution, it is important to keep in mind two different specifications of the pollution equation represented by (2.2). Global pollutants are those which enter the atmosphere and remain for a sufficiently long time to alter its chemical balance. For our purposes, the important characteristic of global pollutants is that the total amount of damage caused is a function of the total volume of the pollutant emitted and is not sensitive to where the emissions are injected into the atmosphere. Global pollutants therefore can be represented by (2.2) when the a parameters are identical for all regions. The implication of this assumption is that the element of $\mathbf{R_m}$ are identical, and this vector can be represented as a scalar. Possible examples of global pollutants are fluorocarbons, which deplete the ozone layer, resulting in a higher incidence of skin cancer and carbon dioxide, and which tends to increase the average temperature of the earth.[4]

In marked contrast is the specification for local pollutants. The damage

---

4. Good descriptions of the problems associated with these pollutants can be found in Bath (1978) and Cooper (1978). Note that we have not ruled out that regional damages from these pollutants may well differ. For both of these pollutants the damage may be rather more severe in some regions than in others.

caused by local pollutants is directly related to the location of the source. Spatially concentrated sources, for example, cause more damage than diffused sources emitting the same amount. Thus, the regional concentration levels will in general differ, and they will be affected by the spatial pattern of emitters.

Technically the global pollutant is a universal public good where all citizens are exposed to the level that prevails regardless of where they reside. The policy target in this case is a scalar and spatial differentiation has no meaning. For local pollutants the efficient level of the ambient concentrations will vary from region to region even though these concentrations are also public goods and even though consumers may care about pollution in areas other than their own. As can be seen in Eq. (2.10), the factors that lead to these regional differences are the number of people who are adversely affected by the pollutant concentration in particular regions, the intensity of their disutility resulting from the pollution, and the costs of controlling emissions in each source region. It would be pure coincidence if the efficient levels of local pollutant concentration were equal in two or more regions.

Although the specification in (2.1) assumes that people receive disutility from the pollutant concentrations in each and every region, it seems reasonable to speculate that they care most deeply about the concentrations in the regions where they reside. If this is so, then population shifts will change the elements in the efficient **R** vector, as will changes in the regional structure of production. In other words, the efficient pollution levels will be temporally differentiated as well as spatially differentiated.

Pragmatically speaking, however, the efficient pollution levels are likely to change slowly. Furthermore, there is reason to believe that the differentials will persist. As Tiebout (1956) pointed out over two decades ago, one solution to the public goods problem occurs as people with homogeneous preferences locate together. Households that are deeply concerned about pollution will tend to migrate to clear air regions, while others will gravitate toward regions with more pollution and higher compensatory wages. If this is an accurate portrayal of the process, the differences among regions in their efficient pollution levels will persist over time.

4. SPATIALLY DIFFERENTIATED POLICY INSTRUMENTS

Let us suppose that the political process has established the ambient standards for the M regions and the next step is to allocate the responsibility for meeting these standards among the various emitters. This allocation can be accomplished by a variety of policy instruments, but I would like to focus my discussion on two that have desirable allocative properties. The first of these, an emission charge, is a per unit charge levied on each unit of the pollutant emitted. The second type of policy instrument is a market for transerable emission entitlements. These entitlements represent the legal right to emit a prespecified amount of the pollutant and are backed by a noncompliance fee for violating the conditions of the entitlement. One of the earliest proposals for using this system can be found in Dales (1968). The general equilibrium treatment of its properties can be found in Baumol and Oates (1971) and Tietenberg (1973).

These policy instruments can be uniformly applied to all emitters or can be spacially differentiated. In discussing how these instruments can be employed, it is convenient to draw a distinction between two types of spatial differentiation: interjurisdictional and intrajurisdictional differentiation. A more detailed description of some of the economic and legal aspects of this distinction can be found in Tietenberg (1978).

Intrajurisdictional differentiation occurs when each receptor region has a unique policy instrument designed specifically to achieve the ambient standard in that region. Thus, using emission charges as an example, while every emitter who contributed to the pollution in that region would pay the same per unit emission charge, emitters contributing to different receptor regions would pay different emission charges. There would be one level of charge associated with each receptor region.[5] Since the levels of these charges would depend on a variety of local conditions, they would not, in the short run at least, be the same across regions.

The transferable entitlements system would similarly be set up so that separate entitlements markets would be established for each receptor region. All emitters which contributed pollutants to that region would be required to buy enough entitlements to cover their emission level. The prices of these entitlements would also vary regionally, reflecting the degrees of control required by the ambient standard and the marginal costs of achieving that degree of control.

It can be shown under conventional assumptions that there exists an M-dimensional vector of emission charges or an M-dimensional vector of transferable entitlement prices that will achieve a reduction in emissions sufficient to achieve the ambient standards in each of the M regions. Furthermore, it can be shown that the particular reduction in emissions achieved is achieved at minimum real resource cost (see Baumol and Oates [1971]).

This degree of differentiation does not achieve the ambient standards at

---

5. Efficiency requires that all emitters contributing to that receptor location pay the emission charge *whether or not they are located in the receptor region*. Furthermore, any emitter contributing emissions to more than one receptor region would pay a separate emission charge for each receptor region.

minimum cost, however.[6]   To accomplish that objective for stationary sources, a further degree of spatial differentiation is necessary. The reason for this is a simple one. The ambient standard must be met everywhere within the region. The binding constraint then is that location where the greatest amount of control is necessary to meet the standard. The charge or entitlement price must be high enough to satisfy the standard at that location. The contribution of any particular emitter to the concentration level at that location is a function of the level of emissions and *the location of the emitter.* For a given level of emissions, emitters that are closer to the receptor location will cause a larger rise in the concentration level than will emitters that are more distant. In other words, a unit of emission reduction by the proximate emitter will result in a larger reduction in the concentration at the receptor location of interest than will an equivalent reduction of emissions by the more distant emitter. The interjurisdictional spatial differentiation is powerless to make this distinction except to the extent that the emitter pays either the uniform rate or nothing at all. Intrajurisdictional differentiation, which allows the location of the emitter to be incorporated into the design of the policy instrument, is necessary to achieve the ambient standards at minimum cost. For emission charges it can be shown that the design that will achieve the objective at minimum cost is of the form:[7]

$$T_k = \sum_{m=1}^{M} a^{\ell m} \cdot \pi_m$$

where T_k is the emission charge per unit of emissions, $a^{\ell m}$ is the parameter that translates emissions at the ℓth source location into concentrations at the mth receptor location, and π_m is the shadow price associated with the mth receptor location. The implication of this design is that in the limit every emitter will face a unique tax rate. These tax rates will differ by virtue of the different meteorological parameters and the number of receptor locations affected by that particular emitter.[8]

---

6. This is formally proven in Tietenberg (1973). The uniform charge results in equalizing the marginal costs of emission reduction across emitters. To achieve the ambient standard at minimum cost, it is necessary to equalize the marginal cost of pollution reduction at the receptor location across emitters.

7. See Tietenberg (1974a). The value of π_m can be obtained iteratively without any information on control costs.

8. Without going into detail here, let it suffice to suggest that arguments that state that meteorological conditions are too unstable to support such a system are wide of the mark. These policy instruments are not changed daily; they are either season specific or held constant all year long. They are there-

The transferable entitlements system can also be modified to meet ambient standards at minimum cost.[9] The modification involves defining the entitlements in terms of standardized emissions. All standardized units of emissions, by construction, have the same marginal impact on the concentration level at the receptor location.

The standardization procedure involves three steps. First, some (arbitrary) *numeraire* emitter is chosen. The emissions of all other emitters are standardized to this *numeraire* emitter. Second, the allowable amount of standardized emissions is computed. This is accomplished by subtracting the background concentration level from the ambient standard and then setting the allowable amount of standardized emissions equal to the maximum amount the *numeraire* emitter could emit (while staying within the ambient standard) if he were the only emitter. Then the meteorological parameters are used to translate a unit of standardized emissions into an amount of actual emissions for each polluter. If the meteorological parameter of the *numeraire* emitter for receptor location m is $a^{\ell m}$ then the entitlement to emit one standardized unit of emissions for the kth emitter entitles him to emit $a^{\ell m}/a^{km}$ actual units of emissions. Because this standardization procedure insures that every standardized unit emitted has precisely the same impact on the concentration level of interest as every other standardized unit, a market can be set up for these entitlements. There will be a single market clearing price for these entitlements. In this system the entitlements are spatially differentiated rather than the price.

When an emitter contributes air pollution to more than one receptor location with a market price of other than zero, he would have to acquire the number of entitlements necessary to legalize this emission rate in every market. Note the similarity here with emission charges, since, *ceteris paribus*, polluters causing problems at a number of receptor locations will have to pay more per unit of emissions than emitters contributing to only one receptor location.

In summary, on a theoretical level efficiency clearly dictates the use of spatially differentiated policy instruments for local pollutants. Furthermore, it dictates that both types of spatial differentiation mentioned above be used. These instruments are sufficient to achieve the desired concentration level

---

fore based on average conditions and the distribution of daily occurrences around that average. This mapping is robust and temporally stable (see Larsen [1971]). Furthermore, in the United States at least, legal authorities have suggested that the diffusion models on which these coefficients are based are sufficiently reliable to withstand legal challenge (see Pierce and Gutfreund [1975]).

9. The exact procedures are described in Tietenberg (1974b). It is worth noting that the control authority does not have to have any information on control costs whatsoever for the correct allocation to be achieved.

without going to complementary policies such as land-use planning. These spatially differentiated instruments provide an incentive for emitters to locate where their emissions cause the least harm.

The question remains, however, whether these distinctions are empirically important. The evidence I have seen indicates that they are. The case for the interjurisdictional differentiation is self-evident. To make the point most graphically, consider the case of Los Angeles. Los Angeles has a topography that severely limits the ability of the winds to disperse and dilute its pollutants. Because of this unfortunate (at least from a pollution point of view) topography, Los Angeles will have to exercise a much higher degree of control to achieve the same ambient standard than would otherwise comparable cities. If their cost-of-control options are similar, this implies that the marginal cost of control for meeting the standard will be much higher in Los Angeles than elsewhere. With no spatial differentiation in order to insure that Los Angeles met its standard, every other emitter in the world would have to pay a charge or entitlement price equal to that high marginal cost of control. Clearly, this forces a much higher degree of control than necessary on the other parts of the world. The absence of spatially differentiated instruments would cause an enormous waste of resources.

The empirical case for the intrajurisdictional differentiation is probably less obvious, although, it turns out, no less important. In a recent study Atkinson and Lewis (1974) have examined the increases in the real resource costs of control that would result from ignoring the intrajurisdictional differentiation. Using data for St. Louis, the authors examined the costs of meeting a predetermined sulfur dioxide ambient standard with and without intrajurisdictional differentiation of the emission charge. Their conclusion was that the cost saving from introducing this kind of spatial differentiation into the emission charge design reduced costs by about 50 percent from the allocation that would have resulted with only interjurisdictional differentiation. This enormous savings, if representative of other areas as well, suggests that it is unlikely that the additional administrative costs that would be incurred in building this differentiation into the policy instrument design would outweigh the benefits to be derived from doing so.

In the long run for both types of spatial differentiation, the differentials in emission charges or in the prices of the transferable entitlements will tend to equalize for each emitter location as emitters seek to reduce their costs by relocating as well as by abating.[10] As long as the ambient standards are

___

10. To avoid possible confusion, it is important to realize that the process of equalization comes about because of the spatial differentiation in the values of the policy instruments. To argue that the efficient policy is to levy a uniform charge, since that is the long-run result anyway, misses the point. A uniform charge does not provide the relocation incentives that are necessary for a uniform charge to ever be efficient.

spatially differentiated, however, this will not result in a uniform level of pollution.

Finally, consider the contrast of the above-mentioned policy implications with the implications for a global pollutant. Since the global pollutant is conceptualized as a single public good and since the level of that good is not sensitive to the location of the emissions, spatially differentiated policy instruments are not appropriate. A worldwide uniform emission charge or transferable entitlements system is efficient.

5. ASSIGNING THE POLICY RESPONSIBILITY

We now come to the question of whether this kind of system has to be administered globally or whether there are some possibilities for national or even local control. Rather than investigate the possibilities for the creation of new optimal jurisdictions, treated later in this volume, I would like to examine the strengths and weaknesses of relying on existing institutional structures. It should be clear that an efficient set of policy instruments could be administered globally if the global authorities had the proper authority and information to implement a control system with as much spatial differentiation as the efficient system would require.

The case for local control arises when the higher levels of government lack the information, the authority, or the motivation to pursue anything but geographically uniform strategies.[11] When the choice is between globally uniform policy instruments and spatially differentiated instruments, regionally implemented and enforced, the tremendous cost savings to be achieved from spatially differentiated instruments would probably dominate the inefficiencies of regional control.

In thinking about jurisdictional responsibilities for pollution control, it is important to differentiate between the responsibility for the ambient standards and the responsibility for the policy instruments. I believe a reasonable case can be made for allocating responsibility for the ambient standards jointly between the national government and local governments, with state or local governments playing the dominant role in controlling the policy instruments.

What I have in mind is the establishment of a national (or international) set of minimum ambient standards, with local areas having the right to establish more stringent standards if they so desired. The rationale for this system is based on a particular concept of the role of information in policy formation.

---

11. In the United States, for example, the Constitution prohibits excise taxes from being levied at different rates in different regions. This provision came about because of a concern when the Constitution was written that the national government would discriminate in its tax policies among the states (see Tietenberg [1978]).

The higher level of government is likely to have a comparative advantage in acquiring information on health effects, material damage, vegetation damage, and so on, that the pollutants cause. This information could be used to set the uniform ambient standard. However, in a number of regions the residents may be unwilling to accept pollution levels as high as the uniform levels allow, either because they wish a higher margin of safety or because their psychic costs from pollution are unusually high. The local areas have better information on these aspects and could therefore translate them into policy more easily than could an international or national governing body. Unless the minimum standard is established at a very low level, this process of shared responsibility is likely to lead to spatially differentiated ambient standards.

There are three possible inefficiencies that can arise from this system. The first arises from the likelihood that the local population will not take into account the value nonresidents place on the quality of the air in their region. Second, the individual regions may not be able to effectively use their discretionary power to the extent that industry is able to play one local area off against another resulting in no ambient standards lower than the nationally uniform level. Finally, local areas may ban certain pollutants from their immediate area while being emphatic about the necessity for the production process that generates these pollutants to be located somewhere within the region. The location of nuclear power plants provides a classic example of this kind of problem.

The first objection is likely to hold strongest for particular areas (e.g., national parks). To the extent that these are easily designated areas there could be a preemption of jurisdiction by higher-level governments, and this preemption could be used to impose a more stringent standard on those specific regions.

The second inefficiency may empirically not be very important, although the evidence is admittedly anecdotal. In the United States several states have already exercised their option to impose more stringent SO_2 standards. They were apparently not dissuaded from their action by the threats of industrial relocation.[12]

The third inefficiency can be limited when the local ambient standards are complemented by regional siting authorities with the power to induce local acceptance of regional plans through the use of tax and compensation schemes. These authorities, however, are needed only for those major emitters and not for the entire range of emitters.

The allocation of responsibilities for establishing the levels of the policy instruments also contains the potential for introducing inefficiency. It is important to be clear about what those inefficiencies are. There are inefficiencies in both the short and the long run. In the short run, when locations

---

12. I am indebted to Ralph d'Arge for calling this point to my attention.

are fixed, inefficiencies result when emitters contributing to a receptor location within a region of interest are outside the taxing jurisdiction of the
regional control authority. In this case, the region has to exercise an inefficiently high degree of control on the emitters within its jurisdiction to
insure that the ambient standard is met.

The long-run inefficiency results from the attractiveness of the border
as a relocation opportunity. By relocating near the border it is possible that
the emitter could avoid affecting the pollution level in his own region and
hence his costs of control. This is inefficient, however, because the emitter
does not bear the full costs of his decision.

Since the problem is caused by an inability to levy charges or to force the
purchase of the appropriate number of entitlements across the border, the
problem can be eliminated if this authority is allowed to extend beyond
the border when necessary.[13] The transferable entitlement system would
appear to offer an option the courts could easily allow to be enforced across
the border. In the United States there is a body of common law that allows
parties whose rights have been infringed upon to collect from the parties who
infringed upon their rights. In these cases the plantiff must usually prove a
causal relationship between the dependent's action and the plaintiff's harm.
The plaintiff must also establish a reasonable basis for the compensation to
be paid. With diffusion models the former objective can be satisfied, and
the entitlement system automatically provides the correct compensation level
(the price of the entitlements times the number of entitlements required).

This case-by-case approach, however, would probably be reserved for large
polluters. Is there any reason to suspect that the problem of transboundary
pollution will prove to be less inefficient than the problem of uniform national policy instruments? While this question cannot be answered adequately without empirical information, there is reason to believe the answer
may be yes. First, as pointed out above, the benefits of spatial differentiation
are large. These benefits are sacrificed with uniform national policy instruments. Second, for many pollutants the effects are quite localized; these
pollutants do not travel long distances. Third, to the extent that particular
control strategies exacerbate the problem (e.g., tall stacks), these strategies
can be prohibited as long as the costs of this prohibition do not exceed the
benefits derived. Finally, in contrast to water pollution, the effects of air
pollution are not unidirectional. The cases where an emitter affects the air
pollution in a contiguous region, but not his own, must be rather rare.

In summary, the demonstration that inefficiencies may arise from local or
regional pollution control is not sufficient grounds for rejecting a regional or

---

13. For a description of how this general kind of approach is working on
the United States–Mexico border see Bath (1978).

local approach. If the higher-level governments demonstrate a proclivity for uniform strategies or lack the requisite authority or information, then the issue becomes the relative inefficiencies of local or regional control versus the inefficiencies associated with a lower degree of spatial differentiation. As we have seen, the latter inefficiency is empirically very large. Furthermore, there are a number of complementary policies that can be adopted to shrink the inefficiencies that may arise with local control. In any case, the claim that a world government approach to the problem of pollution control is essential seems overstated except for the relatively small number of truly global pollutants. Particularly when assigning the responsibility for the policy instruments, a substantial local role seems quite consistent with efficiency.

6. CONCLUSIONS

1. The desirability of spatially differentiated policy targets and policy instruments depends crucially on the nature of the pollutant. For the rather rare global pollutants, globally uniform strategies are efficient. For the much more common local pollutants, efficiency dictates both spatially differentiated policy targets and spatially differentiated policy instruments.

2. For local pollutants the allocation of pollution control responsibility that minimizes the cost of meeting a predetermined ambient standard requires that a unique set of instruments be assigned to each policy target. Furthermore, it requires that the policy instruments assigned to each policy target be differentiated to take into account the location of the emitter vis-à-vis the receptor.

3. If a global authority with perfect information and all-encompassing authority existed, it could clearly design and enforce a policy capable of achieving an efficient spatial allocation of pollution control.

4. When higher-level governments do not have the appropriate authority, the inclination, or the necessary information to build the efficient degree of spatial control in its policy targets and policy instruments, then local control becomes an attractive second-best solution.

5. A policy of minimum national standards complemented by the option for local areas to adopt more stringent standards would appear to represent a means for guaranteeing a reasonable margin of safety for all citizens while allowing legitimate interregional differences in preferences to be reflected in the concentration levels.

6. Although purely local control of the policy instruments will in general be inefficient, this is not a conclusive argument against local control. When higher-level governments show a proclivity toward geographically uniform strategies, this introduces empirically important inefficiencies into the alloca-

tion process that have to be weighed against the inefficiencies associated with local control. In addition, a number of complementary policies are available that tend to mitigate the inefficiencies resulting from local control. These include the prohibition of tall stacks, regional siting authorities for heavy-polluting industries, and the legal acceptance of the idea that receptor regions have the right to sell emission entitlements to emitters that contribute to the air pollution in their region but that are located across the border.

REFERENCES

1. Atkinson, S. E., and D. H. Lewis. "A Cost Effectiveness Analysis of Alternative Air Quality Control Strategies." *Journal of Environmental Economics and Management* 1 (1974): 237–250.
2. Bath, C. R. "Alternative Cooperative Arrangements for Managing Transboundary Air Resources Along the Border." *National Resources Journal* 18 (1978): 181–198.
3. Baumol, W. J., and W. E. Oates. "The Use of Standards and Prices for Protection of the Environment." *Swedish Journal of Economics* 73 (1971): 42–54.
4. Cooper, C. F. "What Might Man-Induced Climate Change Mean?" *Foreign Affairs* 56 (1978): 500–520.
5. Dales, J. H. *Pollution, Property and Prices.* Toronto: University of Toronto Press, 1968.
6. Falk, R. A. *This Endangered Planet.* New York: Vintage Books, 1971.
7. Larsen, R. I. *A Mathematical Model for Relating Air Quality Measurements to Air Quality Standards.* U.S. Environmental Protection Agency, Office of Air Programs. Publication AP-89. Washington, D.C., 1971.
8. Martin, D. O., and J. A. Tikvart. "A General Atmosphere Diffusion Model for Estimating the Effects on Air Quality of One or More Sources." APCA Paper No. 68-148. Presented at the Sixteenth Annual Meeting of the Air Pollution Control Association. St. Paul, Minn. (June 1968).
9. Maugh, T. H. "The Ozone Layer: The Threat from Aerosol Cans Is Real." *Science* 194 (October 1976): 170–172.
10. Mesarovic, M., and E. Pestel. *Mankind at the Turning Point.* New York: New American Library, 1976.
11. Pierce, D. F., and P. D. Gutfreund. "Evidentiary Aspects of Air Dispersion Modeling and Air Quality Measurements in Environmental Litigation and Administrative Proceedings." *Federation of Insurance Council Quarterly* 25 (1975): 341–353.
12. Tiebout, C. "A Pure Theory of Local Expenditures." *Journal of Political Economy* 64 (1956): 416–424.
13. Tietenberg, T. H. "Controlling Pollution by Price and Standards Sys-

tems: A General Equilibrium Analysis." *Swedish Journal of Economics* 75 (1973), 193–203.

14. ———. "Derived Decision Rules for Pollution Control in a General Equilibrium Space Economy." *Journal of Environmental Economics and Management* 1 (1974a): 3–16.

15. ———. "The Design of Property Rights for Air Pollution Control." *Public Policy* 22 (1974b): 275–292.

16. ———. "Spatially Differentiated Air Pollutant Emission Charges: An Economic and Legal Analysis." *Land Economics* 54 (1978): 265–277.

DISCUSSION

Are There Alternatives to the Traditional Economic Paradigms in Regional Environmental Models?

REMY PRUD'HOMME

The first quality of Dr. Nijkamp's paper is that it is ambitious. It aims at no less than providing an "alternative paradigm to traditional economic paradigms," as Dr. Nijkamp puts it, although it restricts itself to the field of environmental economics and policy. More specifically, it describes a new approach to decision-making in this field. It is quite interesting and quite stimulating indeed. But is it convincing?

I do not find it so, and I will try to explain why by discussing what appeared to me as the four basic elements, or steps, of the proposed approach.

The first thing to do, suggests Dr. Nijkamp, is to define a set of Pareto solutions. What he calls a solution is, apparently, a situation defined by the values that a large number of parameters will take as a result of another set of policy decisions. Here comes the first difficulty: there is no model able to relate policy decisions and situations with the degree of detail and of comprehensiveness asked by Dr. Nijkamp. Calling those models "interactive" is not enough to call them into existence. Some models exist, or are being developed, that are able to relate some policy decisions to some environmental magnitudes (and the papers of Allan Kneese and Franz Dreyhaupt refer to such models), but they are limited in scope and do not meet the "relevant criteria which have to be fulfilled by an adequate spacial environmental analysis" and which are listed on pages 55–56. Will the models necessary to generate those many solutions ever be constructed? When one thinks of the time and cost of developing "simple" models, this seems very doubtful indeed.   Then those solutions are classified according to a Pareto criterion, in an elegant and classical manner, thus defining a subset of Pareto or efficient solutions.

Can Table 3-1 be considered as an application of the proposed procedure? I don't think it can. The way pollution is measured (unweighed aggregate of tons of four types of pollutants!) certainly violates the criteria set on pages 55–56 and does not include the ingredients listed on page 64. The solutions that are presented are not related to any policy decision. And I must add that I do not understand how the solution that minimizes pollution is obtained: in a model that assumes constant pollution output ratios (a curious assumption, since the essence of environmental policies is precisely to modify those ratios), the solution that minimizes pollution should be the vector of zero output for each sector; there must be some hidden constraint somewhere.

The second thing to do, in the proposed approach, is to choose, among the subset of Pareto solutions, the best one. This is done elegantly, in two steps. First, define an ideal point. It is a point, beyond the set of feasible solution, that embodies the best characteristics of all Pareto solutions. Second, find the Pareto solution that is "closest" to the ideal point. This is done by looking for the solution that minimizes its discrepancy with the ideal point.

I see two difficulties here. One is that this procedure, which is in effect an optimizing procedure, is arbitrary. It is not based on any explicit criteria. The second difficulty is about the interesting notion of discrepancy. The notion is introduced about the comparison of pairs of regions and used about the comparison of pairs of solutions, but this is not a real difficulty, since the concept can easily be translated. What is more serious is that it implies a weighting of the various (and numerous) parameters that define a solution. To use this concept, one has to decide that an additional 1 percent in employment is worth an additional 5 percent in SO_2 pollution. This is precisely the heart of the matter, the main difficulty of environmental policymaking, and the concept of discrepancy would help hide it rather than solve it.

This is probably the reason why the empirical illustration does not seem to utilize the notion of "ideal" and of optimal solutions. But I may not have understood this properly, and it might be that what is described as a "first compromise solution" is precisely the "optimal solution." It would have been obtained with a nonspecified weighting (which would not matter in any case because of the linear structure of the model).

The third thing to do, according to the proposed approach, is to show this optimal solution to the policymaker and to let him introduce new constraints, which will define new ideals and new optimal solutions.

It should be noted at this point that the procedure changes in nature. Until now, it worked as an optimization model; from now on it works as a simulation model. In an optimization approach, the policymaker intervenes at the beginning by defining what is to be optimized and, in this case, the weights to be attributed to the various (and many) elements of solutions. In a simulation approach, the policymaker intervenes at the end by weighting the outcomes and selecting those he finds best. I find it difficult to see how Dr. Nijkamp combines those two approaches, which seem to be exclusive from each other.

One other difficulty, of course, has to do with the policymaker. Who is he? He must be the prime minister, because he is asked to take decisions that are beyond the responsibility of any minister, let alone high civil servant. But then, the question is: Is it really very realistic to develop models and procedures that require prime ministers as inputs?

The fourth thing to do is to introduce the regional dimension. The approach described so far applies to a country, or to a region. It has to be extended to a multiregional setting. Although this is described as "straightforward" by Dr. Nijkamp, I am not sure I understand exactly how it is done. There are at least two difficulties.

One is that the "intraregional and interregional impact system (e.g., an input-output model, linear emission and diffusion models, etc. . . .)" that would be needed is even more of a dream than in the case of a one-region model. The second difficulty has to do with the role of the policymaker. There must be several—one for each region, at least. How are they to react to the "optimal solution" that will be shown to them? Will they agree on the additional constraints to be introduced? Most probably not. This, again, is at the heart of the matter and is not really tackled by the proposed approach.

Economists should certainly beware of too narrow approaches. On the other hand, trying to encompass everything is equally dangerous. It reminds one of a story told by Jorge Luis Borges about the king who asked his chief geographer to bring a map for him. The geographer came with a map of a 1/10,000 scale. The king asked for a more detailed map. The geographer came with 1/1,000 map. This was not enough, and the king asked for more and more until he was brought a map at the scale of 1/1, which was about the size of his kingdom. This was quite detailed but not very handy.

To get back to the paper, I am tempted to quote an old French saying: "Qui trop embrasse mal étreint" (grab all, lose all).

Dr. Nijkamp did not succeed in convincing me to give up traditional economic paradigms. Are they as bad as he suggests? I don't think so. The old concept of externalities, for instance, which Dr. Nijkamp attacks, appears to me quite useful in spite of all its limitations. There are many cases in real life where externalities can be spotted out and where internalization is possible; carrying that simple message to policymakers would lead to great (or maybe not so great) improvements.

This might lead to a more speculative, and perhaps more ideological, debate. The dichotomy between what Dr. Nijkamp calls old and new paradigms can be seen as a dichotomy between a market and a planning approach. The old paradigm assumes that we operate in market economies, which work automatically and basically well but have to be corrected here and there. The new paradigm rejects such assumptions and the market; it does not aim at improving the market but at replacing it altogether, that is, replacing it by comprehensive planning. This is not a new dream. But it is not an easy task.

Let me conclude by a quotation from Paul Valéry, which applies well to the ambitious effort of Dr. Nijkamp: "All that is simple is wrong, but all that is complex is useless."

CHAPTER 4

Interregional Welfare Comparisons and Environmental Policy

RENÉ L. FREY

1. INTRODUCTION

The interrelations between environmental policy and regional policy can be analyzed from two sides: one may look at the effects a strictly efficiently oriented environmental policy has on interregional equity, or at the effects on economic efficiency when regional equity objectives are pursued along with those of environmental policy.

In this chapter, I want to stress the second aspect. The results of this analysis allow us to draw some conclusions regarding the degree of federal decentralization in environmental policy. My reflections are limited to highly developed market economies.

The questions to be analyzed are:

1. Should one give special protection to some areas, that is, differentiate effluent charges and immission norms regionally? (For a comparison of charges and standards see Lerner [1971] and Osterkamp [1978].) The answer to be found in the literature is yes. The reasons are: (a) the marginal physical damages by effluents differ from region to region owing to different effluent diffusion and spillovers; (b) the evaluation of these damages differs regionally; (c) the different regions do not have the same assimilative capacities; (d) the demand for assimilative services differs; and (e) the marginal costs of environmental protection are not the same in all regions. (See e.g., Siebert [1975, pp. 501ff.; 1976a, Chap. 5; 1976b; 1978a, pp. 130ff; 1978b].)

2. Is it desirable to have regional and local jurisdictions decide on environmental norms and effluent charges because these instruments should be dif-

ferentiated regionally? The answer is mainly no (e.g., Siebert [1975, pp. 504ff.]). It does, however, depend very much on the notion one has of the functioning of politics in a federal system. Therefore, the problem must be analyzed by referring to the economic theory of politics, especially the economic theory of federalism, known as fiscal federalism. This subject will be treated in section 2.

3. What are the effects of the interregional income and welfare disparities when—either on the national or on the regional level—the environmental policy is strictly efficiency oriented, that is, aimed at Pareto optimality? I will go into this question in section 3.

4. What claims to environmental quality and environmental policy will result when interregional equity is accepted as a goal? This question cannot be answered in a general manner. There are great differences from country to country as to what is meant by this goal. In section 4, three different notions of interregional equity will be discussed.

5. What are the welfare losses when environmental policy has to attain not only efficiency but also interregional equity? This question will be treated in section 5.

2. REGIONAL AUTONOMY AND EFFICIENCY

Regional differentiation of environmental policy is considered desirable. Nevertheless, one should not conclude that this must necessarily be a matter decided on by regional and local jurisdictions. Such a solution would be optimal only when a number of prerequisites are met. These prerequisites are quite similar to the conditions necessary in order that the markets for goods and services work optimally from the point of view of economic efficiency. Market systems as well as federal systems can be considered as decentralized decision-making mechanisms (Oates [1972]). The most important prerequisite of decentralization is that there are no technological externalities, that is, no spatial spillovers. This means that the group of people deciding and benefiting must be more or less identical to those having to finance the public good in question (so-called fiscal equivalence, Olson [1969]). Especially in the environmental sector this cannot be assumed. Water discharges, for example, are carried to other regions through rivers without those doing the damage having to compensate those damaged. It is theoretically possible to bring about fiscal equivalence. However, this is must too expensive, because too many environmental goods exist with different spillover radii. The transaction costs are normally prohibitive.

Furthermore, decentralized decisions in environmental policy do not lead to optimal solutions when the regional welfare functions are interdependent. The inhabitants of large cities, for example, are interested in a high environmental quality of the mountain and recreational regions. Because of the great number of jurisdictions involved, the Coase solution fails in this case too. Why should some regions renounce possible economic growth when they do not receive compensation payments from those who benefit? See Knappe (1974) for the possibilities of decentralized environmental policy through negotiations and the creation of property rights.

Decentralization of environmental policy also breaks down because of the free-rider problem. Regional jurisdictions are inclined to let others have precedence in protecting the environment because they hope to benefit from the efforts of other regions without having to bear the costs themselves. Of course, such a free-rider mentality is backed by industry. Most measures to protect the environment are considered as equivalent to a reduction in its competitiveness as long as other firms of the same branch do not have to follow the same injunctions and bear approximately the same costs.

The deficiencies of decentralization mentioned do not necessarily allow the conclusion that environmental policy must lie in the competence of the central government (or even international organizations). Solutions of this kind have their own deficiencies. The greatest danger exists in undifferentiated (schematic) measures. It has to be admitted that national authorities could in principle follow a policy taking account of the specific cost and preference situations of the various regions. But will they do so? In general, the information costs are greater for them owing to the fact that the distance between the citizens or industries and the government is greater than in the decentralized solution. Furthermore, regional differentiations by national authorities are often rejected by groups called federalist because of envy between the various regions. This might be an explanation of why in many federal countries environmental standards and charges are not differentiated regionally— although most economics favor this vigorously.[1] The undifferentiated solution seems to have a greater appeal for lawyers, politicians, and the public than the rather complicated arguments of the economists. This might be called "the normative power of the national average."

Both solutions are therefore associated with disadvantages from the point of view of efficiency: the decentralized solution brings with it the danger that competition between regions could delay or block the realization of environmental protection (free-rider problem); and the centralized solution risks a too schematic course of action.

The problem becomes less acute when it is regarded from a dynamic point of view (cf. mainly Peltzman and Tideman [1971]; Siebert [1975, pp. 503f. and 1978a, pp. 134f.]; Nowotny [1974, pp. 313ff.]). On the condition that

---

1. E.g., the German sewage charges bill (Abwasserabgabegesetz); see Bungarten in the special volume of *Information zur Raumentwicklung* [1976].

the spatial mobility of business and residents is great enough, an adjustment of standards and charges results from decentralization in environmental policy. Residents tend to leave those regions neglecting environmental protection, and industries tend to move in. After awhile the authorities of such regions feel they must take countermeasures. On the other hand, regions making special efforts in the interest of the environment attract residents. If the polluter pays principle is followed, financing does pose problems. It can lead to industry (and jobs) leaving the region, thus slowing down environmental enthusiasm.[2]

Like the mobility of business (capital) and residents (labor), the exchange of goods can, under certain conditions, lead to an optimal environmental policy in the very long run (Siebert [1975, p. 504]). Whether these long-term equalizing mechanisms can be trusted, and therefore a far-reaching federative decentralization in matters of environmental protection is justified, depends considerably on the degree of mobility of resources and people. This again depends on how high costs are for moving location and domicile. Furthermore, the quality of the environment and the costs of environmental protection represent neither the only nor—with the exception of a few industries—very important factors of location. In the case of a selective mobility (higher migration rates of the younger, the better educated, and the richer parts of the population), even a very high global mobility of residents would not induce a convergence of interregional disparities. Finally, the mobility directed coordination of environmental protection might fail because everyone has an option to leave this region when the situation gets too bad, hoping to enjoy a high income today as well as a good ambient tomorrow.

Neoclassical economists tend to rate the mobility of resources and people as satisfactory in order to create an automatic coordination of environmental policy between the regions. Personally, I think that even with very high mobility it takes so many years, indeed decades, to adjust, that such a policy does not have a chance in a world where politicians act in order to gain short- or medium-term success (vote maximization). Therefore the conclusion, according to which in environmental policy fundamental decisions must be made on the highest federal level, does not have to be basically modified even in the long term.

3. EFFICIENCY AND INTERREGIONAL INCOME DISPARITIES

What effects on the interregional income disparities are to be reckoned with, first if a strictly efficiency oriented environmental policy could be followed, and second if the clumsiness of the political system discussed in section 2 waters down efficiency?

If for topographic reasons the regions with a low per capita income are

---

2. Hirschman (1970) calls this reaction the "exit" solution, compared with "voice" (= fighting for a better world).

characterized by high environmental quality and low environmental policy costs, and rich regions on the other hand by grave environmental disruptions and correspondingly high costs, then no conflicts of goals exist between environmental protection and reducing the interregional income disparity. The more vigorously environmental protection is practiced and the more successfully standards and charges are differentiated in accordance with the aim of efficiency, the more strongly environmental protection measures will reduce interregional disparities.

In contrast, serious conflicts arise when the rich regions have small environmental problems and their costs of environmental protection are low; and when the economically poor regions at the same time show ecological problems. The same is true when the less developed regions are burdened with high environmental costs in the interests of maintaining an especially high environmental quality (e.g., recreation areas). Then environmental and regional aims cannot be achieved at the same time. I have the impression that in many countries, the conflict case is very probable for the second reason.

The conflict between environment efficiency and interregional equity can be solved, first, by tolerating or even promoting emigration to rich regions. An alternative solution would be to employ a special instrument to achieve the regional distribution goal. By deliberately compensating the poor regions —for example, with intergovernmental grants-in-aid—their approval of a strictly efficiency-oriented policy could be gained. I would guess that this second solution would be given preference by most economists. In practice, this strategy is rarely used, however. The accompanying visually high costs provoke the opposition of the rich regions. The poor ones, on the other hand, usually fear an impediment of their development possibilities that cannot be made up for later.

Third, a political compromise in such a situation exists when the federal government entitles the poorer regions to a more freehanded environmental policy than the rich ones. This is not because of regionally differing conditions of costs and preferences but because of equity considerations. It should be clear to the economist that this third strategy can be described as inefficient insofar as it brings about an unnecessary loss of income for the economy as a whole. The national product is lower than it could be and would be if one of the other strategies had been chosen. At first glance, this disadvantage is set off by the advantage of the income gap being narrowed between regions. This improvement is not necessarily accompanied by an improvement in those components of welfare that do not enter the GNP, first of all the interpersonal distribution of income, however.

4. WHAT IS INTERREGIONAL EQUITY?

I have tried to show that there is a tendency to burden environmental policy with regional policy objectives when a conflict exists between an efficient environmental policy and interregional equity. In order to explain the differences in solving this conflict, I want to examine what ideas concerning interregional equity. To simplify my argument, I would like to start out from three ideal-typical notions of interregional equity. Behind them there are three different notions of federalism.

Let us first look at *classic federal states*. Today the United States and Switzerland come nearest to this type of federalism. In it regional authorities have the right to solve conflicts of goals according to the preferences of their own population. It is assumed that these preferences differ from region to region, and it is hoped that the welfare of the whole nation is maximized by federative decentralization and competition among regions. As mentioned above, federative decentralization presupposes, first, that no serious spillovers exist. Second, income distribution, here between the different member states, must be viewed as relatively fair. Fulfilling these two prerequisites is the most important task of federal government. In classic federal states the conclusion is *not* drawn that the supply of public goods must be equal (or almost equal) in the different member states. The benefits that can be gained by the inhabitants from the whole set of public and private goods should, rather, not differ too much.

Regional policy in federal countries, therefore, is limited in principle to the following: undertaking redistribution between the regions in the form of income (grants-in-aid); adjusting in this way the realm of possibilities in the regions; and preventing federative decentralization from leading to wrong results in the form of a false level and structure of public goods because of spillovers. For environmental policy, this means that, in a few words, the federal government limits itself, in a skeleton law on environmental protection, to making sure that interregional spillovers of environmental destruction and environmental protection policy are internalized. In it minimal standards must be fixed, above all to prevent the single regions and communities from fleeing into a free-rider role. The regional and local authorities can and should seek those solutions within these basic boundaries that best correspond to their own situation as regards costs and preferences. The choice of environmentally preferential regions in this model does not result from one single political decision but is the result of federal competition.

Whereas in classic federal states the environmental problem is simply considered a spatial public goods problem, in the *federal welfare state* a meritory element comes in. A good example of this type of country is the Federal Republic of Germany. The meritory element lies in the fact that which supply of the various public goods is to be guaranteed in the various regions is politically decided at the national level. Welfare is not understood as a specific level of general welfare but as a specific supply of goods. Legally, this conception takes on the form of so-called social rights: the right to education, the right to health, the right to housing, the right to a clean environment, and so on. In the Federal Republic of Germany this conception of interregional equity has been embodied in the Constitution. The call for "uniformity of living conditions" is derived from articles 72 and 106 of the Constitution. As far as I can see, lawyers do not agree as to whether uniformity of living conditions also means uniformity of environmental quality. As an economist and non-German, I do not wish to interfere in this controversy,[3] but take the liberty of defining my second ideal type of interregional equity, meaning a uniform or almost uniform environmental quality in all regions. What are the consequences for environmental policy?

To begin with, there is a negative one: competition between the regional and local authorities in environmental quality is undesirable. They are only conditionally entitled to use environmental quality intentionally as a factor of location. Environmental protection is much more a matter for the federal government. It decides on the environmental quality objectives, and on the number and geographical position of the regions to which stricter or milder environmental norms apply, and so on. (The problem of the priority zones is treated by Brösse [1978].) It also finances the greater part. The member states and their populations take part in these decisions only within the structure of ordinary participation at the federal level. In the Federal Republic, for example, this happens directly through the Bundesrat (upper house) and indirectly through the election of the members for the Bundestag (lower house). This participation of the regional jurisdictions in the decision-making process at the upper level prevents the central government from regionally differentiating the effluent charges and standards, as should be done from the point of view of efficiency. The member states claim "equality of treatment" and are obviously able to enforce it.

In federal welfare states—as well as in classic federal countries—the enforcement of federal laws on environmental protection, for example, the building of sewage plants, is transferred to the regional and local authorities. This transfer of tasks has nothing to do with decentralization. It is merely a delegation. Although even then a certain scope is given to consideration of regional and local characteristics, the incentives to do this are considerably reduced: first, because they are able to refer only to minor questions; second, because from the point of view of the single regions, a substantial part of the costs is carried by the central government—that is, they can be externalized from the regional point of view.

In *centralized countries*—one might first think of France—regional policies form an essential part of the national plan, that is, national policy. Here, as in the second model of organization, merit notions in the way of an equal or

---

3. For some economic aspects of the constitutional norm of uniformity of living conditions, cf. Neumark (1978).

minimum supply of public goods play a certain role in regional policy. These meritory elements are, however, overshadowed by the endeavor to place regional policy at the service of other economic and social aims. The same is true of environmental policy. In such an ideal-typical system environmental protection is employed purposefully in order to influence the regional structure of population and industry, and thereby also migration. If at the same time a contribution is made to improving the quality of life and diminishing interregional environmental disparities, then this is—somewhat exaggerated— a highly desirable consequence. However, it is not the actual aim of environmental policy. The instrumental employment of environmental policy could explain why a heavily centralized country like France follows an environmental policy more regionally differentiated than the Federal Republic—at least as regards the prevention of water pollution. (My statement is based on Bungarten [1976].)

5. THE OPTIMAL DEGREE OF CENTRALIZATION

Which of the three models outlined is the best? Economists usually attempt to answer this question by examining the costs to the economy as a whole. Statically viewed: By which system is economic welfare least impaired? Dynamically viewed: By which system is economic growth least hindered? These impairments can be understood as the opportunity costs of a regional and environmental policy aimed at decreasing interregional welfare disparities.

As cannot otherwise be expected, these questions cannot be answered generally. This is because of the fact that at least two types of self-compensating costs must be considered and that these costs run differently in the three different systems. On the basis of a diagram developed by Tullock (1969), the problem may be shown as follows. For the sake of simplicity, only two types of costs will be distinguished: spillover costs and meritorization costs.

Spillover costs (*S*) follow when a false level and structure of the efforts to protect the environment result from decentralized decisions. It cannot be said with certainty whether spillovers (or externalities in general) lead to welfare losses. It would be pure chance if the level and structure of public goods were optimal in the presence of uncompensated spillovers, since the decision makers have to consider only those costs they have to bear themselves, and therefore they neglect the other costs in their decisions.

In the purely centralized solution, the spillover costs would be nil if international spillovers could be abstracted from them. Without doubt, these costs increase with increasing numbers of regional and local jurisdictions; they fall with an increasing degree of centralization (see Figure 4-1). In all three types of country considered here, the spillover curve can be assumed to have a similar shape. Its level and slope depend mainly on technological factors

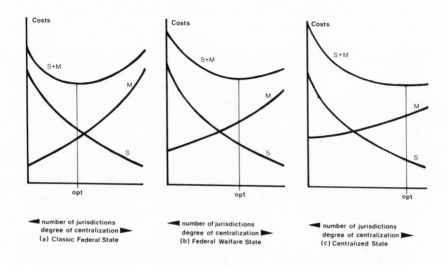

Figure 4-1

such as minimal plant size and economies of scale. Differences in the level of the spillover costs may result from different possibilities of forming the number and geographical boundaries of regional jurisdictions according to ecological regions (Olson's "fiscal equivalence" [1969]). I would not venture to say whether federal, welfare, or centralized countries are more flexible in such adjustments. From a purely theoretical point of view, the centralized system must be favored in this respect. If government failure is taken into consideration, no general conclusion is possible.

Meritorization costs (M) are understood as those welfare losses that result from individual preferences not being satisfied in the best way. A reallocation of resources would increase the welfare of the population—distributive aspects being neglected for the moment. The level of meritorization costs depends on: (a) the information costs; (b) the decision makers' incentives to consider individual preferences in government measures; and (c) the sanctions they must reckon with if they fail in this respect (e.g., no reelection).[4]

_____

4. For information and motivation as fundamental questions of decentralized environmental control, cf. Windisch (1975).

Owing to the great "distance" between citizens and the government, but also to the above-mentioned danger of the "normative power of the national average," the meritorization costs will probably rise with increasing centralization. Even in a distinctly federal country they do not reach the value nil. Political decisions are never unanimous in practice, so that some people are always in the minority and feel themselves violated. In a federal system, however, their number is less than in a centralized one.

It is plausible to assume that centralized countries possess stronger homogeneity in preferences, so that schematic measures taking less consideration of the residents' preferences are not perceived especially unfavorably. The curve for meritorization costs, therefore, runs rather flat in centralized countries. Its level is higher than in classic federal countries because of the generally greater distance between citizens and public authorities. In the classic federal state a steep curve can be assumed, because the usually distinct regional characteristics in such countries can be considered all the less, the smaller the number of regional jurisdictions. The federal welfare state takes a middle place: preferences are spatially less homogeneous than in a centralized country, so that schematic solutions are felt to be outright welfare losses. The fewer jurisdictions there are, the more weight these losses are. On the other hand, politically a much stronger wish for formal equality exists than in classic federal states.

If the spillover and meritorization curves are viewed together (see Figure 4-1), it can be seen that the minimization of the total costs $(S + M)$ in the three systems leads to different optimal degrees of centralization. This is true for environmental policy just as it is for other fields of governmental activity. Unfortunately, without an empirical estimation of both curves, no conclusions can be drawn as to which of the three systems examined leads to the lowest total costs. Such an analysis seems of little importance to me. It is extremely rare that a country discusses whether to change its political system altogether— for example, from a federal to a centralized system or vice versa. What is of interest is in which direction to change the degree of centralization in a specific field of policy.

6. SUMMARY

My analysis may be summarized in eight propositions:

1. Environmental policy should be differentiated regionally if efficiency is to be attained, since costs and preferences differ regionally.

2. From the purely theoretical point of view, the main decisions in environmental policy—also regarding regional differentiation—have to be taken by the federal government. Only thus may the free-rider mentality of the regions be overcome.

3. Government failure is normally considered to be higher on the national level, owing to higher information costs and weaker incentives. Therefore, it is desirable to have a certain regional (and even local) autonomy in environmental policy.

4. Regional and local autonomy is sensible, too, because in the long run a tendency exists to narrow the regional differences in environmental standards and charges—at least if the mobility of business, residents, and good is high enough.

5. Without empirical research it cannot be said whether an efficiency-oriented environmental policy increases or decreases interregional disparities. A conflict exists when the poor regions are identical with the regions having greater environmental problems.

6. In such a situation three solutions exist:

(a) migration from the poor to the rich regions

(b) compensation of the poor regions through intergovernmental grants; and

(c) allowing the poor regions to do less for the protection of their environment than the rich ones.

In reality, the third solution dominates.

7. Different notions of interregional equity and of federalism determine what kind of equity-oriented environmental policy is followed. One may think of three different ideal-typical cases:

(a) classic federal countries consider ecological problems mainly as public goods problems: their effort is directed at internalizing the spillovers and at reducing the interregional income gap by transfers (grants-in-aid);

(b) federal welfare states stress the merit good element: equality of environmental conditions in all regions and formal equality in environmental policy; this aggravates the regional differentiation of environmental standards and charges;

(c) centralized countries use environmental policy in order to attain national goals; for example, to influence migration to arrive at an optimal regional structure of population and industry—optimal from the national point of view.

8. No general conclusions are possible regarding the question of which one of the three systems has the lowest total costs. Two kinds of costs do compensate: spillover costs and meritorization costs. The former speak in favor of a relatively low, the latter of a relatively high degree of decentralization.

REFERENCES

Brösse, Ulrich. "Ausgeglichene Funktionsräume oder funktionsräumliche Arbeitsteilung durch Vorranggebiete als Alternative Konzepte für Regionalpolitik und Umweltpolitik?" *Zeitschrift für Umweltpolitik* 1 (1978): 13–28.

Bungarten, Harald H. "Zur Praxis der Abwasserabgabe und ergänzender Instrumente in der Europäischen Gemeinschaft." *Informationen zur Raumentwicklung* 8 (1976): 391–403.

Frey, René L. *Zwischen Föderalismus und Zentralismus.* Bern and Frankfurt, 1977.

Hirschman, Albert O. *Exit, Voice, and Loyalty.* Cambridge, Mass., 1970.

Knappe, Eckhard. *Möglichkeitn und Grenzen dezentraler Umweltschutzpolitik.* Berlin, 1974.

Lerner, Abba P. "The 1971 Report of the President's Council of Economic Advisers: Priorities and Efficiency." *American Economic Review* 61 (September 1971): 527–530.

Neumark, Fritz. "Bemerkungen zu einigen ökonomischen Aspekten der grundgesetzlichen Vorschriften über die Einheitlichkeit der Lebensverhältnisse in der Bundesrepublik Deutschland." In Wilhelmine Dreissig, ed., *Probleme des Finanzausgleichs I.* Berlin, 1978. Pp. 165–175.

Nowotny, Ewald. *Wirtschaftspolitik und Umweltschutz.* Freiburg in Breisgau., 1974.

Oates, Wallace E. *Fiscal Federalism.* New York, 1972.

Olson, Mancur. "The Principle of 'Fiscal Equivalence': The Division of Responsibilities among Different Levels of Government." *American Economic Review, Papers and Proceedings* 59 (May 1969): 479–487.

Osterkamp, Rigmar. "Standards und Steuern als Instrumente gegen die Verschmutzung der Umwelt." *Kyklos* 31 (1978): 235–257.

Peltzman, Sam, and T. Nicolas Tideman. "Local versus National Pollution Control: Note." *American Economic Review* 62 (December 1972): 959–963.

Siebert, Horst. "Regional Aspects of Environmental Allocation." *Zeitschrift für die gesamte Staatswissenschaft* 131 (1975): 498–513.

———. *Analyse der Instrumente der Umweltpolitik.* Göttingen, 1976a.

———. "Zur Zweckmässigkeit regional differenzierter Instrumente einer Umweltpolitik." *Informationen zur Raumentwicklung* 8 (1976): 367–372.

———. *Oekonomische Theorie der Umwelt.* Tübingen, 1978a.

———. "Räumliche Aspekte der Umweltallokation." In Walter Buhr and Peter Friedrich, eds. *Konkurrenz zwischen kleinen Regionen.* Baden-Baden, 1978b.

Tullock, Gordon. "Federalism: Problems of Scale." *Public Choice* 6 (Spring 1969): 19–29.

Windisch, Rupert. "Coase-Paradigma versus Pigou-Paradigma: Ueber Information und Motivation als Grundfrage dezentralisierter Umweltkontrolle." *Zeitschrift für Nationalökonomie* 35 (1975): 345–390.

DISCUSSION

On Regional Differentiation of Environmental Policy

JEROME ROTHENBERG

This paper constitutes a set of ruminations on regional and group differences in environmental policy intentions and policy consequences, and how they may or ought to be modified. It is motivated chiefly by René L. Frey's "Interregional Welfare Comparisons and Environmental Policy" discussed in this chapter, but it is also in part a response to all of the papers in this volume.

Frey's paper is useful in clarifying a number of the issues in the ambiguous but often conflicted relationship between interregional equity and efficiency in environmental policy. I agree with much that he has to say about them. But they provoke a desire to step back from some of them to ask more anterior questions, to step forward from some to ask further questions, and to step sideward from others to use a different perspective.

ALLOCATIONAL VERSUS DISTRIBUTIONAL GOALS

In large part, the issues raised about allocational and distributional goals in environment policy are similar to those raised in any public area. Almost all public policies designed to rectify market breakdowns and/or deal explicitly with public goods, regardless of the functional area involved, have unequal, nontrivial effects on the distribution of real income among individuals, groups, and regions. Indeed, policies designed primarily for redistributional ends have nontrivial allocational effects too. The two goal dimensions are thus deeply intertwined. While in some cases allocational and distributional impacts are related directly or inversely with respect to political attractiveness (a proxy for socially perceived social welfare), in many other cases a variety of configurations are possible.

It is no longer fashionable to pretend that distributional issues do not exist when allocational programs are considered, or that they are intrinsically less important than the allocational issues that trigger them. In behavioral terms, they sometimes are strong enough to determine the political coalitions that make the difference between political success or failure for the allocational program.

If distributional issues must be faced, how best should this be done? Five types of behavioral strategy seem to be available:

1. Keep the allocational program pure. Achieve distributional goals separately, by means of a specialized set of programs as purely distributional as possible.

2. Link distributional objectives passively with the allocational programs, that is, use compensation techniques for the limited objective of avoiding large net group losses.

3. Link distributional objectives actively with allocational ones, that is, adopt deliberately "impure" programs that compromise distributional and allocational goals.

4. Assemble together under the same "political package" otherwise independent allocational programs that have complementary distributional impacts, that is, develop "logroll" actions that give everyone a piece of the action.

5. Decrease the occurrence and importance of potential distributional impacts of allocational programs by structurally separating population groups and public functions so as to have the exercise of particular functions within jurisdictions that minimize group differences relative to the exercise of those functions, that is, structurally tailor public responsibilities to fit the population scope of each type of rectification of market failure.

The majority of economists have generally favored the last in principle. But there has been recognition that it is an incomplete strategy, since even thoroughgoing federalistic mix cannot create a jurisdictional network in which allocational policies have even approximate unanimity of impact. Distributional issues will continue to arise, and the other strategies are needed. Of the remainder, most economists favor the first in principle. But on practical grounds, the political frictions engendered by the temporal separation between pure allocational and pure distributional programs, and the growing realization that so-called distribution programs have nontrivial allocational impacts as well, make this less obviously preferable than the other strategies. So more and more economists are faced with the need to countenance the less pure, more politically contingent alternative strategy types.

Within this context it is clear that the question of government structure with respect to the balance of centralization and decentralization does bear on whether a regional dimension is relevant for environmental policy, since government structure will influence how much distributional impact is likely to accompany allocationally oriented environmental policy in the context of given regional differences. The greater the regional differences, other things being equal, the larger the distributional nonneutrality of environmental policy is apt to be. But large regional differences with respect to environmental policy are likely to be large with respect to many kinds of public policy as well. Therefore, they will probably in fact elicit an adaptation of government structure to minimize political frictions by just the kinds of decentralization that Frey discusses. So in any period, the structure of government with respect to centralization-decentralization will presumably *already* bear a significant relationship to the size and variety of regional differences.

The structural adaptation is not, however, likely to preclude distributional nonneutrality. It determines which functions are allocated to which jurisdictional levels and how jurisdictional boundaries are drawn between and within such levels. But the variety of public good-externality areas is so great that very few, if any, governmental functions even approach unanimity of impact within the relevant jurisdictions. This holds for historical structural adaptations, and the apparent intractability of the problem of ideal federalism suggests that it will hold also for proposed changes in structure. Environmental— and presumably any other—policy will continue to raise the potential conflict between allocational and distributional consideration. So Frey's analysis of the costs of dealing with the two elements is not to be resolved solely in terms of federal structure.

Even within his own perspective, Frey's detailed treatment in the area lends itself to misunderstanding. The question of which federal structure entails the highest social costs is not really attacked by his analytic procedure. An appropriate design would involve comparison among different alternative governmental structures with the same population. But the curves of Frey's diagrams in Figure 4-1 implicity assume *different* populations, since he treats each structure as a social adaptation to the extent and intensity of population differences within and across the regions of the given nation. The mutual endogeneity of regional differences and government structure frustrates an appropriate analysis.

DISTINCTIVENESS OF ENVIRONMENTAL POLICY

Is there anything special about the environment as a subject for allocation policy with regard to these issues? Yes, there is a typology of environmental problems that has a strong association with the character of distributional impacts. It serves to demarcate problems in which the distributional dimension is critical from those in which such a dimension is nearly absent.

The typology is one I developed in 1970 for the analysis of environmental problems. It consists in seeing a large proportion of such problems as variants of a family of generic congestion ("generalized crowding") situations. Basic to most examples of conventional congestion and pollution is: (1) a public good-common property resource, subject to use by multiple users (of the same or different types); (2) a pervasive externality consisting of interference by some or all uses or some users (either because of volume or type of use) with the quality of the services obtainable by some or all users; (3) the relationship between pattern (magnitude) of use and decline in quality dependent on the size and character of the "assimilative capacity" of the public good relative to the use burden being placed on it; (4) an ability to affect the public good's assimilative capacity and/or the potentially disruptive effect of each use by discretionary human action ("assimilative capacity investment" or "private abatement"). The "crowding" aspect consists in the relationship between the assimilative burden generated by the totality of use and the discretionarily variable assimilative capacity possessed by the system at a given time. An excess burden results in degradation; an excess of capacity results in absence of degradation.

Situations possessing these general characteristics differ in important ways that are relevant to the present discussion. They fall along a continuum, having at one extreme what I call "pure congestion" and at the other "pure pollution." Pure congestion is the situation in which all users contribute equally to the degradation of services from the common property resource and equally share the consequential damages from the degradation. Pure pollution is the situation where one portion of the user population generates degradation of services from the public good but does not suffer any of the damages from such degradation (the "pure polluters"), and the remaining portion of users do not generate degradation but suffer all the damages generated by the pure polluters (the "pure victims"). Real-world situations lie between these two ideal-type extremes, some closer to one extreme, some closer to the other.

The distribution effects of policy designed to correct problems lying in widely separated parts of this continuum will differ markedly. The pure congestion extreme represents situations in which, "We do damage to ourselves." Policy rectifications of these have homogeneous effects: everyone's behavior is similarly re-channeled so that everyone may be made better off on balance. Such policies are almost devoid of redistributional impact. So, on the one hand, a welfare analysis of them is nearly unambiguous; on the other hand, political support for them, when they are properly understood, can be nearly unanimous. The pure pollution extreme is totally different. Intrinsic to rectification of the resource-use distortion is that someone—the pure polluters—must be made worse off so that others—the pure victims—can be made better off. Such policies inherently redistribute real welfare, and the redistribution may be major. Politically, they are likely to be most controversial.

The structure of an environmental problem vis-à-vis this asymmetry continuum enables one to predict the extent to which distributional issues will be most effected. This suggests that where spatial separation or specialization can convert a nearly pure pollution problem to one more nearly pure congestion, such techniques constitute a further method of allaying distributional difficulties without requiring specific regional modifications in otherwise universalistic policy procedures.

GROUP VERSUS REGIONAL REDISTRIBUTIONS

Most of the diversity of impact resulting from environmental degradation and its policy rectification is in terms of individual or group differences, not of regional differences. Moreover, most of the goals of government redistributional policy refer to individual or group redistributions, not to regional ones. Is the region ever the appropriate level on which to deal with distributional problems, or does a regionally defined set of policy modifications invariably conflict with the individual or group basis for dealing with such problems?

In principle the region is at best a proxy for the appropriate individual or group basis of differentiation. But under some conditions it is a good proxy; moreover, under those same conditions an adaptation of political structure is likely to have occurred such that the political system is far more responsive to region-oriented policy differentiation than to any other kind. In other words, political feasibility requires it.

Region-oriented policy differentiation may be an appropriate basis when both of the following conditions are met: (a) differences in population density, industrial mix, technology, and other characteristics of the economy are greater across regions than within them; (b) differences in public tastes concerning environmental quality are greater across regions than within them. Thus, regional differences in the determination of the distributional impact of environmental degradation, the costs of upgrading the environment, and the tastes for environmental trade-offs with other commodities are significant, and more so than idiosyncratic differences in these matters within regions. It is not clear to what extent these conditions are met in different countries, but one does expect substantial differences in the extent to which they are.

REGIONAL EQUITY

The concept of regional equity is central to discussions about regional differentiation of environmental policy. But it is an ambiguous concept. At least three interpretations about what distributional goals should be attached to the primary allocational goals of public policy have gained currency: (a) narrow prior regional disparities in real per capita income via environmental programs; (b) prevent environmental policy from widening prior disparities—in effect, equalize interregional net benefits from these programs; and (c) avoid significant changes in the relative sizes of different regions with respect to population, employment, and business activity.

The first of these is more extreme than most interested parties have been willing to go. Environmental policy is not a particularly good vehicle for carrying a major deliberate redistributional thrust. The second seems a reasonable status quo position and might be suited for linkage with environmental policy; but it seems to have been precluded by serious attention to the third. Simple regional size is often politically considered the proper dimension for evaluating the equity of policy outcomes. This is serious, because the third interpretation conflicts more strongly with allocative efficiency than do either of the other two. It conflicts with an essential component of the efficient adjustment of resource use to imposition of any nonhomogeneous kind of public policy—and certainly to environmental policy, namely: the geographic flow of mobile resources away from less attractive toward more attractive economic opportunities. Environmental programs, whether they are centralized or decentralized, have nonhomogeneous consequences that call for such adjustments. While the other two interpretations can be achieved by partial or complete decoupling from the allocational core of the program, this one, because of its interdiction against necessary spatial flows of resources, is inextricably embedded into that core. The welfare evaluation of different environmental programs will be most distorted from its conventional allocational basis if this interpretation of regional equity is politcally influential.

REGIONAL POLICY AND INTERREGIONAL RESOURCE MOBILITY

Interregional resource mobility is, indeed, an important aspect of environmental policy. It has wider ramifications than the issue of regional equity and raises issues more complex than those dealt with by Frey.

A key to the issue lies in the degree of heterogeneity in the impact of environmental policy—the degree to which such policy is not distributionally neutral both within and across regions. Suppose that a particular type of policy has, in every region, in addition to the positive impact on the group that the policy is designed to help, group A, a negative net impact on some group B, and that the balance of positive and negative impacts differs across regions. This will set up tendencies for *both* groups A and B to migrate interregionally—the first to maximize their net gains, the second to minimize their net losses.

But the migration patterns will be more complicated than this suggests because of functional linkage between groups A and B. Suppose group A consists of households generally and group B consists of a set of industries. If the environmental policy improves water quality, for example, by imposing significant costs on many business firms, the initial migratory tendencies will be modified by the fact that household location is strongly influenced by the location of jobs. If substantial business out-migration occurs in a region due either to especially high water quality standards established there, or to especially high compliance costs on business because of the particular nature of the businesses or the particular physical-spatial configuration of watercourses, and business and population concentrations there, this out-migration will decrease the initial population inclination to move there. In serious cases, the region in question may lose both business activity and population–may experience a loss of per capita income and total economic activity.

Regions will thus generally try to avoid generating strong locational disincentives on such salient activities. If a single national policy sets environmental standards and/or constraints, whatever changes in interregional locational incentives occur are beyond the control of individual regions. But if the individual regions set policy for themselves, they may well engage in a competitive dilution of standards and constraints to capture–or avoid losing-business activity in the interregional contest, with an end result perhaps no different in location patterns but weaker in environmental protection.

Thus, in the face of a given set of externalities with a distinctive interregional distribution of particularities, the interregional mobility of resources can induce a competitively oriented interregional configuration of policy that differs substantially from what would have been forthcoming from a single national policy. A Coase-type theorem about equivalence between a completely centralized and completely decentralized policy in general fails. Indeed, it is likely to fail on both static and dynamic grounds. On static grounds, as I have just argued, a comparison of decentralized and centralized equilibrium suggests that the former will represent a weaker, incomplete internalization of environmental externalities relative to the latter–a suboptimal outcome. On dynamic grounds, there is some possibility that no competitive general equilibrium will even be realized by the decentralized scenario. The separate regions are essentially oligopolists and must consider the policies set by each other in devising policies most beneficial to themselves. The resulting conjectural variations stemming out of the strategic interplay can quite conceivably lead to continued instability or to various noncompetitive equilibria. Certainly there is no guarantee of a general optimum. This problem is absent in the centralized policy scenario.

The foregoing consideration raises a further question about the optimality of regionally initiated policy. It concerns the very nature of regional collective choice. The competitive market analogue presupposes that each region can select its desired resource allocation, not solely in terms of desired level and character of environmental quality, but of this *relative to* per capita market goods income. Yet the region may have no way to control the bundle of these two "commodities" that it can receive by setting environmental policy: nor may it even be able to predict closely what bundle will follow upon a particular policy choice. The implicit tradeoff between environmental and market goods results from a complex composed of: (a) the actual induced resource mobility stemming from any set of regional policy disparities;(b) what induced mobility is believed to exist by the different regional policy authorities; and (c) how these authorities from other regions strategically respond to their beliefs about mobility and their outcome preferences. Given the formidability and effective indeterminacy of this intervening machinery, the commodity bundle *intended* by a specific region when it makes its policy choice may diverge widely from what actually results. So the rationality of each region's choice—the building block of the normative interpretation of competitive theory—cannot be presumed.

What is really wrong with interregional policy competition as an efficient "allocative" process is that the regional decision makers are not directly competing for resources or commodity bundles; rather, they are competing in terms of how environmental externalities are to be internalized. Most of environmental policy deals with quality degradations that are unintended byproducts of intended primary activities, not intended commodity bundles. So the control question is how much of the externalities is to be internalized and in what manner. The regional competition enters because of policy-induced resource mobility; but this mobility itself generates externalities within the economies of the regions. So there is a form of free-rider incentive for each region, and this distorts the competitive regional policy process in the predictable way previously suggested: namely, by *weakening* the policy on the average. This does not simply provide a variety of environment–per capita income packages among which the population may choose to distribute themselves (the presumed normative competitive analogue à la Tiebout)—it represents rather differential degrees of failure to repair private market breakdowns among the regions. It can by no means be guaranteed to provide an overall efficient allocative or even distributive policy configuration.

SOCIAL COSTS OF INDUCED MOBILITY

This discussion of interregional resource mobility is not intended to suggest that such mobility is undesirable—not at all. The warnings are quite limited. An essential part of the internalization of environmental externalities consists in correcting the allocational distortion due to market failure. A new allocational configuration is the whole point of such policy. Part of the change involves—requires—a spatial reshuffling of resource use, and some of this entails interregional shifts. There are, however, regional distributional consequences of these shifts that may be deemed unsatisfactory. Moreover, if it is desired to avoid such consequences directly by allowing the regions to formulate policy for themselves, some possibly serious allocational aberrations may occur because of similar—but a different set of—such shifts.

There can be, however, in addition to these problems, direct allocational costs arising from the primary adjustment to internalization. These stem from a possibly important asymmetry in major spatial migration of population. A significant shift of population from regions B to A (and even more when there is a concentrated rise in A fed by smaller flows from B, C, D, etc.) will generally necessitate additional infrastructure investment in A but without releasing even approximately equal amount of real resources due to a smaller infrastructure use in B (and C, D, etc.). Large fixed-cost elements in infrastructure services (highly durable capital, rigid administrative apparatus, etc.) mean that B (and C, D, etc.) simply experiences excess capacity with little saving in real resource cost (although this can generate *fiscal* problems on those remaining in B: if use charges are based on average cost those who remain will face higher charges). So the population shifts make the total infrastructure cost of the total population larger than it was previously. This is a real resource cost. It is an *efficiency* ground on which to consider modification in internalization policies that call for especially large spatial (not simply interregional) adjustments.

DISCUSSION

Sociopolitical Aspects of Regional Welfare Comparisons

JEAN PHILIPPE BARDE

First, I wish to state that Professor Frey's paper explains in a clear and systematic manner the problems associated with various national and regional environmental strategies. In fact, I fully agree with his conclusions, in particular about the need to differentiate environmental policies on a regional basis while insuring proper coordination at national, central level. Therefore, in my comments I would like to present some complementary remarks by elaborating a little on the sociopolitical aspects of the issue, as I can see them from my international "observatory."

The problem of a welfare-environmental policy must be analyzed from two viewpoints: that of the objectives and that of the instruments. Both have different scope and meaning at the national and regional levels.

THE OBJECTIVES OF ENVIRONMENTAL POLICIES

The National Level. Environmental objectives must be and are actually set at the national level for the following reasons: (i) they are part of the overall socioeconomic policy; (ii) they can be a means to alleviate inequalities; (iii) they are needed to avoid interregional spillovers; and (iv) they are needed to fit in an international setting.

At the national level, environmental objectives are essentially a component of the overall aims of a nation. These, in fact, express the need for a national consensus on broad issues such as "economic growth," "access to education," "good quality of life," and so on. At this level, environmental policy is part of the socioeconomic policy of a nation and, as such, is viewed as a general "quality-of-life policy," broader than pollution control, *stricto-sensu.*

Indeed, this quality-of-life policy is considered as an element of the general welfare policy, and its public expenditure component can be important. Remember that the welfare component of public expenditures is the most important part of total public expenditures in OECD member countries: in 1974-76, total public expenditures were about 41 percent of the growth domestic product (GDP); (OECD average), whereas total welfare amounted to 18.8 percent of the GDP; about 50 percent of the increase in public expenditures over the period 1960-70 was due to welfare expenditures (OECD, 1978). Now, although public environmental expenditures are a tiny part of overall public expenditures (varying between 0.8 and 1.5 percent according to the country), these are a major part of overall (private plus public) environmental expenditures (between 30 and 40 percent).[1] Part of these expenditures is regional and part is national, but national coordination is always required. Thus, environment is part of the national welfare objectives; hence the need for national environmental objectives.

The reduction of inequalities constitutes a major element of welfare policies. Environment, or rather quality of life, is an important factor of inequality. In France, studies have been made about what is called inegalités écologiques (ecological inequalities). Not only does this cover geographical variations in pollution levels, natural resources; and so on, but it also covers socioeconomic inequalities,—for example, ease of access to natural resorts, quality of life in relation to income levels, and so on.

Clearly, central governments must make explicit that they are trying to reduce these inequalities: everybody has a right to education, health, labor, minimum revenue, and the like. Similarly, everybody has a right to a harmonious, satisfactory, or unpolluted environment. These rights are often

---

1. In several countries, water pollution control is the major part of public environmental expenditures (about 80 percent).

constitutional, and "environmental rights" also tend to be written in national laws.

Here again, environmental objectives, as a means of social policy, will be set at the national level. But the central government is confronted with two classical contradictory requirements: one is equality the other is efficiency (i.e., maximize "national efficiency"). Striving for an equivalent environmental quality all over a country can lead to prohibitive costs. Professor Frey has shown that economic efficiency requires regional differentiation and that equity consideration entails a welfare loss for the national economy. Politically, the central government must show that it is striving for equality; economically, it has to take full account of regional disparities.

Thus, two sets of objectives will be fixed: (a) *national minimum objectives* such as minimum quality standards for water, air, and noise, and (b) *regional objectives* (but fixed by national authorities), aiming at maximizing something like a "national welfare function," taking advantage of the relative resources of each region—for example, the "stand-still principle" (Netherlands) in nonpolluted regions; "recovery objectives" for specific rivers (France); "rehabilitation zones" for noise (Netherlands); and so on. Also, during the present (and probably future) unemployment situation, the government might tune its environmental policy as a regional job-creating mechanism. For instance, the EEC has considered a "package" of individual environmental labor-intensive projects, adapted to particular situations (it was estimated that a total expenditure of about $500 million dollars would create 20,000 jobs). During the period 1971–1974, Sweden also deliberately used environmental policy as a job-creating mechanism (20,630 jobs were created out of a 1.9 billion SKr [kronor] program).

Interregional pollution spillovers must obviously be taken into account at the national level because of pollution transfers from basin to basin, or state to state, and also a management of national assets (*gestion patrimoniale*).

Finally, *international constraints* must be considered, and this can be done only at national level. Some environmental standards are harmonized at the international level (in particular in the EEC); non-tariff barriers represent a permanent concern for governments; also international agreement on policy principles is gaining in importance (the polluter pays principle, principles on transfrontier pollution, consultation procedures, banning of toxic substances etc.).

The Regional Level. When we come down to the concrete on-the-field problems, objectives have to be set in a very precise way. This can be done reasonably only at the regional-local level. I need not elaborate too much on this point which is dealt with in other papers of this volume. Obviously, objectives have to be closely adapted to regional, natural, economic, and social conditions.

In this respect, the size and the internal variety of countries is a major factor. In fact, I think this factor is even more important than the politico-administrative structure. The typology (classical federal state-welfare federal state–centralized state) presented by Professor Frey is very useful, but more important is the fact that countries may be big (United States) or small (Switzerland) even if both have a federal structure; more important also may be the fact that environmental conditions may be fairly uniform over the national territory (Netherlands, Denmark), or are subject to wide variations (France, Italy, Sweden). Thus, the concept of region has very different meanings (a U.S. state is not a Swiss canton nor a German *Land*; the Italian *Mezzogiorno* is completely different from northern Italy; and so on) and needs to be precisely defined not only as to its politico-administrative aspect but also as to its geographical, sociological, and environmental dimensions.

The more geographical and cultural differences there are, the more variations in objectives there will be. Social preferences can vary enormously within a single country (e.g., Spain and Italy, and, to a lesser degree, France and the United Kingdom). What is important is that only at the regional level will the demand for environmental quality be revealed; this can be very localized. For instance, in France not only are regions demanding more and more autonomy, but there are growing claims for independent management of city districts (*comités des quartiers*). On the occasion of political elections, specific regional environmental claims are expressed (e.g., the "ecological party" in France).

THE INSTRUMENTS

Instruments of environmental policy also can have a national and a regional dimension.

At the national level, the instruments and strategies must be adapted to other, related strategies: physical planning, transport policy, urban policy, and so on. Also, the instruments must obey a national "philosophy" and/or fundamental politico-administrative choices. For instance, some countries are definitely in favor of charges (Netherlands); others (so far) are deliberately against them (United States, Sweden); some are in favor of technologically based standards, and others are not.

National and international constraints require uniformity of certain standards, in particular *product standards*—automobiles and other durable goods, detergents, etc.—[2] although the concept of regional differentiation of product standards is appealing for the economist, and notwithstanding the fact that

---

2. This aspect has been treated in the author's contribution to Walter (1976).

product standardization brings important economies of scale, there exists an overriding need to avoid nontariff barriers to trade.

Finally, national objectives require national emission limits (minimums).

At the regional level, emission standards will be adapted to regional objectives and conditions. But most product standards cannot be differentiated.

For example, in France there are specific zones in river basins according to which emission standards and charges are differentiated. There are air quality zones in the United States, noise rehabilitation zones in the Netherlands, and so forth.

CONCLUSION

To conclude, not only does economic efficiency require regional differentiation, but it also requires very fundamental sociopolitical considerations. Environmental policies do have their roots in regions, and only regional needs can make explicit the demand for environmental quality. But a national (central) impetus and coordination is also essential, since environmental is part of the socioeconomic policy of a nation. Apparently the delicate balance between national and regional settings has not yet been achieved. Things are evolving; for instance, in the field of water management, countries with a traditional centralized structure such as France and England have implemented decentralized water management institutions and policies (river basin agencies in France, river authorities in England). Conversely, more decentralized countries (United States, Germany) have a tendency to reinforce centralized management.

One final remark: conflicts will obviously arise between regions; one possible solution is compensation. This has been mentioned by Professor Frey, and some examples are given by M. Potier. This approach seems to me very important and promising. It should be related to the so-called new conservation approach that aims at keeping the national stock of natural resources constant and as such is a component of a national welfare policy. Also, damage compensation is an essential element of environmental law.

REFERENCES

OECD. *Public Expenditures Trends—1978.* Paris, 1978.

Walter, I, ed. *Studies in International Environmental Economics.* New York: Wiley, 1976.

CHAPTER 5

Dynamic Aspects of Regional Environmental Policy

FINN R. FØRSUND[1]

1. INTRODUCTION

In a very summary fashion one can say that the objective of regional environmental policy is to achieve a certain spatial distribution of environmental services. These services are assumed to be produced by the various regionally located recipients in competition with residual disposal services. The specific regional element of environmental policy is that policy measures are tailored according to the different natural characteristics or assimilative capacities of the recipients.

A natural distinction can be made between intraregional and interregional environmental policy, that is, considering a region as the unit of analysis, and considering interactions between regions as regards, for example, transportation of residuals.

As regards dynamic aspects, a distinction can be made between the economic activities generating primary and secondary residuals and the natural systems of the recipients "processing" the discharged residuals and producing environmental services. The standard dynamic feature of economic activities is the accumulation of capital. Purification or "modification" capital constitutes an additional capital category. When considering natural systems, the choice of the unit of time is important, that is, a dynamic ecological model can yield stationary solutions for variables that are then used in static economic models based on a more aggregated time unit.

---

1. I am indebted to Knut Sydsæter for helpful comments.

In section 2 some dynamic aspects of environmental policy in general are surveyed. It is not our purpose to go through the results obtained but to give an exposé of the basic relationships utilized in the trade. A dynamic problem of allocating investments on two regions is set out in section 3. The environmental aspect enters as current pollution and as accumulating pollutants.

2. SOME DYNAMIC ASPECTS OF ENVIRONMENTAL POLICY

A standard environmental management model specifies: (i) how primary and secondary residuals are generated by economic activities; (ii) the link between discharge of residuals and the environmental services yielded by the recipients; (iii) how the changes in these environmental services are evaluated; and (iv) the policy instruments available and their impact on economic and environmental magnitudes.

It is in the second element we may encounter dynamic problems specific to environmental problems. Time may here enter "in an essential way" owing to time lags between the discharge of residuals and the resulting change in environmental services and also to the fact that the current flow of environmental services is influenced not only by current discharge of residuals but also by previous discharges; that is, environmental services are functions of *stocks* of residuals (interpreted in a general way). Ecological models can, of course, contain both features. Such dynamic ecological models developed to function within the framework listed above are found in Russell (1975). They are all aquatic models containing various food chains, such as the ones leading up to the production of phytoplankton biomass.

The well-established "oxygen-sag" model illustrates the importance of the time unit chosen. The prediction of steady-state levels of dissolved oxygen derived from a dynamic model of decomposing organic residuals can be linked to a static environmental management model where the variables relate to a more aggregate time unit than is relevant for the oxygen-sag model.

Ecological or environmental models need to be numerically specified in order to yield solutions. As a habitual occupation, economists have tried to derive qualitative results of interest for environmental policy. Such undertakings have naturally been on a very high level of aggregation. I will here review the main types of models formulated in such a way that the theory of optimal control can be applied. In the context used the models can be interpreted as intraregional models.

Dynamic aggregate environmental models. In its most simple form, variations on the following dynamic problem has been posed (Haavelmo [1971]; d'Arge and Kogiku [1973]; Plourde [1972]; Smith [1972]):

$$\max_{c,e} \int_0^T A(t) u(c, e) dt$$

subject to

$$e = d(Z), \qquad d' < 0$$
$$\dot{Z} = g(c), \qquad g' > 0 \tag{2.1}$$

where

$u(c, e)$ = the social, or representative, preference function
T = the planning horizon
$A(t)$ = discounting function
c = rate of consumption
e = flow of environmental services
Z = stock of pollutants

The flow of environmental services from Nature depends on the accumulated stock of pollutants. This is the case of pure waste accumulation, or on this high level of aggregation one could say that the accumulation aspect represents the notion of entropy.

The model has naturally been expanded to include accumulation of production capital and a more general growth equation for pollutants (Keeler et al. [1971]; Nijkamp and Paelinck [1973]; Mäler [1974]):

$$\underset{c,e}{\text{Max}} \int_0^T A(t) u(c, e) dt$$

subject to

$$e = d(Z), \qquad d' < 0$$
$$x = f(K), \qquad f' > 0$$
$$c = (1 - s) x \tag{2.2}$$
$$\dot{K} = sx - D_x(K)$$
$$\dot{Z} = g(x, c, Z),$$

where the additional variables are:

x = rate of output
s = saving ratio
K = production capital
$D_x(K)$ = depreciation function for capital

The stock of pollutants can now "depreciate" if $\partial g / \partial Z < 0$; for example, the natural decomposition of organic waste. Model (2.2) can be further extended by introducing "purification" out of the current output rate (Keeler et al. [1971] and Nijkamp and Paelinck [1973]).

However, it seems more realistic to assume that current purification depends on the stock of purification capital (Strøm [1972]). The growth equation for the stock of pollutants then reads:

$$\dot{Z} = g(x, c, Z, K_p), \qquad \partial g/\partial K_p < 0$$

where K_p, the third state variable, is purification capital. The two controls in this model are the saving ratio and the share of investments to the purification activity. (In Gruver [1976]), purification and production capital are considered together with current pollution only.)

These basic models have been combined in various ways as regards depreciation and purification assumptions, terminal conditions on the state variables; and the length of the horizon, T; for example, whether it is finite or infinite. In d'Arge and Kogiku (1973) the horizon is determined endogenously as the extinction time. The population grows with an exogenously given rate right to the time of extinction.

This somewhat strange feature has been criticized in Strøm (1974), formulating a model where the population growth rate and the fraction of the working population of the total population are functions of the stock of pollutants. The pollutant is a current input (positive productivity) in the macro production sector. (Output is a function of the stock of pollutants [negative productivity] in Nijkamp and Paelinck [1973].)

Other dynamic aspects. It may also be instructive to consider dynamic aspects from the point of view of the environmental managers.

(i) Lack of information. Damage functions and abatement cost functions are seldom known explicitly by the decision makers. Therefore, a dynamic adjustment problem may arise. For example, discharges are restricted stepwise until the corresponding damages are regarded as optimal. The dynamic adjustment problem is to minimize the costs of achieving the final level of pollution; that is, the adjustment cost of the polluters in question must be taken into consideration.

Adjustment algorithms from the theory of economic planning can profitably be applied to this adjustment problem; for example, as in the use of iteration procedures such as introduced by Kornai-Liptak et al. (see Heal [1972]) concerning the allocation of a common resource to several units by a central planning authority.

A variant of this problem is the following setup. The central authority imposes certain quality standards as regards the recipients in question, but the authority does not know the exact connection between the current discharges of pollutants from various sources and the quality characteristics, which are conceptually *stock* variables. If, for instance, effluent charges are used to curb discharges of pollutants, the dynamic adjustment process of changing the charges until the desired quality standards are obtained will be similar to the well-known cobweb model (see Johannesson [1972]).

(ii) Impact of instruments.   In a dynamic setting the choice of instruments may have importance even though the different instruments solve the same short-run problem.   The fact that the different instruments can have a different impact on the net profit of firms when solving the same short-run environmental problems implies that the optimal expansion paths of firms depends on the instrument chosen.   Therefore, long-run objectives for the firms as regards growth in output, employment, and the like, must also be taken into consideration when deciding on instruments.

Consider the case of direct regulation restricting the assimilative capacity available for polluters, or fixing the total load—for instance, based on threshold considerations.   The problem then arises of how to utilize this fixed capacity over time within the existing legal framework of licensing.   Will it be optimal to allocate the total capacity now, or keep a certain reserve for the future arrival of a firm with a higher rate of profit than average (given the assumption that a license cannot be withdrawn too abruptly)?

One important aspect of introducing a charge is the incentive of actively developing new technology.   To the extent that technical change is endogenous, it is of special importance that the decision-making units face the *time path* of the prices, including the charge. (See Førsund [1975] for an analysis of the time path of the charge.)   Direct ad hoc regulation can result in increased costs to the society of achieving certain environmental qualities, because investments in technological development do not get the correct price signals.

A dynamic decision problem of the society is how to allocate resources between known abatement techniques now and investments in the developments of new technology reducing abatement costs at future dates.

The impact of regulation versus a charge on technological change in production and abatement activities has recently been analyzed on the firm level in Magat (1978).   The firm faces a certain return on R&D investments in terms of "augmenting" technical progress and can costlessly choose between getting abatement- or production-improvement within a given transformation relationship.   One of the main conclusions is that with a fixed tax rate over time the rate of residuals discharge will increase when output grows under reasonable assumptions.   A related model can also be found in McCain (1978).

(iii) Transitional problems.   The usual time lag between concrete action and the recognition of the necessity of adjusting the present pattern of economic development implies an initial effort of moving off the present growth path and onto the new one. A natural objective of the society is to minimize the costs of the initial catching-up effort, given the desired environmental qualities. This is a dynamic problem of at least two reasons.

(a) A putty-clay production structure.   The possibilities of changing the

production technique of a plant as regards factor proportions and discharge of pollutants may be more or less minimal *after* the concrete investment in a plant has been undertaken. The substitution possibilities are mostly present *ex ante* but not *ex post*. The capital structures have certain physical durabilities, which depend on price developments. The choices of present factor proportions and residual discharge technology have been made according to the firm's past price predictions. This implies that the present structure is not on the path of growth that is optimal when taking into consideration environmental qualities.

The dynamic adjustment problem is how to transform this given structure to a structure that is on the optimal path. It may well be optimal in a transitional period to treat already existing plants differently compared with the new investments, because the options are limited. When investing in new plants, the future time paths of all relevant prices, including effluent charges, should be taken into consideration by the decision-making units.

The impact of adjustment cost on the optimal application of an effluent charge has been studied in Harford (1976).

(b) Social costs of adjustment. The more rapid structural change due to the new environmental policy may cause local and regional problems as regards employment, migration, income distribution, and so on. Such social costs must be taken into consideration in the transitional period of reshaping the technological structure of firms. Regional economic objectives may constrain the pace of structural change.

3. POLLUTION AND OPTIMAL REGIONAL ALLOCATION OF INVESTMENT

Allocation of investment on regions is a central problem in dynamic regional analyses. In order to derive qualitative results a very simple model has to be considered. The analysis will be based on a model introduced by Rahman (1963) and analyzed in Intriligator (1964), and Takamaya (1967, 1968, 1974). There are two regions with one production sector each. Capital is the only explicit factor of production in the linear production functions. Given an objective function of maximizing the discounted total consumption within the horizon, how should total investment be allocated between the regions? The regional saving ratios are fixed. Owing to the linearity of the model, the optimal value of the investment share is either 0 or 1, and, most interesting, we may have a switch once from one to the other of these values. The switch can occur if the region with the highest product of the capital productivity and the saving ratio also has the highest saving ratio.

Current pollution. Let us now consider the introduction of environmental services into this model and start with only current discharge of pollutants having a negative impact on the flow of environmental services. The objective function to be maximized is:

$$\int_0^T e^{-rt} W(c_1(t), c_2(t), e_1(t), e_2(t)) \, dt \qquad (3.1)$$

where $c_i(t)$, $i = 1, 2$, is the rate of consumption, $e_i(t)$, $i = 1, 2$, is the rate of environmental services in region i at time t, T is the time horizon, and r is the societal discount rate.

The production system is:

$$x_i = f_i(K_i) = f_i K_i \qquad (3.2)$$
$$(i = 1, 2)$$
$$z_i = g_i(x_i) = g_i x_i \qquad (3.3)$$

where x_i is the output rate of region i, K_i the capital stock, and z_i the rate of pollutants. (The time index is omitted for notational ease.) The relationships are linearized directly using as fixed coefficients the same symbols as those that represent the general functions.

The flow of environmental services is related to the discharges of pollutants:

$$e_i = d_i(z_1, z_2) = - \sum_{j=1}^2 d_{ij} z_j \qquad (i = 1, 2) \qquad (3.4)$$

The maximal attainable flow of environmental services, $d_i(0, 0)$, is normalized to zero in the linear version. The pollutants are in general transported between both regions. In the linear case $[d_{ij}]$ is the "diffusion" matrix. The coefficients d_{ij} have the dimension environmental service units per unit of pollutant, that is, they show the impact on environmental services in region no. i of pollutants generated in region no. j. Thus, the specific features both of regional recipients and conceptualizations of environmental services are reflected in the unit impact coefficients d_{ij}.

The regional investments, $\dot{K}_i$, are made out of total savings:

$$\dot{K}_1 = \beta s \sum_{i=1}^2 x_i \qquad (3.5)$$

$$\dot{K}_2 = (1 - \beta) s \sum_{i=1}^2 x_i \qquad (3.6)$$

where s is the common saving ratio of the regions and β is the investment share of region 1. Obviously, $\beta \in [0, 1]$.

We will consider the linear versions of the relations and simplify the objective function to a simple sum of consumption and environmental services. It is assumed that these variables are measured in the same unit. (It would be straightforward to introduce linear weights to accomplish this.) Eliminating the current variables, we have the following optimal control model:

$$\underset{\beta}{\text{Max}} \int_0^T e^{-rt} \sum_{i=1}^2 \left[f_i\left(1 - s - \sum_{j=1}^2 d_{ji}g_i\right)K_i \right] dt$$

subject to

$$\dot{K}_1 = \beta s \sum_{i=1}^2 f_i K_i, \qquad K_1(0) = K_{10} > 0, \quad K_1(T) = \text{free}$$ (A)

$$\dot{K}_2 = (1 - \beta)s \sum_{i=1}^2 f_i K_i, \quad K_2(0) = K_{20} > 0, \quad K_2(T) = \text{free}$$

$$\beta \in [0, 1]$$

The Hamiltonian for the system is:

$$H = e^{-rt} \sum_{i=1}^2 f_i s_i K_i + p_1 \beta s \sum_{i=1}^2 f_i K_i + p_2(1 - \beta)s \sum_{i=1}^2 f_i K_i$$

$$= e^{-rt} \sum_{i=1}^2 f_i s_i K_i + (\beta(p_1 - p_2) + p_2)s \sum_{i=1}^2 f_i K_i, \qquad (3.7)$$

where p_1, p_2 are the adjoint variables, and

$$s_i = 1 - s - \sum_{j=1}^2 d_{ji}g_i$$

can be interpreted as the "social" rate of consumption of good no. i. Since environmental services and the produced goods are measured in the same unit, the reduction in the amount of environmental services in both regions generated by increasing the production in region no. i with one unit,

$$\sum_{j=1}^2 d_{ij}g_i,$$

can be subtracted from the common rate of consumption, $1 - s$. We will assume $s_i > 0$ ($i = 1, 2$) for all choices of β. (Since there are no restrictions on the terminal values of the state variables, the multiplier associated with the maximand is positive and normalized to 1 according to the transversality conditions.)

Model (A) is formally very close to the model versions presented in Intriligator (1964) and Takayama (1967, 1968, 1974). However, their approaches cannot be utilized directly owing to erroneous analyses on crucial points.

According to the maximum principle, the auxiliary variables satisfy the following differential equations:

$$\dot{p}_i(t) = \frac{\partial H}{\partial K_i} = -e^{-rt} f_i s_i - (\beta(p_1 - p_2) + p_2) s f_i \qquad (i = 1, 2) \qquad (3.8)$$

Combining these two relations an expression for the difference between the adjoint variables is obtained (utilizing the transversality conditions $p_i(T) = 0$ to determine the integration constants):

$$\frac{\dot{p}_1 + e^{-rt} f_1 s_1}{\dot{p}_2 + e^{-rt} f_2 s_2} = \frac{f_1}{f_2}, \qquad \dot{p}_1 = \frac{f_1}{f_2} \dot{p}_2 + e^{-rt} f_1(s_2 - s_1)$$

$$p_1(t) - p_2(t) = \frac{f_1 - f_2}{f_2} p_2(t) + f_1(s_1 - s_2) \frac{1}{r} (e^{-rt} - e^{-rT}) \qquad (3.9)$$

By maxamizing the Hamiltonian (3.7) with respect to β, we obtain

$$\beta = 1 \qquad \text{for} \quad p_1 > p_2$$

$$\beta = 0 \qquad \text{for} \quad p_1 < p_2 \qquad (3.10)$$

$$\beta \in [0, 1] \quad \text{for} \quad p_1 = p_2$$

As regards sufficient conditions for an optimal solution of model (A), we have that for each t, the Hamiltonian (3.7) maximized with respect to the control variable β is linear, and hence concave, in the state variables K_1, K_2. Therefore, according to the Arrow sufficiency theorem (see Seirestad and Sydsæter [1977, theorem 3, p. 370]) a solution satisfying the necessary conditions is indeed optimal.

Equation (3.9) shows that if $f_1 > f_2$ and $s_1 > s_2$, then $p_1(t) > p_2(t)$ for all $t \in [0, T]$. (It is easy to see that $p_i(t)$, $i = 1, 2$ are positive in $[0, T]$). For $t = T$ we have $p_i(T) = 0$ and from (3.8) $\dot{p}_i(T) < 0$. Thus, $p_i(T) > 0$ in an interval to the left of T. In that interval the term $(\beta(p_1 - p_2) + p_2) s f_i$ must be positive, and from (3.8) we have again $\dot{p}_i(t) < 0$, etc.)

Hence, for $f_1 > f_2$ and $s_1 > s_2$, $\beta(t) \equiv 1$ on $[0, T]$. If $f_1 > f_2$ and $s_1 < s_2$, the sign of $p_1(t) - p_2(t)$ is not necessarily constant on $[0, T]$, and there is a possibility for a switch in the optimal value of β.

From the definition of s_i we have that

$$s_1 - s_2 = -\sum_{j=1}^{2} d_{j1} g_1 + \sum_{j=1}^{2} d_{j2} g_2 = D_2 - D_1$$

that is, the difference in "damage" generated by a unit of output in regions 2 and 1, respectively. Even if the pollutant-generating technologies (3.3) are equal, that is, $g_1 = g_2$, the unit damage coefficients D_i may differ due to differences of the recipients and so on. Thus, the possibility of a switch of investments occurs when the region with the highest capital productivity has the highest damage coefficients. Note that this does not necessarily mean that the high productivity region is the most dirty, since the damage coefficients relate to the reduction in environmental services in both regions. This seems to be empirically relevant enough to warrant a closer examination.

Let us therefore now assume that $f_1 > f_2$ and $s_1 < s_2$. From (3.8) the difference between the growth rates for the adjoint variables is obtained:

$$\dot{p}_1 - \dot{p}_2 = -(\beta(p_1 - p_2) + p_2) s (f_1 - f_2) + (f_2 s_2 - f_1 s_1) e^{-rt} \qquad (3.11)$$

Since we have assumed $f_1 > f_2$ and $s_1 < s_2$, $f_2 s_2 - f_1 s_1$ may be positive. The condition is that $f_1 D_1 > f_2 D_2 + (f_1 - f_2)(1 - s)$, where D_i is the unit damage coefficient for output from region no. i. Let us assume that this is the case. We then note that at $t = T$, $\dot{p}_1 - \dot{p}_2$ is positive, implying that $p_1 < p_2$ on an interval to the left of T. One possibility is that $p_1(t) < p_2(t)$ on all of $[0, T)$. Then $\beta = 0$ is the optimal control on $[0, T)$. If this is not the case, let t^* be the maximum value of t for which $p_1(t) \geqslant p_2(t)$. Then $p_1(t^*) = p_2(t^*)$, and we have a switch from $\beta = 1$ to $\beta = 0$ at t^*. In order to investigate this possibility, let us find the functions for $p_i(t)$ on $[t^*, T]$. We then know that on this interval $\beta \equiv 0$. Starting with $p_2(t)$, the solution of the differential equation (3.8) is

$$p_2(t) = \frac{f_2 s_2}{s f_2 - r} e^{-rt} (e^{(s f_2 - r)(T - t)} - 1), \qquad t \in [t^*, T], \qquad (3.12)$$

where the transversality condition $p_2(T) = 0$ is used to determine the integration constant. The time function for p_1 then follows directly from (3.9).

The switching time t^* can now be found by inserting (3.12) in (3.9) and setting $p_1(t) = p_2(t)$ and solving for t.[2] On implicit form we have.

---

2. As mentioned above, the analyses in Intriligator (1964) and Takayama (1967, 1968, 1974) contain several errors. Since it is a rather unusual birth of a model, a short recapitulation may have some merit. In Intriligator (1964), Rahman's (1963) original model is reformulated to continuous time, and an objective function of total discounted consumption of the type used in this article is introduced in addition to Rahman's objective function of maximizing the terminal values of consumption. However, when solving for the time functions of the auxiliary variables mistakes appear for both types of objective functions, thus leading to erroneous conclusions. Takayama (1967) tries to correct these but makes mistakes himself in the very same equation. Then, when he tries to correct himself in Takayama (1968), he involves himself in a new type of error when deriving the expression for the switching time. This error is repeated in Takayama (1974) in more detail. Since I am not aware that this erroneous line of reasoning has been corrected elsewhere, let me just hint at the crux of the matter. When deriving the switching time, Takayama (1968, 1974), in addition to $p_1(t) = p_2(t)$, also implicitly imposes the restriction $\dot{p}_1(t) = \dot{p}_2(t)$. This last restriction is clearly not relevant.

$$\frac{(f_1 - f_2)s_2}{sf_2 - r} e^{-rt}(e^{(sf_2 - r)(T - t)} - 1) + f_1(s_1 - s_2)\frac{1}{r}(e^{-rt} - e^{-rT}) = 0$$

$$(3.13)$$

The impact on the switching time of changes in the various parameters can be studied by implicit differentiation of (3.13).

Can we have more than one switch? Remembering the property of p_1, p_2 being positive, it follows directly from (3.9) that if there is a switch, it can only be once.

On the interval $[0, t^*]$, $\beta \equiv 1$, and solving (3.8) for $p_1(t)$ yields:

$$p_1(t) = \left(p_1(t^*) + \frac{f_1 s_1}{sf_1 - r} e^{-rt^*}\right) e^{sf_1(t^* - t)} - \frac{f_1 s_1}{sf_1 - r} e^{-rt}, \qquad t \in [0, t^*],$$

$$(3.14)$$

where $p_1(t^*)$ is determined by inserting (3.12) in (3.9) and setting $t = t^*$. The solution for $p_2(t)$ follows directly by inserting (3.14) in (3.9). A numerical solution is provided as an illustration in Figure 5-1 for reasonable values of the parameters.

Summing up, a switch may occur in the optimal investment allocation policy if there is a conflict between capital productivity and generation of pollution in the production activity of a region. Intuitively, the switch can be explained by reasoning that greater consumption possibilities are obtained by allocating investments to the high productivity region, but when production in this region generates sufficiently more pollution, it pays eventually to switch all the investments to the low pollution sector because the gain in less pollution outweighs the loss of production potential built up by investments in the high productivity sector.

Accumulating pollutants. Let us now consider the case of the flow of environmental services depending on the accumulated stock of pollutants. Instead of Eq. (3.3) we now have:

$$\dot{Z}_i = g_i(x_1, x_2) = \sum_{j=1}^{2} g_{ij} x_j \qquad (i = 1, 2) \tag{3.15}$$

where $\dot{Z}_i$ is the flow of pollutants to region no. i generated by the production activities in both regions, and Z_i the stock pollutants in region no. i. The matrix $[g_{ij}]$ is now a dispersion matrix in physical units. Equation (3.4) becomes:

$$e_i = d_i(Z_i) = -d_i Z_i \qquad (i = 1, 2) \tag{3.16}$$

where in the linear version the flows of environmental services is again normalized to zero when the stock of pollutants is zero. The coefficients d_i reflect the characteristics of the regional recipients and the conceptualization of environmental services. For simplicity, any natural depreciation of the stocks are disregarded. On the basis of the linear version of Eqs. (3.1), (3.2), (3.15), (3.16), (3.5), and (3.6), the following control problem is formulated:

$$\text{Max}_{\beta} \int_0^T e^{-rt} \sum_{i=1}^{2} ((1 - s) f_i K_i - d_i Z_i) \, dt$$

subject to

$$\dot{K}_1 = \beta s \sum_{i=1}^{2} f_i K_i, \qquad K_1(0) = K_{10} > 0, \quad K_1(T) = \text{free}$$

$$\dot{K}_2 = (1 - \beta) s \sum_{i=1}^{2} f_i K_i, \quad K_2(0) = K_{20} > 0, \quad K_2(T) = \text{free}$$

$$\dot{Z}_i = \sum_{j=1}^{2} g_{ij} f_j K_j, \qquad Z_i(0) = Z_{i0} > 0, \quad Z_i(T) = \text{free}, \qquad i = 1, 2$$

$$\beta \in [0, 1]$$

(B)

It is assumed that both terms of the sum in the maximand are positive for all choices of β.

The Hamiltonian is:

$$H = e^{-rt} \sum_{i=1}^{2} ((1 - s) f_i K_i - d_i Z_i) + (\beta (p_1 - p_2) + p_2) s \sum_{i=1}^{2} f_i K_i$$

$$+ p_3 \sum_{j=1}^{2} g_{1j} f_j K_j + p_4 \sum_{j=1}^{2} g_{2j} f_j K_j, \qquad (3.17)$$

where p_3, p_4 are the auxiliary variables associated with the state variables Z_1, Z_2. According to the maximum principle, the auxiliary variables satisfy the following differential equations:

$$\dot{p}_i = - \frac{\partial H}{\partial K_i} = -e^{-rt} (1 - s) f_i - (\beta (p_1 - p_2) + p_2) s f_i$$

$$- f_i (p_3 g_{1i} + p_4 g_{2i}) \qquad (i = 1, 2) \qquad (3.18)$$

$$\dot{p}_{i+2} = - \frac{\partial H}{\partial Z_i} = e^{-rt} d_i \qquad (i = 1, 2) \qquad (3.19)$$

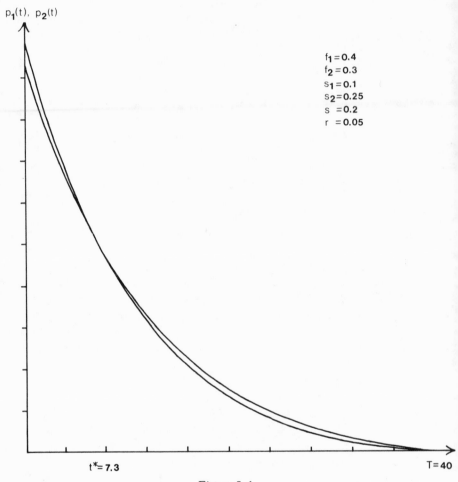

Figure 5-1

Since $Z_i(T)$ is free, $p_{i+2}(T) = 0$, so integrating (3.19) yields:

$$p_{i+2}(t) = -\frac{1}{r}(e^{-rt} - e^{-rT})d_i = -\frac{1}{r}e^{-rt}(1 - e^{-r(T-t)})d_i \qquad (i = 1, 2)$$

$$(3.20)$$

The shadow prices on the pollution stocks are negative and monotonic increasing to zero at time T. Combining (3.18) and (3.20) yields:

$$\dot{p}_1(t) = \frac{f_1}{f_2}\dot{p}_2(t) - \frac{f_1}{r}e^{-rt}(1 - e^{-r(T-t)})\left(\sum_{j=1}^{2} d_j g_{j2} - \sum_{j=1}^{2} d_j g_{j1}\right)$$

Integrating and using $p_i(T) = 0$, we obtain:

$$p_1(t) - p_2(t) = \frac{f_1 - f_2}{f_2}\, p_2(t) + (D_2 - D_1)\, E(t), \qquad (3.21)$$

where

$$D_i = \sum_{j=1}^{2} d_j\, g_{ji}, \qquad i = 1, 2$$

$$E(t) = \frac{f_1}{r}\left(\frac{1}{r}\, e^{-rt} + t \cdot e^{-rT} - e^{-rT}\left(T + \frac{1}{r}\right)\right)$$

The interpretation of D_i is the instantaneous damage caused in both regions by a unit of production in region no. i.

As for model (A) we have that the optimal allocation policy is described in (3.10). As regards sufficiency conditions, we have again that the Hamiltonian (3.17) maximized with respect to the control variable β is linear, and hence concave, in the state variables K_1, K_2, Z_1, Z_2. A solution satisfying the necessary conditions is therefore indeed optimal (Seierstad and Sydsæter [1977]). If $f_1 > f_2$ and $D_2 > D_1$, Eq. (3.25) shows that $p_1 > p_2$ and hence $\beta = 1$ when $E(t) > 0$. Since $E(T) = 0$ and $dE(t)/dt < 0$, $E(t)$ is positive. Furthermore, $E(t)$ is strictly convex since $d^2E(t)/dt^2$ is positive. If the instantaneous damage is highest for the region with the highest capital productivity, a switch in the optimal policy may again be the case. From Eqs. (3.18) and (3.20) we get:

$$\dot{p}_1 - \dot{p}_2 = -\left[\beta(p_1 - p_2) + p_2\right](f_1 - f_2)s$$

$$+ e^{-rt}\left[\frac{1}{r}\left(1 - e^{-r(T-t)}\right)(f_1 D_1 - f_2 D_2) - (f_1 - f_2)(1 - s)\right] \qquad (3.22)$$

Consider now $t = T$. Equation (3.22) then yields that $\dot{p}_1 - \dot{p}_2 = -(f_1 - f_2)(1 - s)\, e^{-rt}$ independently of the values of the instantaneous unit damage coefficients. This implies that on an interval to the left of T the optimal value of the control β must be 1 when $f_1 > f_2$. It seems intuitively obvious that if the difference in the D_i coefficients is sufficiently large when $D_1 > D_2$ we will have a switch from zero to 1. Proceeeding as in the analysis of model (A), we can start by finding the maximum value t^* of t for which $p_1(t) \geqslant p_2(t)$. When $f_1 > f_2$ we have $\beta \equiv 1$ in the first interval to the left of T. Solving (3.18) for $p_1(t)$ when the solutions (3.20) are inserted yields:

$$p_1(t) = \frac{D_1}{rs}\, e^{-rT}(e^{sf_1(T-t)} - 1) + \frac{f_1 D_1 - (1-s)f_1 r}{(sf_1 - r)r}$$

$$\cdot\, e^{-rt}(1 - e^{(sf_1 - r)(T-t)}), \qquad t \in [t^*, T] \qquad (3.23)$$

The solution for $p_2(t)$ follows from inserting (3.23) in (3.21). The maximal switching time t^* can now be found by solving for t from the following equation:

$$\frac{f_1 - f_2}{f_2} \frac{D_1}{rs} e^{-rT} (e^{sf_1(T-t)} - 1) + \frac{f_1 - f_2}{f_2} \frac{f_1 D_1 - (1-s)f_1 r}{(sf_1 - r)r}$$

$$\cdot e^{-rt}(1 - e^{(sf_1 - r)(T-t)}) + (D_2 - D_1) E(t) = 0 \qquad (3.24)$$

Could we have more than one switch? If it is optimal to start with $\beta = 0$, it does not, intuitively, seem possible to have more than one switch. The reason for switching is that the accumulation of pollutants does not count that much toward the end of the planning period; the higher productivity in the provision of current consumption matters more. To have two (or more) switches before the last switch is therefore implausible. However, it could be optimal to start out with $\beta = 1$, then switch to $\beta = 0$ when the burden of the accumulated pollutants is too much to carry with us for the rest of the planning period, and then switch to $\beta = 1$ toward the end when the accumulation does not have time enough to make itself felt.

Let us assume that there is a second switching time, $t^{**} < t^*$. On the interval $[t^{**}, t^*]$ we then have $\beta = 0$. To find the switching time t^{**}, the time function $p_2(t)$ for $t \in [t^{**}, t^*]$ can be found by solving (3.18):

$$p_2(t) = p_2(t^*) e^{sf_2(t^* - t)} + \frac{D_2}{rs} e^{-rT}(e^{sf_2(t^* - t)} - 1) + \frac{D_2 f_2 - (1-s)f_2 r}{(sf_2 - r)r}$$

$$\cdot e^{-rt}(1 - e^{-(sf_2 + r)(t^* - t)}), \qquad t \in [t^{**}, t^*], \qquad (3.25)$$

where $p_2(t^*)$ is found by inserting $t = t^*$ in the time function for $p_2(t)$ on $[t^*, T]$. Setting $p_1(t) = p_2(t)$ in (3.21) and inserting (3.25), we have the implicit equation for determining t^{**}.

The time functions for p_1, p_2 and the implicit expressions that determine the switching times are so complex that it is difficult to draw conclusions without numerical analyses.

In comparing the investment allocation policy for the two cases of current pollution and accumulating pollutants, we have found a difference as regards the last period. If we have a switch in the former case, it will be from plowing all investments into the most productive and "dirty" region to the least productive and "clean" one. In the latter case it is the "dirty" and high productive region that will always be allocated all the investments in the last interval of the planning period. Moreover, we can have only one switch in the current pollution case, whereas we might have two in the accumulating pollutants case.

REFERENCES

d'Arge, R. C., and K. C. Kogiku. "Economic Growth and the Environment." *Review of Economic Studies* 60, no. 1 (January 1973): 61–77.

Førsund, F. R. "The Polluter Pays Principle and Transitional Period Measures in a Dynamic Setting." *Swedish Journal of Economics* 77, no. 1 (1975): 56–68.

—— and S. Strøm. "Industrial Structure, Growth and Residual Flows." In J. G. Rothenberg and I. G. Heggie, eds., *The Management of Water Quality and the Environment*. London: Macmillan, 1974.

Gruver, G. W. "Optimal Investment in Pollution Control Capital in a Neoclassical Growth Context." *Journal of Environmental Economics and Management* 3, no. 3 (1976): 165–177.

Haavelmo, T. "Forurensningsproblemet fra et Samfunnsvitenskapelig Synspunkt." *Sosialøkonomen* 25, no. 4 (April 1971): 5–8.

Harford, J. D. "Adjustment Costs and Optimal Waste Treatment." *Journal of Environmental Economics and Management* 3, no. 3 (1976): 215–225.

Heal, G. M. *The Theory of Economic Planning*. Amsterdam and London: North-Holland, 1972.

Intriligator, M. D. "Regional Allocation of Investment: Comment." *Quarterly Journal of Economics* 73, no. 4 (1964): 659–662.

Johannesson, M. "Dynamic Aspects on the Use of Prices for Protecting the Environment." *Swedish Journal of Economics* 74, no. 2 (June 1972): 286–291.

Johansen, L. *Production Functions*. Amsterdam and London: North-Holland, 1972.

Keeler, E., M. Spence, and R. Zeckhauser. "The Optimal Control of Pollution." *Journal of Economic Theory* 4, no. 1 (1971): 19–34.

McCain, R. A. "Endogenous Bias in Technical Progress and Environmental Policy." *American Economic Review* 68, no. 4 (1978): 538–546.

Magat, W. A. "Pollution Control and Technological Advance: A Dynamic Model of the Firm." *Journal of Environmental Economics and Management* 5, no. 1 (1978): 1–25.

Mäler, K. G. *Environmental Economics. A Theoretical Inquiry*. Baltimore and London: The Johns Hopkins University Press, 1974.

Nijkamp, P., and J. H. P. Paelinck. "Some Models for the Economic Evaluation of the Environment." *Regional and Urban Economics* 3, no. 1 (1973), 33–62.

Plourde, C. G. "A Model of Waste Accumulation and Disposal." *Canadian Journal of Economics* 5, no. 1 (February 1972): 119–125.

Rahman, Md. A. "Regional Allocation of Investment." *Quarterly Journal of Economics* 77 (1973).

Russell, C. S., ed. *Ecological Modeling*. Resources for the Future. Washington, D.C., 1975.

Seierstad, A., and K. Sydsæter. "Sufficient Conditions in Optimal Control Theory." *International Economic Review* 18, no. 2 (1977): 367–391.

Smith, V. L. "Dynamics of Waste Accumulation: Disposal versus Recycling."
    Quarterly Journal of Economics 80, no. 4 (1972): 601–616.
Strøm, S. "Dynamics of Pollution and Waste Treatment Activities." Memo-
    randum. Institute of Economics, University of Oslo, May 10, 1972.
———. "Dynamics of Pollution." Unpublished manuscript (1974).
Takayama, A. "Regional Allocation of Investment: A Further Analysis."
    Quarterly Journal of Economics 81, no. 2 (1967): 330–337.
———. "Regional Allocation of Investment: Corrigendum." *Quarterly Jour-
    nal of Economics* 82, no. 3 (1968): 526–527.
———. *Mathematical Economics.* Hinsdale, Ill.: Dryden Press, 1974.

DISCUSSION

Some Extensions of the Theory of Regional Growth and Environmental Policy

ALAN EVANS

What is meant by "the regional dimension of environmental policy"? It is evident from the various papers in this volume that environmental policy can be given a regional dimension in various ways. The concept can be interpreted narrowly or widely. In my view, Finn Førsund interprets the concept fairly narrowly, with the result that some important "dynamic" aspects of regional environmental policy are not discussed by him. I believe they deserve further analysis, so I shall briefly introduce these aspects.

To begin with, however, it would seem worthwhile to set out the various ways in which environmental policy can be given a regional dimension, for I believe the authors of these papers may be unaware of these conceptual differences.

First, it is possible to argue that, from the individual's point of view, improvements to the environment are relevant to his welfare only if they are made in the region within which he lives and works and are irrelevant elsewhere. Moreover, an improvement to the environment such as a reduction in smoke emission will usually affect only those living or working in the immediate vicinity of such a reduction. Thus, environmental policy is perforce regional, indeed intraregional, in nature. This is the narrowest interpretation of the concept, but it is one that occurs very frequently in these pages (see, e.g., papers of Thoss, Dreyhaupt, and Førsund).

Second, it may be observed that pollutants emitted in one region may affect the population located in another. Therefore, environmental policy has interregional effects. As an example of this, the attempt to reduce pollution in the United Kingdom by making factory chimneys taller has apparently caused an increase in pollution in Norway and Sweden on the other side of the North Sea. A common example is the pollution caused by industry in the upper reaches of a river affecting the population living nearer the sea. In such a case, it has sometimes been argued that the whole river basin should be treated as one region, but this argument appears less plausible in the case of air pollution, as the example cited above shows. Interregional dimensions of this kind, or spillover effects, are discussed here, for example, by Førsund, Cumberland, and Nijkamp.

Third, the population of one region may have an interest in the environment in another region because they visit that region. For example, the peoples of northern Europe have an interest in the quality of the environment in southern Europe because they go there on holiday. People in the rest of the United States have an interest in air quality in Arizona because they hope to visit that state and see, among other things, the Grand Canyon. This is implied in the paper by Kneese and Williams; I discuss the problem briefly in the last section of this paper. The visitors may have no direct political voice in the controls imposed on the environment in the region they visit. Moreover, although they have an indirect say, through the money that it is anticipated they will spend there, this indirect voice is inadequate, as I have shown elsewhere (Evans [1978]). Their wish to visit this location will, in the absence of specific controls, result in its deterioration.

Fourth, the widest interpretation of what is meant by a regional dimension of environmental policy is in my view the most interesting, but one that is touched on very little (but see the papers by Frey and Potier). Instead of the pollutants moving between regions or the people moving between regions, as in the second and third cases outlined above, the activities emitting the pollutants may move between regions. Environmental policy may, therefore, also refer to the choice of location by activities that affect the environment. Moreover, this wider interpretation is important because only water- or air-borne pollutants can be carried between regions, but the location of a factory or other activity may affect the environment not only through the emission of pollutants but also visually and aurally. These latter factors are unlikely to be considered under normal circumstances in any study of interregional pollution.

Thus, Finn Førsund in his paper, considers pollution only in the form of emissions. In his interpretation, the problem becomes dynamic because as the extent of current pollution is changing, the "stocks" of pollutants resulting from past emissions affect the present. The reasons for the change in the level of pollution are largely unstated, but this change would appear to be due mainly to changes in regional environmental policy.

In my discussion, the dynamic element occurs largely because of regional growth, whether latent or actual. It is assumed that there is an interrelationship between the growth of a region and the state of the environment. By "growth" I tend to mean changes in the prosperity of a region relative to other regions. I assume that increases in the relative prosperity of a region will tend to lead to in-migration and that decreases in the relative prosperity of a region will lead either to out-migration or to unemployment.

It may be noted that interpreting "the regional dimension" in the widest sense allows us to consider the environment as a whole, including the state of the physical environment as well as the level of pollution. Economists tend to concentrate on the latter rather too much, in my view, since I would think that the state of the physical environment is usually considered equally important by the ordinary citizen. Moreover, it probably varies a great deal more than the level of pollution, largely because the latter, in most developed economies, is respectably low.

ENVIRONMENTAL PLANNING CONTROLS IN INDUSTRY

Of fundamental importance when considering the dynamic aspects of regional environmental policy is the way in which the rate of growth of the region will affect the political will of those charged with the enforcement of environmental controls. In the United Kingdom, as in most mixed economies, environmental planning is carried out mainly by negative controls. Positive planning is difficult and has to be carried out mainly by using subsidies or incentives, as in the case of the financial incentives used to encourage firms to locate in the less prosperous regions. It is extremely difficult to force a firm to do something it does not want to do. It is far easier to prevent a firm from doing something it wants to do. Indeed studies of the effectiveness of regional policy have generally shown that the controls that have prevented firms locating in the more prosperous regions have been more successful in making firms set up plants in the Development Areas, although unwillingly, than have the various financial incentives.

Both environmental planning and regional policy are, however, carried out by means of negative controls. When and where they reinforce each other this causes no problems, but where they do not things are more difficult. Thus, in the prosperous regions, regional policy is designed to prevent firms from locating there unless they can give very good reasons for doing so. In the less prosperous regions, regional policy is intended to encourage firms to locate there. Environmental planning is intended to prevent firms from locating in particular locations in any region where their presence would be detrimental to the environment. Thus, a firm wishing to locate a plant in a prosperous region would stand little chance of obtaining planning permission for a location in which there was an attempt to preserve the environment, and if it wished to remain in the region it would be forced to choose the location thought to be the most environmentally desirable by the planning authority.

On the other hand, a firm that wished to set up a plant in a region in decline would be encouraged to do so, and it might get permission to locate in a position that was detrimental to the environment in order to ensure that it located in that region. This would be even more likely to occur if there were several regions in decline, each therefore desiring additional employment, and if environmental planning were under local control. A firm could then play one planning authority off against another by saying that unless environmental controls were weakened in one region it would locate in another. Similarly, the various planning authorities would be more likely to weaken environmental planning controls in order not to drive away possible employment. One would therefore expect environmental planning controls to be stronger and implemented more conscientiously and more effectively in growing regions than in declining regions, and thus that their effectiveness would be correlated with the rate of growth of the region. Could this be, in some sense, optimal? Or should controls be implemented centrally so it would be not possible for regional governments to weaken controls to attract industry?

In the situation I have described it seems possible that the relaxation of controls may be a second-best policy even if it is not a first-best policy. Why does the unemployment occur? One reason might be that wage rates are laid down through national bargaining, with the result that there is little incentive to move from one region to another and because housing policy may restrict people's mobility. One way of encouraging industry to move to a high unemployment region might be a form of labor subsidy such as the Regional Employment Premium operated in the United Kingdom between 1966 and 1978. The cost of implementing this is borne by the United Kingdom as a whole. If environmental policy is relaxed in the high unemployment region, this can be seen as a way of granting a form of subsidy in which the costs falls wholly on the residents of that region. Thus, such a policy may be optimal.

It has been mentioned in discussion in this volume that central governments regard the relaxation of environmental controls by regions with suspicion if not with disfavor. If the foregoing analysis is correct, why should this be so? What is it that they fear? The costs of the policy are borne by the regions, and therefore there would seem to be no obvious objection. One possible answer is that there may be a fear that such a policy might be irreversible, so that it would become impossible for the regional government to improve the environment once industry had been attracted and the unemployment rate had fallen.

In a recent paper, Ray Richardson and I have put forward a theory to explain the fact that unemployment in British cities is highly correlated with the proportion of the population that is unskilled (Evans and Richardson [1978]). Metcalf (1975) has argued that this is because the unskilled are more likely to be unemployed. We argue that the direction of causation is more likely to be in the other direction. Suppose the employment situation in a town or region worsens, say because of a decline in the demand for the product of a local industry; it is clear that the more skilled find it easier to migrate. Thus, the unemployment rate of the skilled tends to be almost constant over the whole country, but the unemployment rate of the unskilled varies. As a result, we argue, the firms or plants that can be attracted to areas of high unemployment are those employing a high proportion of unskilled labor. Therefore, the population that moves out will be relatively skilled, but the jobs that move in will be relatively unskilled, so that the skill structure of the population will tend to diverge from the national average.

In the context of the present volume this divergence is important. Environmental quality is not an inferior good. We would expect that people would be willing to spend more on environmental quality if their incomes were higher. For example, there is some evidence quoted by Walters (1975) that the income elasticity of demand for peace and quiet may be about 2.0. Thus if, as we argue above, the population becomes less skilled in a depressed region so that average incomes fall, the population will become more willing to allow governments to reduce environmental quality, particularly if this means that jobs will be encouraged. But the problem may now be that because environmental quality is low, the more skilled will become less willing to move to the area, or more likely to move away if they are already there, thus setting in motion a further sequence of environmental deterioration. Moreover, the initial policy may fail to achieve its aim of attracting industry if environmental quality becomes so low that it is difficult to attract the few managers and other skilled people who must be employed in the factories even when the labor force may on average be less skilled.

Thus, it is possible both that deliberate environmental deterioration may become cumulative and difficult to stop and also in the end fail to achieve its policy objective. If this is so, central governments would be right to discourage regional authorities from deliberately relaxing environmental controls to encourage industry.

ENVIRONMENTAL POLICY AND REGIONAL POLICY

If the argument set out at the end of the previous section is correct, it would explain not only why central governments are unwilling to allow regional environmental deterioration but also why they may take positive steps to improve the environment in less prosperous regions. If this is done, the more skilled may be encouraged to return to these areas and the process of cumulative deterioration reversed.

In Britain it has been thought that the slag heaps and wasteland left by mining and industry have discouraged firms from locating plants in some regions because managers have been unwilling to move to these areas. Even if the managers may been willing to move, it has been widely believed that their wives have not wished to go! As a result, the improvement of the physical environment has been incorporated into regional policy.

Grants are available towards the costs of acquiring and cleaning unsightly or neglected derelict land in the assisted areas where this is expedient with a view to contributing to the development of industry. Grants are at 85 per cent in Development Areas and Special Development Areas and 75 per cent in Intermediate Areas. Grants at 75 per cent are also available throughout the remainder of the North West and Yorkshire and Humberside and parts of the North Midlands, designated as Derelict Land Clearance Areas, under the Local Employment Act 1970 (EFTA[1971, p. 160]).

This means that environmental improvement of this kind is subsidized by central government everywhere in the United Kingdom outside the South East, East Anglia, and most of the Midlands, the latter composed of areas where there is relatively little derelict land anyway.

It may be noted that it is also part of regional policy to improve the infrastructure in order to encourage the in-migration of industry.

Grants of up to 30 per cent are available throughout the assisted areas for the improvement of basic services (transport, power, sewerage, etc) where this is deemed expedient for the development of industry. (EFTA[1971, p. 160]).

It is of course arguable whether these improvements to the infrastructure constitute an improvement to the environment. The policy does mean that there is greater public investment in the assisted areas than in the nonassisted areas than would be justified on a strict calculation of current costs and benefits, and therefore although congestion may be greater in the nonassisted areas, there will be greater environmental intrusion in the assisted areas through public investment in, say, roads.

THE RURAL REGION

The discussion in the two preceding sections describes the situation in regions that are already industrialized; the example I had in mind in writing were West Central Scotland and South East England. A different situation arises when one is talking of a rural region. There the environment is usually considered most beautiful (by the town dweller) if the region is picturesquely in decline. Even a region that remains rural but where agriculture is prosperous may be regarded by townsfolk with disfavor. In the more prosperous parts of the English countryside, for example, either the traditional small fields with hedgerows are being replaced by hedgeless farms more suited to modern agricultural machinery, or animal husbandry of a traditional kind is being replaced by factory farming with the birds or animals in long, low, almost windowless, gray concrete buildings. In neither case do the visual effects find favor with the urban population, which regards the agricultural areas as an environmental amenity.

An even more difficult situation arises if the growth in the region is likely to occur because of industrialization, for this may completely change the area. In this situation latent growth is clearly bad for the environment, while gentle decline will be good for it. The clearest example of this situation in the United Kingdom is the recent pressure on the Highlands and Islands of Scotland for development connected with the exploitation of North Sea oil. Sites for the location of terminals or for the construction of oil rigs have had to be fitted into an environment where almost any location will spoil some unspoiled aspect. Fortunately, the Highlands are large, so that the development has been small in relation to the total land area, but the discovery and proposed exploitation of new English coalfields in Yorkshire, Leicestershire, and Oxfordshire are raising the same problems but in areas that are small, so that it would be difficult to make industrial development unobtrusive. Which do we value more highly? Economic growth or the environment?

GROWTH AND DECLINE AND ITS IMPACT
ON THE ENVIRONMENT

In this section we draw on an argument I presented some time ago in a book on the economics of residential location (Evans [1973]). I showed there that in an area in which rents are increasing, property is likely to be newer, or rather have a shorter economic life, than in an area in which rents are decreasing. I have since developed the argument using growth theory (Evans [1975]), but since the earlier argument, based on comparative statics, is more general and easier to understand, I shall recapitulate it here. Suppose we indicate the quantity of space that can be developed on a particular site, that is, the density of development, on the horizontal axis in Figure 5-2, and costs and prices on the vertical axis.

Now, the relationship between the marginal cost of increases in density is likely to be as shown by the curve MM in the figure. If, therefore, the price

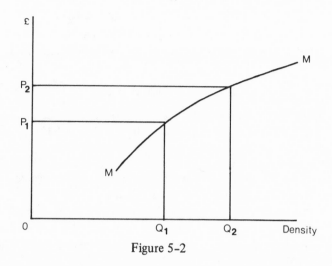

Figure 5-2

of space is P_1, the profit-maximizing density for a newly constructed building will be Q_1. If the price were P_2, the optimal density will be Q_2. Suppose now that the price is initially P_1, that buildings of density Q_1 are constructed, but the price of space increases to P_2. Given that the buildings are already in existence, does the owner have an incentive to redevelop? It is obvious the incentive is fairly strong, since if he does not redevelop his income is $P_2 Q_1$ and if he does his income is $P_2 Q_2$, a clear gain of $P_2(Q_2 - Q_1)$. Suppose, on the other hand, that the rent as initially P_2, that buildings of density Q_2 were constructed, but the price of space fell to P_1. If he does not redevelop the site, his income will be $P_1 Q_2$, and if he does his income will be $P_1 Q_1$, a clear loss of $P_1(Q_1 - Q_2)$. Thus, if the rent is falling the developer has no incentive to redevelop, but if it is increasing he does. If we now make allowances for both the capital cost of redevelopment and for the fact that as the building ages and becomes obsolete the net rent obtainable would not be constant but would tend to decrease over time, the implication is clear. The faster the price of space rises, the quicker the buildings will be demolished and replaced. The slower the rate of increase, the more likely it is that the built environment will be old, obsolete, and decaying. Since the price of space in a region will be a function of the demand for space, and hence of the rate of growth of the region, we can see that this is another instance of the way in which the rate of growth of the region will be related to the state of the environment.

The fact that buildings are likely to be replaced earlier in the faster-growing region is also likely to affect the environment if technical progress that improves the environment is incorporated, or embodied, in the newest buildings. If this is the case, then since the faster-growing region has the newest buildings, environmental improvements, whether brought about by market forces or by the law as an instrument of policy, will be more quickly effective in the faster-growing region than in the slower-growing region.

ENVIRONMENTAL CLUBS

In a recently published paper, which, however, results from a conference on the quality of life held nearly four years ago, I argued that the theory of clubs, or consumption with externalities due to congestion, was formally similar to the theory of common property resources, or production with externalities due to congestion, and went on to prove various results relating to market failure in the control of entry to clubs.

In brief, a club-type situation arises where a good of some kind is consumed in common with other people, but the consumption of the good by others reduces the enjoyment obtained from consumption of the good. I cited as examples tourist attractions or national parks, where the low cost of entry means that entry is virtually uncontrolled. Where there exists what could be regarded as a system of such clubs, some will be regarded, in the absence of congestion, as more attractive than others. Therefore, more people will visit these "better" clubs. There will therefore be greater congestion in these "better" clubs, and this will make them less attractive. The equilibrium situation will come about when all the clubs are equally attractive to consumers choosing between them, the natural attractiveness of the "better" clubs being balanced by greater congestion.

I went on to show that the same arguments are applicable even when the club is an environment that can be consumed only by purchasing or renting a site within it, unless the land is owned by a single landowner, or unless planning controls restrict the amount of development. In the absence of either of these alternatives, the amount of development would be greater than the Pareto—optimal level. In the areas with the naturally better environments, development would tend to be excessive, resulting in environmental deterioration. Once again, the equilibrium situation is one where the attractiveness of environments in different areas will tend to be equalized through overdevelopment in the "better" areas. Obvious examples of this occurring are tourist resorts, but the argument is also applicable to regions; for example, consider the impact of migration on California: the migration happens because of the favorable environment but itself results in a deterioration of that environment.

The relevance of this argument to the problem of regional economic policy is obvious. In the absence of a battery of controls, and *ceteris paribus*, the improvement of one area or region relative to another may result in migration into the "improved" area, and this in-migration will lead to a deterioration of the environment in that area until the amenity of the two areas is equalized.

CONCLUSION

In this discussion I have attempted to show the way in which regional economic growth and regional environmental policy are interlinked. First, a region with low growth prospects, may weaken environmental controls to encourage plants to move there; second, it may attempt to improve the environment in order to encourage people to move there, particularly the owners and managers of plants. Third, a region that is growing rapidly is likely to have newer buildings and newer technology, while a region that is not growing rapidly is likely to have older buildings and an older technology to monitor and control the environment. Finally, in-migration is likely to cause a deterioration in the environment, so that (a) in the absence of controls, environmental improvements may be self-defeating, and (b) the environment in growing regions may deteriorate.

On balance, I feel that the low growth region will be the one with a poorer visual environment and higher levels of pollution, while the residents of the high growth region will suffer more from congestion.

REFERENCES

European Free Trade Area Secretariat. *Regional Policy in EFTA: Industrial Mobility*. Geneva: EFTA, 1971.

Evans, Alan. *The Economics of Residential Location*. London: Macmillan, 1973.

_____. "Rent and Housing in the Theory of Urban Growth." *Journal of Regional Science* 15, no. 2 (August 1975).

_____. "Neighborhood Externalities, Economic Clubs, and the Environment." In Lowden Wingo and Alan Evans, ed., *Public Economics and the Quality of Life*. Baltimore: The Johns Hopkins University Press, 1978.

_____ and Ray Richardson. "Unemployment in Urban Areas: a Critical Survey." Unpublished manuscript. University of Reading (1978).

Metcalf, David. "Urban Unemployment in England." *Economic Journal* 85 (September 1975): 578–589.

Walters, Alan. *Noise and Prices*. Oxford: Clarendon Press, 1975.

DISCUSSION

Dynamic Aspects of Regional
Environmental Allocations:
A Comment

HORST SIEBERT

In the Førsund model the dynamic aspects of regional environmental policy are considered from the point of view of the planner who maximizes a welfare function for a two-region system subject to constraints. The intertemporal characteristics of the model are given by capital accumulation and the accumulation of pollutants. I would like to put the problem of the intertemporal allocation into a broader perspective.

Following Førsund and assuming perfect foresight of the planner into the future, the following aspects should be pointed out that may complicate the problem considerably.

Spatial structure, that is, the distribution of economic activities over space at a given moment of time, influences location decisions and spatial structure in the future. This is, for instance, the case with infrastructure (social overhead capital) determining the location of firms. This is also the case with housing and cultural infrastructure influencing the mobility of labor. Spatial structure is a rather rigid variable that can be changed only over a long time horizon.

Regions are not only interrelated to each other via interregional diffusion and the competition for a given investment fund. Capital may be mobile, in the sense that depreciation may make "rigid" capital interregionally mobile. Labor is mobile among regions to some extent, and also technical knowledge may be diffused over space. (Compare, for instance, the studies of diffusion analyses.) Mobility takes time, but the time-consuming adaptations should eventually be included in our considerations.

Mobility of people refers not only to a factor of production but also to an alteration of residency. As new voters in a region, the newcomers have an impact on the political demand for environmental quality.

Besides factor mobility, regions do interact among each other by trading. Though we may interpret interregional trade as an example of arbitrage, the development of trade may follow historical (time-consuming) patterns such as proposed in the export base theory (North [1955]). Also, trade and interregional specialization have implications on environmental quality (Siebert [1978]).

Preferences may shift over time, especially through interaction among regions. Demonstration effects may occur in the sense that environmental quality in one area will eventually influence the achievement levels of environmental policy in another area. Preferences may change because of purely regional phenomena. Since regions are also interrelated in the sense that environmental quality in one area is an element in the welfare function of another region, preference shifts can also occur if the inhabitants of one area change their evaluation of the other region's environmental quality.

The factors mentioned—namely, spatial structure, mobility of factors, changes in residency, trade, and shifts of preferences—will influence the time path of regional environmental allocation. Other factors are conceivable, such as the underlying philosophy of environmental policy, the type of institutionalization of environmental policy, and others, all having a feedback on the time path of environmental allocation over space.

Assume now that our planner does not have perfect foresight. Then the planner has to consider all potential adaptation processes in order to get an "optimal" time path for the accumulation of capital and pollutants and for the development of spatial structure, sectoral structure, and the like. The problem is to determine these "rigid" structures in such a way that they are on (or not too far away from) the optimal path (defined for perfect foresight). Any deviation from the optimal path causes social costs of adjustment and consequently a misallocation of resources.

The planner's dilemma can be nicely illustrated by the over- or undershooting problem. Consider a context without spatial considerations and let the planner set a too high emission tax. Then this overshooting will imply a too strong buildup of purification capital, too many resources being used in R&D for abatement, and a sector structure being eventually biased in the form of less pollution-intensively producing sectors. These variables are more or less "rigid" and can be changed only at social costs if overshooting is corrected.

In a regional context, the above-mentioned variables, especially spatial structure, enter the scene. Assume a two-region system, with area A being densely populated, industrialized, and heavily polluted, and region B being the opposite. There is an interregional diffusion of pollutants to the less polluted area. In this initial situation spatial structure is biased in favor of region A in the sense that region A attracts more economic activities than is optimal. Let environmental policy be enacted and let a too strong emission tax be set (overshooting). Comparative advantage of region A is reduced, and specialization of production toward pollution-intensive commodities occurs in region

B. Eventually factors will migrate to region B. One can assume that part of the agglomeration economies of region A have not been "real" but were only "perceived," since the environmental costs of agglomeration were not considered. Consequently, environmental policy will reduce these perceived agglomeration economies. Eventually spatial structure will be changed in favor of region B. If overshooting occurs, the spatial structure of region B is too strongly developed; in the long run, spatial structure has to be changed in the other direction. Overshooting has caused social costs of adaptation.

The overshooting problem in a spatial context may be extremely severe if we look into the problem how rigid different variables are. We can assume that commodities are interregionally mobile and that commodity markets react quickly to a change in environmental policy. Investment funds (savings) are quite mobile, but capital embodied in machines can be made mobile only by depreciation. Infrastructure capital is completely immobile. The mobility of labor is impeded by social intergration in a given region. Since the spatial structure at a given moment of time influences future location decisions of economic units and since spatial structure can be considered as very rigid, the overshooting has strong long-run effects on the spatial structure. A similar result is obtained if one considers that polarization of regional growth will occur if at least one regional growth factor is immobile and attracts other growth factors (Siebert [1969]). According to this interpretation we can expect polarizing effects of the spatial structure; that is, overshooting is aggravated by these interdependencies.

The problem discussed so far may seem academic in the sense that the optimal path can be determined only with perfect foresight and that over- or undershooting and the implied social costs of adaptation can be recognized only as mistakes *ex post*. For practical policy decisions, however the same problem appears as the question whether environmental policy should be oriented with respect to the short or the long run. The debate by Stein (1971) and Peltzman and Tideman (1972) documents this issue. In the very long run, quite a few mechanisms are working toward an equalization of emission charges between regions. (i) Assume region B has a higher assimilative capacity than region A. Then firms in region B will specialize toward the production of the emission intensively produced commodity. *Ceteris paribus*, the emission tax will tend to equalize in the long run. (ii) A similar result is obtained if pollution intensively producing firms migrate to region B. (iii) How the mobility of residents affects the long-run equalization of emission taxes between regions will depend on what influence an individual will have on emission taxes. If we assume that an individual will influence the level of emission taxes, migration will reduce the political demand for environmental quality in the polluted area and increase the demand for environmental quality in the less polluted area. Then emission taxes will tend to equalize in the long run.

The problem for practical environmental policy is whether the long-run adaptation processes are relevant for the planning horizon. If these adaptation processes take more time than the planning horizon permits, that is, if the spatial structure is rather rigid and cannot be changed in a desired time lapse, environmental policy cannot set emission taxes that are optimal in a long-run setting with perfect mobility but must use such taxes that take into account partial immobility of information, commodities, factors, and firms.

The problem of whether environmental policy has to be regionalized can be considered on three different levels. First, from the (static) economic allocation aspect, we ask whether environmental policy instruments should be differentiated between regions or applied uniformly for a nation. Second, from the institutional-political aspect the problem is whether environmental policy, if it is to be regionalized, should be undertaken by national or regional agencies. Third, the problem of regional differentiation of environmental policy is also related to the time orientation of environmental policy. A long-run orientation implies a weaker regional differentiation of emission taxes.

REFERENCES

North D. C., "Location and Regional Growth". *Journal of Political Economy* 63 (1955): 243–258.

Peltzman, S., and T. N. Tideman. "Local versus National Pollution Control: Note." *American Economic Review* 62 (1972): 959–963.

Siebert H., *Regional Economic Growth: Theory and Policy*, Scranton, Pa., 1969.

———. *Ökonomische Theorie der Umwelt*. Tübingen, 1978.

Stein, J. C. "The 1971 Report of the President's Council of Economic Advisers: Micro-Economic Aspects of Public Policy." *American Economic Review* 61 (1971): 531–537.

CHAPTER 6

The Institutional Setting of Regional Environmental Policy

D. EWRINGMANN and K. H. HANSMEYER

It is surely a commonplace statement that environmental systems always have a spatial dimension, that there are interregional economic and ecological exchange relations; consequently there is the possibility of regionalizing environmental policy. These interdependencies often are summarized by economists as follows (Siebert [1978, pp. 123–140]).

1. As emissions have unequal spatial extent, environmental use in one region can influence environmental quality of other regions irrespective of possible political interdependencies among them.

2. Environmental use and environmental policy of one region have effects on environmental quality and economic efficiency of other regions, not only by direct emission-immission linkage, but also because of induced migration of people, goods, and factors. These regions, with a high standard of environmental quality and a severe application of environmental policy, generate high residential value, but they also, on the other hand, discourage business. Factors, jobs, and emissions are transferred interregionally, leaving the final result of this migration process in abeyance.

3. The environmental policy of one region may be outlined taking into account the environmental quality management of other regions, thereby raising the compensation problem within the context of a functional specialization and differentiation between regions.

These interdependencies result in questions concerning regional environmental policy as they were formulated, for example, by H. Siebert (1976, p. 80) and on which the present paper is focused: Should the environmental quality targets be defined and fixed uniformly or regionally differentiated? Should identical tools of environmental policy be applied over the whole economy, or should they be differentiated regionally? Should local, regional, or national agencies be responsible for environmental policy? Is the regionalization of targets and instruments practicable?

By taking a purely theoretical view and a long-term perspective, the problem of regionalizing environmental policy becomes less important. Assuming total mobility, the shadow prices for environmental uses or pollutants will be equalized interregionally.

1. If the factors of production are really mobile, they will leave regions with high environmental protection standards as long as there is an environmental differential profit in other regions. This migration process comes to an end as soon as the respective returns/costs are adjusted.

2. The same effect will occur if one assumes that the factors are immobile but free trade takes place between the regions; the less strained regions can produce and export emission-intensive goods. This cost advantage ends as soon as the immission capacity of the concerned region is exhausted, which has to manifest itself in the application of the instruments of environmental policy.

3. This adjustment can be brought about by population migration as well. As migration moves toward regions with better environmental quality, environmental policy in those regions has to be intensified *ceteris paribus*. On the other hand, policy measures can be relaxed in the inmigration regions as the demand for environmental quality is reduced in correspondence with personal preferences.

Taking these aspects into consideration, regionalization of environmental policy theoretically would be only a short-term task, which would become less important as adjustments occur over the long term. Likewise, environmental policy could be left to regional authorities, as they are subject to a mechanism of correction, which adjusts their action. If the assumption of total mobility is abandoned and the actual, at least partially existing immobility of resources is taken into account, the above-mentioned calculation evidently changes. This aspect renews the significance of the problem of regionalization of environmental policy and its institutional framework.

Economists concerned with environmental problems tend to justify and affirm the need for regionalization of environmental policy instruments, but normally reject the delegation of political competence to the regional level, because:

1. A definite delimitation of environmental regions would generate nearly insolvable problems of coordination. The environmental media differ from each other by their spatial extent, which necessarily means that the planning regions will overlap. The resulting coordination problems would be unsolvable.

2. Regional agencies would not be prepared to take into consideration the

interdependencies of regional welfare functions. Likewise, the level of welfare of region 1 affects the level of welfare of region 2, and so on.

3. Regional agencies would not be prepared to take into account the interregional diffusion of pollutants, resulting either in locational advantages or in locational disadvantages, thus creating competitive distortions.

4. The success of solutions achieved by bargaining has to be considered negligible. H. Siebert, for example, believes that the solution normally reads: "Der Geschädigte zahlt" (the victim pays). So in toto is it summed up: environmental policy can not be left to independent regional agencies or authorities.

THE FRAMEWORK FOR THE INSTITUTIONAL SETTING

The above answer and the underlying arguments have to be examined as to whether the basic assumptions are valid for all environmental media indiscriminately, as do which criteria offer themselves for regional delimitation—institutional as well as instrumental—and whether the constitutional framing of environmental policy and the necessity of coordination with other areas of politics and integration of different aims does not lead to other consequences for the institutional setup of environmental policy.

Considering the actual nuisances within different media and the concentration of different pollutants in particular regions, regionalization of environmental policy could possibly be called for if the external effects of environmental utilization were regionally concentrated, thus influencing preferences homologously resulting in the possibility of a special environmental policy even on this level.

Besides, it may be possible that specific external effects cannot be exported and therefore that local or regional policy has to be carried out. This might lead to the attempt to set up "optimal" regions that are appropriate to certain sectors of environmental policy. This will be done later. In doing so, action has to be adjusted to the media from the very beginning and has to be removed from the area of global discussion that is the concern of many of the papers in this volume.

During the earlier phases of environmental discussion, environmental nuisances and hazards were looked upon almost exclusively as a worldwide, interdependent phenomenon.

The institutional consequence therefore was quite obvious: environmental policy should be implemented on the national level; or even better, it should be harmonized internationally or delegated to supranational organizations. Indeed, environmental spheres that call for centralized control exist; purification of the oceans, for example, can be realized only on an international level. But this consideration must not be generalized. The "environment" comprises several subsystems, which differ a great deal in respect to their interdependencies, their spatial extent, and their consequences. Many environmental goods are limited public goods, which are restricted regionally in respect to their utilization.

Hence it can be seen that environmental policy should not be organized homogeneously across all media; and, on the other hand, that regionalization of environmental policy—concerning quality targets as well as use of instruments—seems to be advisable. The regionalization of environmental policy appears to be even more necessary, the more the functional division of labor is performed, or aimed at, between the separate regions and the more ecological criteria determine the functional differentiation of regions.

On the other hand, the existence of regionalization does not answer the question of how political and administrative competence is to be delegated. Regionalized environmental policy can be centrally planned and implemented; it can be made to fit an overall frame; or can be left to regional units altogether. How far the regional approach is meaningful as well as possible will be examined in the following paragraphs. In this context, the question of the "optimal" region of reference in respect to medially differentiated environmental policy is of most importance.

The preceding must be followed by the question of how the above units are to be adjusted to environmental policy in particular and to regionally oriented policy in general with respect to their organizational and institutional shaping.

It must be pointed out that different general competences within a federal state can urge regionalization and therefore may constitute restrictions for environmental policy. It cannot be the function of environmental policy to wear itself out in fighting regional constraints, but rather to make use of regional structures. Only in those cases where centralized solutions cannot be renounced is the principle of federalism to be substituted (principle of subsidarity). Within the Federal Republic of Germany the *Länder* are in a very strong position in all areas relevant to environmental policy, especially in those cases where problems of regional planning and landscape conservation are of significance. Likewise, water regulations are mostly State law.

The competences of the Federal Republic are mainly restricted to "skeleton" laws, which can only establish a rough framework, which has to be filled out *by* the *Länder*. The new federal antipollution law (Bundesimmissionsschutzgesetz) certainly offers possibilities of action for a central anti-air pollution and anti-noise pollution policy. Nevertheless, the Federal Republic even there is dependent on the *Länder,* as they dispose of the implementing agencies. Environmental policy does not dispose of a central agency that has the power to direct these implementing agencies of lower hierarchical standing. The communal level controls the planning rights within the construction sector. Therefore, it has many possibilities of influencing and modifying environmental policy. Communal associations also have important tasks within the field of environmental policy. The task of regional conservation (Landeskonservierung), for example, lies with the Landschaftsverband in North Rhine-Westphalia. Furthermore, there are numerous intercommunal associations (Zweckverbände) that are occupied with different environmental policy functions—in particular, the associations for the purification of sewage.

"OPTIMAL" ENVIRONMENTAL REGIONS

Designing environmental competences and responsibilities and assigning environmental functions to local, regional, and central authorities represent problems that—like deciding on the degree of regional homogeneity or heterogeneity of environmental quality targets and how to use environmental protection instruments—can be dealt with only in a global political context.

Whole rational and efficient solutions to these problems cannot be found from an exclusively ecological or economic perspective, let alone implemented. Nevertheless, it seems possible to derive criteria for assigning environmental functions and designing competences from ecological system relationships and approaches of economic theory—especially if they have become part of the theory of federalism. In a second step, however, the results that are based on these criteria have to be checked for their compatibility with the requirements of other policy areas and with the invariant conditions of the respective political-administrative system.

From an exclusive ecologico-economic perspective, there are, to begin with, the following criteria—already suggested by K. Zimmermann elsewhere (1977)—which may help to solve institutional problems of environmental protection policies.

Spatial diffusion of emissions and their harmful effects. The possibility of internalizing external effects within the local, regional, or national unit is dependent on this primarily ecological criterion. Under the aspect of efficient supply of public goods, an "optimal" environmental region should be dimensioned in such a way that it encompasses all individuals who are being affected by the production costs of environmental goods and who are, at the same time, consuming these environmental goods. Thus, the appropriate environmental region would minimize regional and interregional spillovers. Considering the different modalities of diffusion, it is evident that the regional approach must be tuned to the specific environmental media.

Degree of homogeneity of preferences concerning environmental goods and environmental utilizations. The welfare effect of regionalized environmental decisions and jurisdictions is due to the greater consideration of individual preferences within smaller regional units, since one can assume that preferences in smaller regional units are more homogeneous than those in larger units. With respect to individual environmental media—though to varying degree—regional homogeneity of preferences can be assumed all the more as preferences are influenced by actual dangers or existing damages or degradations, while the level of danger and degradation varies from region to region. The higher the degree of existing environmental pollution and damages is and the more visible degradations are, the more homogeneous preferences will be within a region. Preferences of individual regions will be relatively homogeneous with respect to the minimal supply of public goods; in other words, they will be indentical concerning the avoidance of immediate health damages. In other respects, however, they will differ depending on the actual pollution and degradation that exist in the region. Furthermore, they will differ to the extent that variations in regional prosperity and income influence the estimation of environmental benefits. Such differences concern, in particular, the "luxury share" of the public supply of environmental goods.

This leads to the following conclusion: the prevention of direct health dangers requires, owing to high interregional conformity, nationwide minimal standards. However, more far-reaching decisions on environmental protection should be left to smaller regional units, whereby the concrete dimensioning of regions should be done for separate environmental media according to the respective preference structure.

Cost advantages of larger units of environmental goods production. One can assume economies of scale for numerous technical facilities of environmental protection. From an economic perspective, larger organization and production units are, in this case, preferable to smaller ones. However, it should be recognized that the analysis of the economies of scale must not be confined to the cost curves of single technical facilities—for example, refuse incinerators or sewage treatment plants. Of course the costs of facilities per damage unit (*Schadeinheit*) or per damage unit abated (*vermiedene Schadeinheit*) tend to decrease with as the size of facilities increases. But the evaluation should be based on whether the total production costs of a public environmental good per capita of the population being supplied with the good (including additional costs of transportation, collection, administration, and information which are typically caused by larger units) actually decrease with the increase of the supply unit.

In what follows these criteria will be used for a closer examination of the situation in four environmental protection areas, that is, four sectors of environmental policies: noise abatement policy, water quality management, anti-air pollution policy, and waste management.

NOISE ABATEMENT POLICY

Sources of noise generally have only locally limited effects. This means that nuisances, annoyances (*Belästigungen*), and damages can be caused only within the near vicinity of a source.

Noise—especially such dominating types of noise as that of traffic and industry—will pose environmental problems only if divergent utilization demands on a narrowly defined area are locally colliding. This is, therefore, a specific problem of location, which, at least in part, can be controlled by local planning.

Locally restricted solutions in anti-noise policies are also supported by existing causal relationships. While emissions in other environmental areas are often not perceived despite acute danger or damages, or are perceived only after damaging effects have taken place, the conscious perception of emission plays a decisive role with respect to noise. Except for auditory damage, such as noise deafness, and the influence of noise on sleeping behavior, the effects of noise are always realized through annoyances. The levels of annoyances are dependent on noise tolerances and situative factors and therefore differ widely. Conditions of weather and climate are among the influencing factors; for example, it is possible to speak of a typical noise climate of a region.

One of the strongest moderators of reactions to annoyances is the individual sensitivity to noise that contributes more strongly to interindividual variations of annoyance than differences in noise emissions that can be measured objectively (Der Rat von Sachverständigen [1978, pp. 238-242]). Sensitivity to noise varies very much at the national level, though the same thing holds true at the regional and local levels. Consequently, it is not at all surprising that in communities with a higher measured noise level sometimes a smaller percentage of people feels annoyed than in communities with a lower measured noise level. Local preferences concerning the level and structure of noise abatement will possibly vary correspondingly.

Since subjective factors are dominant, it is impossible to draw the line between "acceptable" and "considerable," that is, nontolerated annoyance, with the help of generally binding immissions standards. Regional differentiations become necessary and are appropriate; they require taking into account the dominating functions of a region—existing pollution, expectations of the population concerning the noise level in the area, social stratification, and other factors. Under this aspect it is advisable to make the decision on what is "acceptable" at the local level, where the people concerned are more likely to articulate their conceptions of "tolerance."

Besides that, the local level is able to control at least new noise emissions with its own planning instruments in a way that is oriented toward immission standards in the sense of local quality objectives. It is true, however, that the regulation and abatement of existing noise nuisances and annoyances following partly from planning errors of the past (Hansmeyer [1977]), and partly from different norms and value standards of the past, may exceed the control capacity and especially the financial resources of a community. This fact does not necessarily require transferring competences to a higher institutional level.

It also seems possible to solve the problem through special mechanisms of financial compensation by means of a grants-in-aid system.

What has been said so far applies only to immobile noise sources, that is, to industrial noise and the noise of living, as well as to the area of passive noise abatement measures. Local solutions and competences, however, are hardly appropriate to reduce emissions of mobile noise sources, a fact that is equally true with respect to the abatement of traffic noise, leaving out of account the local possibilities of traffic and transportation planning and the above-mentioned passive noise abatement measures. Although communities have some control parameters to influence demands for passenger car and truck traffic—for example, by concentrating traffic, limiting parking areas and pedestrian zones, and so on—more comprehensive solutions based on the market system, such as road pricing or other pricing systems, are either not amenable to implementation or eventually conflict with national goals if implemented by communities. Consequently, directly attaching noise abatement measures to emissions sources—such as noise pricing by effluent charges or emissions standards—does not represent a viable solution for autonomous communal implementation.

Summarizing the discussion, the question of what the most appropriate institutional structure and regional differentiation are may be answered as follows:

1. Since the effects of noise are connected with perception, subjective annoyance plays the main role. The annoyances are influenced by a great many factors that vary from region to region. Hence, it follows that regional differentiations of antinoise policies are advisable. It is a specific characteristic of noise "that regional standards of 'tolerance' can be determined by taking into account advantages of location, the customary situation in a place, and existing pollution" (Der Rat von Sachverständigen [1978, p. 234]). This must show up in immission standards, which are regionally differentiated.

2. Local competences are advisable for the implementation of noise abatement policy, since it is possible to locally internalize external effects of noise, which is to say that all costs and benefits of noise emissions and of noise abatement measures can be ascribed to the inhabitants of the community that has caused them.

3. The preference structures are locally different. Taking them into account does not lead to conflicts with the national welfare function. This holds true, at least, with respect to immobile noise sources and passive noise abatement. Apart from a general minimum immission standard that could be fixed at a national level, these areas of noise abatement policy can be left to local authorities.

4. Measures concerning the reduction of emissions of mobile noise sources should, on the other hand, be regulated nationwide, preferably in the context

of international harmonization processes. This would help to avoid welfare losses and trade barriers that are usually caused by local (and regional) differentiations.

5. Economies of scale do not play any role in this context. Likewise, cost calculations do not lead to a different structure of competence.

WATER QUALITY MANAGEMENT

Water sources usually have different functions at the same time; for example, they serve to supply water for drinking and domestic purposes, and for fishing, recreation, shipping, agriculture, and generating energy. But they also are used in flood control and to transport waste water. In individual regions very different sorts of usage are dominant: there are waters that are exclusively reserved for drinking, others that are exclusively used for discharging waste water, for navigable waterways, and so on. Since the particular uses depend on different kinds of water quality, a regionally differentiated policy of water quality is appropriate.

To establish the competence and institutional consequences of water management that is not centralized, there are of course other aspects to be taken into account than in the field of noise abatement. As opposed to the noise medium in the medium "water," the local delimitation is usually passed over by discharging waste water in the respective *Vorfluter*. Sometimes, the pollution spreads out regionally by means of other river systems to other regions or countries, whereas pollution of the groundwater usually is regionally limited. Hence, internalization of externalities in the local area to minimize spillovers is not possible. The producers of waste water and their locations are not directly concerned. They receive no direct benefits from their own abatement activities, due to their upstream location.

The regional "catching" of externalities in the area of water protection seems to have the best chance on the level of river systems. It is on this level that a differentiated system of immission targets and a differentiated enforcement of water management measures should be implemented (Der Rat von Sachverständigen [1974]). But river systems are also qualified as delimitations for administration units of a regional and autonomous water management. A regional solution of this kind should be preferred in particular if the competence for the treatment of the waste water—meaning water purification—included the capacity to supply water as well; in this case, the external benefits of water protection measures could best be regionally internalized.

Water management of this regional kind with different kinds of organization has already proved workable in many countries. It meets revealed preferences of a relative homogeneous structure, especially if there is an assignment of responsibility for the water supply in the delimitation of the region, at least if compared with those of other scales of delimitation.

In this context, to what extent economies of scale play an important role is not as evident as is usually supposed—nor is it evident if they are an appropriate criterion for a certain size of the unit that should be supplied with the limited public good, "water." Undoubtedly the specific costs for the abatement of one pollutant unit decrease with increasing sizes of the purification plants and with increasing passage of pollutants (Hoffmann and Ewringmann [1977]). However, cost advantages of the larger plants will at least partially be compensated by higher transportation and sewer costs in the case of a local administration union (Interkommunaler Zweckverband); the additional costs depend especially on topographic characteristics, numer of inhabitants per s.m., and so on. Hence the cost advantages of larger and centralized purification plants cannot be the only essential argument for the establishment of regional water management.

The cost advantages of regional associations, like the German Wasser- und Bodenverbände, are based on the fact that they are the most appropriate means of differentiating the purification requirements by means of emission standards and/or waste water charges by taking into account the total amount of discharge points, the respective relevance of the kinds of pollution, and individual cost situation of the polluters. Thus, they are able to produce an optimal cost structure of purification capacities and performances.

Even in the case of an overall system of Wasser- und Bodenverbände the individual unit should not be able to decide quite autonomously in the area of relevant water quality measures. There should at least be some fixed centralized minimum standard in the sense of interregional diffusion norms that could define the maximum amount of pollutants a region would be allowed to export to another water region (Siebert [1974]). Such a standard will be necessary because there are interdependences between water systems and river regions. Whether it will be convenient to do this by means of uniform diffusion standards or by means of differentiated standards that will pay attention to the specific function of the river region in a spatial concept of functional differentiation depends especially on the concrete federalistic structure of the respective country.

AIR QUALITY POLICY

Emissions in the air are characterized by a high degree of spatial diffusion of the emitted pollutants—especially dependent on climatic factors—and by the fact that there are no measures of pollution abatement as they exist, for instance, in the field of sewage purification (*Mündungsklärwerke*). From this point of view, a local competence for air purification policy cannot be founded. It is true that polluters cannot take a pure *Oberlieger* (upstream) position because they themselves are usually concerned about their emissions; they benefit from their own abatement activities as well. Nevertheless, there are externalities that cannot be internalized on a local level. Hence local competences would suggest solutions that are not optimal. From this point of view, the installation of a competence below the central level could be founded at best within the borders of airfields, but managing these airfields by administrative units will generate problems.

On the other hand, an analysis of the preferences seems to affirm a delimitation in this way, because harmful and dangerous effects diffuse relatively homogeneously within an airfield. Hence the homogeneity of revealed preferences could be expected first of all in an area where a significant environmental degradation exists or is suspected. That is why a relatively homogeneous preference structure will be suggested in areas of agglomeration where nuisances and harmful effects are manifested most evidently. In this context, the air quality control regions (*Belastungsgebiete*) of North Rhine-Westphalia, for example, could be mentioned as an example for regions with homogeneous preferences.

The need for a central or national competence can be deduced only from preference argumentation with reference to minimum standards for the avoidance of immediate health damages. On this point one can assume an interregional identity and a nationwide homogeneity of preferences. This means, of course, that regional competences and jurisdictions for air purification policy could be concerned only with setting quality targets and gradations extending beyond the minimum standards. Economies of scale cannot be expected to be very important in this context.

In sum, the situation pleads for a central framework competence with the capacity to fix minimum standards of air quality in all regions; the regions, however, should have after that the authority to differentiate their immission targets above the general minimum level and to vary their instruments. The best regional environmental units would be the airfields.

SOLID WASTE MANAGEMENT

Solid waste management has as its object harmless refuse collection and disposal as well as improving and increasing the recycling of waste or waste treatment. The harmful effects of waste dumping—as an environmental problem in a restricted sense—take place by causing pollution of water, air, and soil. The effects, as a rule, are restricted to the local or regional level. Interregional negative external effects ordinarily do not occur as result of refuse collection and dumping. But different consequences can be assumed in the case of special waste with high toxicity, which—depending on the specific ingredients and the technical methods of dumping—possibly pollute waters or airfields to a greater extent and could be injurious to the health of people in a larger spatial unit. Furthermore, special waste components may have interregional importance as causative agents of infectious diseases. Special waste products therefore require specific treatment and call for a waste management competence at a higher level.

A central planning competence in the field of toxic and radioactive waste is also indicated because of the interregional preferences that can be assumed to be very homogeneous with reference to the avoidance of direct health damages; furthermore, the decision problems in locating special waste dumps call for national management. On the other hand, the preference argument results in a local or regional competence for collecting and disposing of typical urban waste. Nevertheless, economies of scale in the use of modern refuse incinerator plants should lead to regional solutions in the form of intercommunal associations for waste disposal and treatment with a sufficiently dimensioned catchment area.

As the degree of concentration of refuse disposal plants as well as the appropriate economical delimitation of waste management regions depend on costs in relation to environmental quality targets, one can generally suppose that these plants should be planned to be more decentralized the more harmless waste products are; the more harmful and dangerous waste products are, on the other hand, the more centralized waste management has to be and the higher the degree of plant concentration should be (Mertens [1977, pp. 47–48]).

In market economies the progress and improvement of using the resource and energy content of waste products by recycling is not primarily a policy problem. As far as technological preconditions make it possible and application is economically efficient, recycling will be put into practice (Mertens [1977, p. 49]). As far as the markets for raw materials and the technology of waste treatment do not allow an economically efficient waste recycling, policy has to enter the picture if unproductive and unremunerative recycling could avoid environmental damages that could not be avoided by normal refuse disposal. In that case, environmental policy on the central level should seek especially to implement a specific research and development program.

EXTRA DEMAND FOR CENTRALIZATION

The institutional consequences of the foregoing analysis needs a completion and an adjustment from the point of view of a whole national and political perspective. Environmental policy cannot be enforced as an isolated skilled policy, and it cannot be efficiently realized if there is a strict institutional separation between the different environmental policy areas. The indispensable integration of the different sectors of environmental policy and the essential inclusion of environmental policy into the whole political planning process lead to an extra demand for centralization of the environmental management organization.

It has become evident that an identical distribution of competence and a coincident regional delimitation cannot exist over all environmental policy areas. The appropriate regional delimitations for parts of a noise protection policy will be different from those of an air purification policy; the regional-institutional framework of water quality management must differ from that of air purification policy because river basins are geographically quite different from air basins. This means that because of the overlapping of planning regions and of the differently limited competences of the "appropriate" regional units, national authorities will be necessary. Without such authorities, the interdependencies between the environmental media would hardly be taken into consideration within the political decision process in the different regional units. The "water regions," for instance, should accomplish a bargaining process, with the "air regions" being organized with regard to quite another set of criteria; they ought to take into consideration that waste water abatement techniques, just like sewage sludge incineration, substitute air pollution for water pollution. Of course, such bargaining processes will not take place.

Even national authorities will not perfectly solve these problems, but there they are basically and earlier resolvable under the aspect of information and organizational theory.

Furthermore, the need for coordination of environmental policy and other policy sectors with reference to the efficient supply of public goods generates an additional demand for centralization. A rational environmental policy—in the economic sense—has a chance to be realized only if it enjoys real priority and if there are no conflicts with other policies. These requirements, however, do not exist. There are, for instance, permanent conflicts with economic stabilization targets, which should take into consideration environmental policy. Environmental protection also needs national authorities fitted with at least a framework competence, because individual regions will not take into account national goals.

In this context, the relation between a regional decentralized environmental policy and a regionally differentiated but in the last analysis centrally controlled spatial-functional structure represents a special problem. The regional division of labor leads to a spatial separation of certain emission-intensive and less emission-intensive activities, so that externalities, which could possibly reduce the functions of the individual regions, will be avoided. If the national welfare position is taken into consideration, the functional structure of the whole region will be available only by given national policy patterns, by a given delimitation of the regions, by an assignment of functions to the regional units, and by formulating and fixing regional environmental quality objectives that correspond to the specific regional functions.

SUMMARY

A regionalization if immission targets will become the more necessary, the more intensively a spatial-functional division of labour is practiced.

Environmental policy instruments—whether they are emission standards or monetary-fiscal mechanisms as effluent charges—have to be regionalized even if there is no differentiation on the target level.

Regional environmental authorities or agencies should not be completely autonomous. As a rule, nationally uniform minimal imission standards have to be fixed by a central national authority, which has to manage the above-mentioned coordination process. Exceptions to this rule are indicated if it is possible—according to the very specific preconditions of pollutant diffusion and/or to the technical abatement measures—to avoid conflicts with other target areas.

This will be the case, for instance, in the field of water quality management, where regional institutions should not be obliged to care for an identical minimum level of water quality in each spatial point of the region, if it is assured by centrally fixed diffusion norms that water of inferior quality will not be transmitted to other regions. Intraregional gradations of water quality and intraregional differentiations of the measuring out of environmental policy instruments then could be left to regional water authorities or intermediary associations.

As to noise abatement policy with reference to immobile sources of noise and to passive noise protection, local or regional competences are as recommendable as they are for the collection and disposal of ordinary urban waste. On the other hand, general maximum emission standards should be centrally normalized with reference to mobile sources of noise. A higher level of competence also has to be required for special waste management.

In the sector of air purification policy a lot of criteria plead for a regional solution in accordance with that of water quality management. But as it is much more difficult to implement and to control interregional diffusion norms for air quality and as air purification policy becomes of much greater importance within a spatial-functional conception of regional planning, it is advisable to centralize air quality management. This does not mean renunciation of the regionalization of immission targets and policy instruments.

REFERENCES

Der Rat von Sachverständigen für Umweltfragen. *Die Abwasserabgabe.* Stuttgart: Wassergütewirtschaftliche und gesamtökonomische Wirkungen, 1974.

Der Rat von Sachverständigen für Umweltfragen. *Umweltgutachten 1978.* Stuttgart, 1978.

Hansmeyer K. H.: "Umweltpolitik, finanzielle Stabilität und wirtschaftliches Wachstum." *Verkehr und Umwelt.* Cologne: Schriftenreihe der Deutschen Verkehrswissenschaftlichen Gesellschaft. Vol. B 35, 1977.

Hoffmann, V., and D. Ewringmann. *Auswirkungen des Abwasserabgabengesetzes auf Investitionsplanung und -abwicklung in Unternehmen.* Bonn: Gemeinden und Abwasserverbänden, 1977.

Mertens, B. "Abfallwirtschaft auf Landesebene." In E. Keller, ed., *Abfallwirtschaft und Recycling.* Essen, 1977.

Siebert, H. "Regional Aspects of Environmental Policy Instruments." Paper prepared for the OECD. *Beiträge zur angewandten Wirtschaftsforschung.* Institut für Volkswirtschaftslehre und Statistik. Universität Mannheim, 1974. No. 49.

_____. *Analyse der Instrumente der Umweltpolitik.* Göttingen, 1976.

_____. *Ökonomische Theorie der Umwelt.* Tübingen, 1978.

Zimmermann, K. "Regionale Dimensionen in der Umweltpolitik." Unpublished manuscript. Berlin, 1977.

DISCUSSION

Criteria for an Appropriate Institutional Structure

GARDNER BROWN, JR.

Professor Hansmeyer and Mr. Ewringmann have tackled what I believe is the most difficult topic treated in this volume—the proper institutional structure for regional environmental management. The generic problem is an old one, going back several decades, for example, to the time when there was a great deal of discussion in the United States about the watershed or river basin as the proper unit for water resources management. The issue extends further back in the U.S. resources literature to the debate over the appropriateness of the Tennessee River Valley Authority as a management entity. In this case, an institutional structure spanning a geographic region, with powers extending beyond those necessary for water resource management alone, was the subject debated. And of course the essence of the matter—centralization versus decentralization,—is as old as civilization.

Pieces of the controversy, as it applies to water or environmental management, could be picked out because they were "instructive." But on the whole, it has been an indecisive, unproductive quest. Studies sort themselves out into two types. Either they pertain to such particular circumstances that the concluding prescriptions cannot be used confidently elsewhere; or the discussion is so general that the recommendations sound like slogans (internalize the externalities), cannot be of much applied use, and may even be dangerously costly if not artfully put into practice.

A good institutional structure is one that satisfies criteria springing from legal, economic, political, geographical, technical, and natural resource considerations. I think the reason that we have not come up with simple but at the same time productive results regarding a regional institutional fabric is that even a simple and elegant model contributed by one discipline, when necessarily aggregated over all disciplines, becomes a very complex model indeed. Therefore, studies of institutional structure conducted by members of a single discipline or from the viewpoint of one discipline, as is the present one, lack sufficient professional breadth to treat so comprehensive a problem. But then I can think of no other study regarding the proper institutional structure for an environmental agency that takes a suitable breadth of view. Before, commenting on the problems arising from a foreshortened view, let me summarize the paper.

The authors conveniently summarize the scope of their paper in four questions: (1) Should the environmental quality target be defined and fixed uniformly or should they be regionally differentiated? They should be regionally differentiated. (2) Should identical tools of an environmental policy be used without regard to location? Don't use identical tools. (3) Should local, regional, or national agencies be responsible for environmental policy? All of the above. (4) Is the regionalization of targets and instruments practical? It all depends.

There is more to the Hansmeyer and Ewringmann paper than this. If I read the first few pages correctly, a regionally independent set of environmental policies theoretically can be found that will work in the long run if there is free trade or mobile factors of production. It might take some tinkering in the short run, but after the common vector of shadow prices for environmental services is established for each region, the independent system could be left on its own. The authors then point out the many difficulties such a plan would encounter: regional interdependent welfare functions; technological interdependencies; overlapping regions for different natural resources; strategic bargaining; and so forth. Thus, independent regional agencies in general are unacceptable, although there might be some special cases where regional autarchy would work and we should be alert to these possibilities. On the other hand, institutional restrictions such as limited competence in the case of the Federal Republic of Germany necessarily shape the domain of possible policies and regional management agencies. We should further acknowledge that current institutional fabric is insufficiently complex at the local and regional level so that the least-cost means of coordinating environmental policies will require a regional agency. These are important points well made by the authors.

In the next two sections, the authors establish three criteria by which to appraise the optimal environmental region for four protection areas: noise, water, air, and solid waste. The three criteria are: (a) the level of spatial diffusion of the pollutants—the larger the area of effect, the larger the control region; (b) the homogeneity of preferences—the greater the homogeneity, the more aggregate can be the management region; (c) economies of scale—interpreted broadly to include the cost of administration (presumably including enforcement) and information gathering. They argue that waste such as rubbish and most noise can be handled at quite a low level of aggregation. Ambient air quality poor enough to affect health requires a national response. Water can be handled by river system regions.

The authors state that in the long run the problem of regionalizing environmental policy may grow less important. This follows if factors are mobile—we vote with our feet—or free trade exists. This may or may not be true, but there is insufficient structure given to the problem setting to know. The authors cannot mean that in the long run it is optimal for every region to look alike; to have the same standards or charges. This could happen only if all regions had the same natural endowments, were governed by the same description of the dynamics of the ecology, and in short all demand-and-supply equations were alike. Perhaps the authors mean that the payoff of acknowledging regional distinction is greater now than in the future. To prove this, the authors would have to show, at least figuratively, that the ratio of the initial values of the control variables in two regions, say the ratio of regional charges for BOD in the initial period is greater than the regional price ratio for BOD in a later or final period.

The authors say that regional policies are more important the more immobile are the resources. If the authors are simply using the Le Chatelier principle, I of course agree with them. Payoffs are always higher when one has more freedom to optimize; that is, when there are fewer restrictions. I may have overlooked a more substantial point that can be argued more persuasively, in which case it should be set forth more clearly.

There follows next a question followed by a suggestion for further research. I agree that existing institutions, such as the federal competence in West Germany, restrict certain options. But the federal government in the United States had its hands bound also by the power of states to manage water quality. The United States got around these restrictions by offering enormous subventions to the states if they would go along with the central government's desired water quality policies. Could the federal government in West Germany do the same or have done the same insofar as its Constitution is concerned? This train of thought suggests to me that institutions, like other organisms, can be characterized by difference equations. How much they change today is a function of where they are, perhaps where they have been recently, and where they ought to be going. We have not written these conservation equations for institutions into our models. For example, as general as Professor Nijkamp's presentation is, he still doesn't have the institutional component in explicity, although he has introduced some of the ingredients. Therefore, building a better institutional structure in our analysis is likely to have a fairly high payoff.

Consider now the criteria for choosing an optimal environmental region. The major problem with these criteria is that they are too imprecise. The problem with the spatial diffusion criterion is obvious. When the region is extended to cover all environmental externalities, too much is covered. There are airsheds intimately connected through substitution possibilities and technical relationships with watersheds, which spill into water basins and groundwater aquifers. The larger basins flow into tidal estuaries and thence into oceans. The authors know this, but they have failed to solve the fundamental problem—trading increasing comprehensiveness for decreasing management feasibility.

The second criterion—homogeneity of preferences—has promise but is treated too superficially. One cannot assume that preferences in a smaller *geographic* region are more homogeneous than those in larger units. Perferences can usefully be aggregated within use groups, the members of which can be worlds apart. Sociologists are given to remark about the differences within (in this case a geographic region) being greater than the differences across regions. People in the flooding area along the Sacramento River valley, two thousand miles from those in the Mississippi valley, have more in common than different and competing water-user groups in the Sacramento River valley. The small irrigationists in the United States may have more in common with the utility manager than the large irrigationists, given certain U.S. policies explicity acknowledging distribution objectives. Thus, homogeneity of preferences is an admirable criterion, but it may be of limited use in the common instance when multiple, conflicting resource-using groups are in the same geographic region.

I'll now comment briefly on the section where the criteria are applied to the different receiving resources. Barde and Pearce, specialists on noise, did comment effectively on the authors' oversights when reaching conclusions about the appropriate level of regionalization and noise management. As for water, criteria such "catching of externalities" are too imprecise to be operational. This, plus size economies and homogeneity of preferences, cannot explain the number and scope of regional water management institutions in England, the Netherlands, Hungary, and France. For example, these criteria don't explain why all the parts of Wales that supply water to England are not part of the water authority in England receiving the water. The reasons why France has six regional basin authorities have little to do with the three criteria. Any specialists of French water quality management can corroborate that assertion. These three criteria won't help the authors very much to break up the Netherlands or Hungary into regional water management units that, in fact, mirror the actual geographical extent of the regional agencies in 1978 or 1968 or 1958, for that matter. Nor will knowledge of preferences, costs, and technical interdependencies permit an accurate prediction of the powers and responsibilities delegated to these "basin" agencies. Surely the extent of powers and responsibilities is as critical as the geographic determination of a regional management unit.

Three final remarks close the paper. Tony Scott, in previous discussions, itemized nicely some cost factors. They are organizational costs, bargaining costs, monitoring costs, the costs of jurisdictional negotiations, and so forth. These are the costs of running an organization effectively. How, in fact, do they vary with size, however one defines size? Does anyone know of an empirical study of these matters? Until we do know these data, we are simply chatting about optimal size of regional organizations. Penultimately, I want to underline a point made by Jean Philippe Barde. We have observed that centrally administered economies such as France had to introduce basin agencies to make environmental policies work better; and decentralized economies such as the United States have had to introduce centralized activities. These are terribly vague terms, but the point to make is a clear one. Water quality management now is sufficiently complex that it requires both regional authorities and central authorities.

Finally, there is an unmistakable trend toward comprehensive management. That is a vague term, too. But to get a grip on it, one can think of actions such as planning, financing, construction, managing, and enforcing. One can think of use groups such as water supply, drainage, water quality, recreation, navigation, flood control, hydroelectric power. One can think of policies such as taxing, charging, subsidizing, setting standards, issuing permits. One can aggregate over space and time as well as location. We can quibble about the meaning of "comprehensive," but just think about these facts. Since reorganization in England in 1963, the number of water management agencies has fallen from more than 1,550 to 10. In the Netherlands, the number has been reduced from 1,200 to about 29 in about the same period. The march toward aggregating functions, powers, and so forth into fewer management entities, though not as dramatic as these cases cited, is a very widespread phenomenon that I expect will continue. It would be exciting to have a theory that predicted the pace and specific direction of this trend. Professor Hansmeyer and Mr. Ewringmann have provided in their three criteria some of the ingredients of such a theory.

DISCUSSION

Political and Jurisdictional Systems for Regional Environmental Policy

GIDEON FISHELSON

In most countries when the environmental issues approach the margin at which they become equivalent in importance with the conventional economic objectives (e.g., GNP per capita, growth of GNP, unemployment, inflation, deficit in the balance of payments) by that time the structures of the political and jurisdictional systems are already fully developed. Over the development period of the economy the solutions with regard to the environment are practically corner solutions, that is, the environmental issues are almost a priori inferior relative to the economic issues. From the functional point of view, the political and jurisdictional systems are structured to serve the socioeconomic system in the best way. Getting out of the corner thus requires corresponding modifications in these systems.

Any modification, even when disregarding the constraints it would enable the government to impose on the other sectors in the economy, is economically not costless. Given the advanced stage of the economies at which the need for "corrections" with regard to the attitude toward the environment becomes apparent, in principle the economy "can afford it." The extent of this effort is limited by the criteria of optimal policy, that is, social marginal costs = social marginal benefits. This criterion is a universal law. Yet, when applying it to environmental policies it seems that the new political-jurisdictional systems were implicitly considered to exist; therefore, the costs of replacing the existing systems by the new ones was never considered. Thus, the "true" social costs were underestimated.

The economic studies that investigated the properties and suggested environmental policies (e.g., standards versus taxes) also disregarded the need to define the boundaries within which the policy is imposed. They implicitly defined economic boundaries that were always sufficiently flexible to encompass "all those on which the policy is to be imposed."

When subjects related to environmental policy were analyzed, such as a differential emission tax (Fishelson [1977] and Tietenberg [1973, 1978]), and uncertainty (Fishelson [1976]; Adar and Griffin [1976]; Keeler et al. [1971]), the possible conflicts with the political system are not even mentioned. An exception is Fishelson (1977), which examines the constraint of uniformity of policies and concludes that "a standard, regardless of the way it is specified, if it is forced to be uniform, would always be inferior to an optimal uniform tax."

In regional benefit-cost studies, the boundaries of the region were a priori determined (Cohen et al. [1974] and Zerbe and Croke [1975]). The last study is of interest in the regional context, since it suggests two levels of emission standards for automobiles: urban and rural. A minor generalization leads to a by-state standard. Yet, as far as we know, specific emission standards were applied only by California. A relevant question is why. Neither in the economic literature nor in legislative debates can we find an answer. This is surprising, since a two-level standard is in the benefit of both automobile manufacturers and consumers. It is thus conceivable that the only ones that are disadvantaged are the policymakers. They might not be able to manage and control this new system. The contrary, however, seems to be true for stationary sources, but various side effects might arise.

If different, by-location emission standards (or emission taxes) were imposed on stationary sources, the existing sources would either lower emissions through the installment of control devices, fuel switching, minor technological changes, lowering output, or even relocating to other regions. Potential producers who consider entering the market in a specific area (the markets for factors of production or output) would change initial decision and would be more likely to locate across the quota (tax) boundaries (see technical Appendix to this paper, which treats some of these issues). The move to a location that was suboptimal prior to the environmental policy is positive from the environmental quality point of view. It might, however, have negative effects on the regional economy. Furthermore, if across the border there are no regulations at all, the region with regulation might bear the entire economic negative effects while gaining little in terms of improved environmental quality. These situations have to be an integral part of the decision process. Hence, the policy enacted by one region is not independent of the policies imposed by the neighboring regions, a situation that calls for a *joint determination of the differential policies*. Thus, by definition an overall objective function (for all regions or countries within a subcontinent) is needed to determine the differential policy structure to be applied simultaneously over the whole area. This procedure contains the essentials of regional environmental policy, the first being the definition of the policy boundaries and the second being the optimal regulation for each locality. It misses the third element, which is the optimal path over time of borders and regulations.

The joint determination of regional environmental policies is required *only* when there are spillovers of pollutants across regional borders. If the regions' borders are also pollution borders (a closed airshed, or a closed river [lake] basin), each region should enact its environmental policy independently of the others. This is the only case for which interregional competition in attracting polluters is allowed. As long as the pollution does not affect other regions, if the region has (or the citizens agree to) a comparative advantage in absorbing pollutants, it should be allowed to utilize it as it does any other advantage (this holds only in a static sense; the intergeneration issue still remains). The spillover does not have to occur physically. Hence, if citizens in other regions do have interests in the closed region and they want to protect these interests (e.g., a national monument), an implicit spillover occurs and the privilege of independent determination of environmental policy is not to be granted.

The flexibility of regulations and boundaries is needed owing to the dynamics of urban structure, technological innovations, and the changing social attitudes toward environmental quality. These "natural" events raise the need for defining optimal time spans for policies, given that switching from one policy to another is not costless. A minimization of these adjustment costs requires a flexible system. However, flexibility sometimes leads to noncompatibility with regional differentiation; the reason is that the more flexible the regional framework is, the more power is assigned to the central government, which is obligated to treat all regions uniformally. The flexible-uniform conflict is a synonym for the federalism-regionalism conflict. The optimal degree of federalism (regionalism) cannot be found by economic conventional (mathematical) optimization models. First, the formulation of the problem is nonfeasible; second, many of its components are not quantifiable. Thus, common sense, assisted by economic facts and figures, is the tool for assigning political responsibilities and powers for improving environmental quality.

The optimal regional setup is thus a compromise among economics, desired environmental amenities, and the political-jurisdictional structure. The statistical rule of grouping such that the total variance within the regions would be as small as possible relative to the variance among regions is the guiding rule.

Let us define the now established regions—environmental regions. In order to avoid congestion of environmental authorities, over one geographical area only one environmental authority is to be defined. This regional authority controls all forms of environmental issues. The joint responsibility over all pollutants is needed both because of the interphase of pollutants and because of economies of scale in management.

Regional differentiation is achieved by a hierarchy of constraints and regulations. The pryamid of regulations is toward stringency. This system takes care of specific issues (national monuments, highly dense populated areas). Its major characteristic is vertical responsibility. Vertical differences in the stringency of regulations (or taxes) are positively related to potential damages. Since the effective authority is that ranked highest in the pyramid, there is no double control. It also assures that the entire area is covered (see Figure 6-1). The figure describes two possible pyramids. (1) The constraints imposed by the authorities for the *AEIFJH* area are the lower limit for those imposed by the authorities of the *IFJ* area, and the latter are the lower limit for the authorities of the *M* area. Furthermore, given the across-the-border externalities, the authorities of the *IFJ* area consider area *M* when setting their constraints for the entire area. (2) Region *M* is a low density area (desert); thus it hardly requires environmental policies for its own sake, but does require some owing

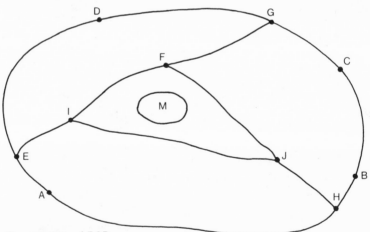

The country − ABCD.
Three basic regions− EFH, FGH, EDG.
The first is divided into two subregions, AEIJH and IFJ.
In one subregion there is a national monument, (M can be partly in
   IFJ and partly in AEIJH).

Figure 6-1. The hierarchy of environmental regulation—pyramid a.

to externalities. Region *IFJ* is more populated, and thus the policies there are more stringent. The most stringent policies are in the *AEIFJH* region.

An examination of environmental control agencies in various countries indicates that they are constructed according to the first pyramid. Since optimality in terms of the structure of stringency was never applied across regions, the second pyramid cannot be a priori "rejected." Furthermore, combinations of the two might arise that will form different shapes of the environmental structure.

Professor Hansmeyer and Mr. Ewringmann suggest that there are environmental issues that are definitely local—noise around airports. Our view is that these cases should still be controlled by the wider-area environmental authority, since the airport users reside (work) within a large radius of the airport and any decision might affect them, even to a larger extent than those currently damaged by the noise. Hence there are lower limits below which there are no more subdivisions, since both environmental quality and the implications of its control are generated and spilled over long distances.

CONCLUSIONS

Based on the foregoing discussion, and the relocation model (in the Appendix), predictions regarding land-use patterns and regional economic growth could be made. Differential air quality standards are likely to strengthen the suburbanization process with attempts to locate in areas that are predominantly rural (e.g., Muth [1961]). Policies such as "nondegradation" might slow or prevent such changes (e.g., U.S. EPA [1973]). The "nondegradation" policies, once they become effective, would give rise to externalities that did not previously exist. We might witness new types of negotiations among firms—for example, between those that already have pollution rights and newcomers. Newcomers might finance the installment of pollution control devices on existing plants in order to keep ambient air quality below standard (e.g., 80 μg/cm of SO_2 annual average in class III areas). In regions that are close to the allowed pollution level, the monopoly of existing firms would increase and they would be able to extract environmental rents (Buchanan and Tullock [1975]). It was also shown elsewhere that air quality standards would change land-use patterns (Tolley and Cohen [1976]). Shortages of clean fuels (especially natural gas) make the fuel-switching options less attractive and sometimes not feasible. Hence, relocation is the almost single way to meet *local* air quality standards. Economically is not a cheap solution. Furthermore, it solves local air quality problems but not global ones. This again implies the need for an integrated interregional environmental policy, that is, regional differentiation within closely defined boundaries.

APPENDIX

Optimal Location-Relocation of
Air Polluters
A Suggestive Model

The regional aspect is introduced in the second section. The idea of several regions is illustrated by many reference points. As shown, the decision by a single firm is reached simultaneously with respect to constraints imposed by all regions.

1. A SINGLE RECEPTOR POINT

Let us assume a "two-centers city." For one center, the residential section, the air quality standard is determined. In the other center, n polluting firms are located. Each of the polluters is sufficiently large such that its contribution to ambient air quality at the reference point is measurable. The current air pollution level at the reference point is A^0 where

$$A^0 = a + \sum_{i=1}^{n} F(E_i, D_i) \tag{1.1}$$

where:

   a = is the background level of the pollutant, i.e., it would prevail also when the n firms were shut down

   E_i = is the emission rate of the i polluter. This emission rate is assumed to be steady (e.g., tons of SO_2 per day)

   D_i = is the distance of the i polluter from the reference point

   $F(E_i, D_i)$ is the contribution of the i polluter to air quality at the reference point

Relation (1.1) can be simplified by assuming proportionality between emission rate and contribution to ambient air quality.[1]

---

   1. Wind direction, wind speed, and other atmospheric conditions are disregarded. The incorporation of a dispersion model, for example, the one lately described by Busse and Zimmerman (1973) into the economic model would further emphasize the issues raised in this paper, but at relatively high costs of making the analysis more complicated.

$$F(E_i, D_i) = E_i \cdot g(D_i); \quad g_{Di} < 0 \tag{1.2}$$

The air quality regulation specifies an upper limit on pollution at the reference point, a level of $A^*(A^* < A^0)$. Kohn [1969], and later in a series of articles, presents an optimization model for this problem. The means available to the firms in Kohn's model are emission control devices and fuel conversions. Kohn disregards the relocation option.

The economics of relocation is based upon this substitution between costs of emission control (C_i) and relocation costs (M_i). The annual cost of installing and employing a control device or of fuel switching is C_i, such that $\partial E_i/\partial C_i < 0$ and $\partial^2 E_i/\partial C_i^2 > 0$. The relocation costs, M_i, depend upon the final distance from the reference point. Denoting the initial (present location) distance by D^0 and that of the optimal solution by D^1 the relocation costs, M_i, are

$$M_i = h_i(D_i^1 - D_i^0) = \bar{h}_i(D_i^1) \tag{1.3}$$

where

$$\partial M_i/\partial D_i^1 > 0 \quad \text{and} \quad \partial M_i^2/\partial^2 \partial D_i^1 < 0 \tag{1.3a}$$

(For $D_i^1 \leq D_i^0$, $M_i = 0$.) M_i is the sum of the annualized costs of relocation and the annual costs resulting from the greater distance beween the plant and the city (e.g., transportation costs).

The contribution of firm i to air quality at the reference point is a function of the expenditures on control devices and of relocation costs

$$A_i = E_i(C_i) \cdot \ell_i(M_i) \tag{1.4}$$

where

$$\ell_i(M_i) = g(D_i^1) = g(h_i^{-1}(M_i)) \tag{1.4a}$$

The economic problem of a centralized economy (for the n firms) is

$$\underset{C_i, M_i}{\text{Min}} \sum_{i=1}^{n} (C_i + M_i)$$

subject to: $\tag{1.5}$

$$\sum_{i=1}^{n} E_i(C_i) \cdot \ell_i(M_i) \leq A^*$$

The first-order conditions are

$$1 + \lambda E_{iC} \cdot \ell_i(M_i) \geq 0 \qquad i = 1, \ldots, n \tag{1.6a}$$

$$1 + \lambda \ell_{iM} E_i(C_i) \geq 0 \qquad i = 1, \ldots, n \tag{1.6b}$$

Hence, an internal equilibrium for firm i for both options $(C_i > 0, M_i > 0)$ implies

$$E_{iC}\ell_i(M_i) = \ell_{iM}E_i(C_i) = 1/\lambda \qquad (1.7)$$

The interesting case is that for which some firms move, some change production technology, some do both, and some do none. The Kuhn-Tucker conditions imply that for the firm that relocates $(D_i^1 > D_i^0)$, the marginal costs of one unit of expenditure equals the product of the reduction in air quality times its shadow price at the optimal use of control devices. For the firm that does not relocate $(D_i^1 = D_i^0)$, the marginal cost of moving of an initial distance already exceeds the value of the marginal improvement of air quality $(1 > \lambda^*E_i(C_i^*) \cdot \ell_i)$.

The important message of the above, simplified model is the possibility that instead of each firm investing in emission control or relocation there are firms that are relatively efficient in improving air quality and they should specialize in doing it.

2. TWO (AND MORE) RECEPTOR POINTS

For the single reference point, the direction of relocation was assumed to be away from the receptor point along the line that connects the reference point and the present location. Once there is more than one receptor point, this simplifying assumption is no longer valid. The relocation has to be defined in terms of both distance and direction.

In order to appreciate the results obtained later, we digress to a simple location model. The model is a simplified version of the Eaton-Lipsy (1976) model. We assume that the residential locations are fixed, with populations $P_1, P_2 \ldots P_m$. A new firm is coming into the area. Its cost of production is a function of the distance to each residential location. Let the function be a linear weighted sum of the distances (the weights, d_i, might be proportional to population size). Hence, supply costs are

$$M = \sum_{i=1}^{m} d_i((x - a_i)^2 + (y - b_i)^2)^{1/2} \qquad (2.1)$$

where a_i, b_i are the coordinates of location of city i, x and y denote the coordinates of the location of the firm. The first-order conditions for cost minimization are

$$\sum_{i=1}^{m} d_i [(x - a_i)^2 + (y - b_i)^2]^{-1/2}(x - a_i) = 0$$

$$\sum_{i=1}^{m} d_i [(x - a_i)^2 + (y - b_i)^2]^{-1/2}(y - b_i) = 0 \qquad (2.2)$$

The general solution to these equations is

$$x = D^x(d_1 \ldots d_m, a_1 \ldots a_m, b_1 \ldots b_m)$$
$$y = D^y(d_1 \ldots d_m, a_1 \ldots a_m, b_1 \ldots b_m) \qquad (2.3)$$

where we know for sure that

$$\partial x / \partial d_i > 0 \qquad \partial y / \partial d_i > 0 \qquad (2.4)$$

Once air quality regulations, R_i, are introduced (they too might be proportional to population), the previous optimal location decision is altered. First, note that the contribution of a firm located at x, y to air quality at a residential location i, A_i, depends on distance and angle (e.g, wind direction), thus:

$$A_i = E(C) \cdot h \left[((x - a_i)^2 + (y - b_i)^2)^{1/2}, \ \frac{x - a_i}{y - b_i} \right] \qquad (2.5)$$

where C, as before, denotes expenditures on emission control devices. Define supply costs as above, M; then the location decision of the firm is determined by the optimization model

$$\underset{x, y, C}{\text{Min}} \ z = C + M$$

$$\text{s.t.} \quad E(C)h \left[((x - a_i)^2 + (y - b_i)^2)^{1/2}, \ \frac{x - a_i}{y - b_i} \right] \leqslant R_i \qquad i = 1 \ldots m$$

$$(2.6)$$

The first-order conditions are

$$\frac{\partial z}{\partial C} = 1 + \sum_i^m \lambda_i E_c h[\cdot] \geqslant 0$$

$$\frac{\partial z}{\partial x} = \sum_i^m d_i [B_i] (x - a_i) + E(C) \cdot \sum_i^m \lambda_i h_x \geqslant 0 \qquad (2.7)$$

$$\frac{\partial z}{\partial y} = \sum_i^m d_i [V_i] (y - b_i) + E(C) \cdot \sum_i^m \lambda_i h_y \geqslant 0$$

where B_i and V_i are the square brackets in the $\partial M / \partial x$, $\partial M / \partial y$ expressions, for example, (2.2), respectively. In addition, there are the m equations of the constraints (sign reversed).

Note that h_x, (h_y) is the sum of the two components, h_{1x} and h_{2x}, since any change in location changes either/or the distance and direction angle.

We are now ready for the initial problem. The n firms are located at x_0, y_0, which historically is the industrial section of the city. The environmental constraints imposed by the authorities $\overline{R}_i$ are effective for at least one residential location. Hence, a firm located at x_0, y_0 is either to install control devices (annualized costs are C) or relocate to x_1, y_1. For simplicity, the annualized relocation costs are assumed to be independent of distance of relocation. The annual production costs are changed by ΔM_j owing to relocation where

$$\Delta M_j = M_j^1 - M_j^0 = M_j(x_1, y_1) - M_j(x_0, y_0) \tag{2.8}$$

The problem of the economy is

$$\text{Min} \sum_{j=1}^{n} (\partial M_j + C_j)$$

$$C_j, x_j, y_j$$

subject to:

$$\sum_{j}^{n} E_j(C_j) \cdot h\left[((x_j - a_i)^2 + (y_j - b_i)^2)^{1/2} \frac{x_j - a_i}{y_j - b_i}\right] \leqslant \overline{R}_i \qquad i = 1, m$$

$$\tag{2.9}$$

The difference between this constraint and the one specified for a single firm is the additional options of substitution, that is, between C_j and C_j', C_j and x_j', and C_j and y_j', while before it was only between C_j and the pair $x_j, y_j (j, j' = 1 \ldots n)$. The solution to (2.9) is a generalized version of the solution to problem (1.5). As before, some firms will relocate, some will install control devices, some will do both, and some will do none. The net effect, however, is an overall improvement in air quality.

REFERENCES

Adar, Z., and J. M. Griffin. "Uncertainty and the Choice of Pollution Control Instruments." *Journal of Environmental Economics and Management* 3 (1976): 181–188.

Buchanan, J. M., and G. Tullock. "Polluters, Profits and Political Response: Direct Controls versus Taxes." *American Economic Review* 65 (1975): 139–147.

Busse, A. D., and J. R. Zimmerman. *Users for the Climatological Dispersion Model.* U.S. Environmental Protection Agency, Research Triangle Park, North Carolina (December 1973).

Cohen, A. S., G. Fishelson, and J. Gardner. *Residential Fuel Policy and the Environment.* Cambridge, Mass.: Ballinger, 1974.

Eaton, B. C., and R. G. Lipsy. "The Non-Uniqueness of Equilibrium in the Löschian Location Model." *American Economic Review* 66, no. 1 (1976): 77–93.

Fishelson, G. "Taxing Emissions, A Theoretical Note." *Air Pollution Control Association* 24, no. 1 (1974): 43–47.

_____. "Emission Control Policies Under Uncertainty." *Journal of Environmental Economics and Management* 3 (1976): 189–197.

_____. "Some Basic Considerations for Policies Aimed at Improving Environmental Quality." Unpublished manuscript (1977).

Keeler, E., M. Spence, and R. Zeckhauser. "The Optimal Control of Pollution." *Journal of Economic Theory* 4 (1971): 19–34.

Kohn, R. E. "A Linear Programming Model for Air Pollution Control in the St. Louis Airshed." Ph.D. dissertation. Washington University of St. Louis, Missouri, 1969.

Muth, R. F. "Economic Change and Rural Urban Land Conversions." *Econometrica* 29, no. 1 (January 1961): 1–23.

Stein, J. L. "The 19th Report of the President's Council of Economic Advisers, Microeconomic Aspects of Public Policy." *American Economic Review* 61 (1971): 531–537.

Tietenberg, T. H. "Controlling Pollution by Price and Standard Systems: A General Equilibrium Analysis." *Swedish Journal of Economics* 75 (1973): 193–203.

_____. "Spatially Differentiated Air Pollutant Emission Charges: An Economic and Legal Analysis." *Land Economics* 54 (1978): 265–274.

Tolley, G. S., and A. S. Cohen. "Air Pollution and Urban Land Use Policy." *Journal of Environmental Economics and Management* 2 (1976): 247–254.

U.S. EPA. "Prevention of Significant Air Quality Deterioration." *Federal Register* 38, no. 135. Washington, D.C.

Zerbe, R. O., and K. Croke. *Urban Transportation for the Environment.* Cambridge, Mass.: Ballinger, 1975.

DISCUSSION

On Regional Pollution and Fiscal Equivalence

MANCUR OLSON

The paper by Professor Hansmeyer and Dr. Ewringmann is, to my mind, a constructive and sensible one. It puts forth an approach which deserves close attention, but it is not the approach I personally would think the best. It is perhaps unlucky or unfair for the authors that I happen to be a partisan of a point of view that is somewhat different and which I shall try to persuade you is better. This is a point of view I have advocated before with indifferent success.

In 1969, I published an article on "fiscal equivalence."[1] Although it has been embraced by a few economists, in general the concept has not attracted very much attention. This failure has encouraged me to press on and repeat the argument once again and try and see, finally, if I could make some progress. My argument has something in common with that of Professors Hansmeyer and Ewringmann in that both start with the view that environmental problems have spatial dimensions and that these spatial dimensions—the geographical boundaries of each environmental problem—are usually fairly clear. In almost all cases water pollution is confined to particular watersheds. Though air pollution is sometimes more diffuse, it often is confined to particular airsheds (or air fields, as I think Professor Hansmeyer put it)—that is to say, air pollution is typically more or less coincident with the boundaries of metropolitan areas or of certain industrial zones. Noise pollution is normally confined to the areas around airports or highways or other determinate locations. Of course there are some problems that, although well defined in their spatial extent, nonetheless involve different regions or countries. At the extreme we have the ozone layer; it seems to me that the emission of fluorocarbons anywhere in the world may affect the ozone layer that protects the entire world. Here we have an environmental problem with the widest possible scope, yet the area of impact remains well defined.

Now if it is generally agreed that environmental problems for the most part have fairly well defined spatial dimensions, what follows from this? What behavior ought we to expect from the various governments and jurisdictions that deal with such environmental problems? One problem is that sometimes a jurisdiction, when it acts to deal with the environmental problem, will create externalities. If the domain of an environmental problem extends beyond the boundaries of a jurisdiction, whatever that jurisdiction does to reduce pollution will benefit citizens of other jurisdictions. It follows that the jurisdiction will engage in a smaller than optimal amount of environmental protection— i.e., it will neglect the spillover, and so we get a familiar nonoptimal result if we have a local jurisdiction dealing with an environmental problem that transcends its frontiers.

There are other problems that occur in this sort of case, most notably what I like to call "the exploitation of the great by the small." If there is, for example, air pollution over the whole of a metropolitan area, and if that metropolitan area is governed by many different jurisdictions, the largest of these jurisdictions—let's say the city-center government—is likely to bear a disproportionate share of the burden of air pollution control. The reason is that

---

[1] *American Economic Review, Proceedings Issue* (May 1969), pp. 479-487.

when the biggest jurisdiction has produced that amount of pollution control which is optimal for itself, inevitably the whole metropolitan area will enjoy the better air quality that results, so there will be no incentive for the lesser suburban jurisdictions that share the problem with it to do anything; their marginal costs of pollution abatement are presumably just as high as in the city-center, but they get a smaller share of the benefits. But this is a subordinate matter: the crucial point is the underprovision of environmental goods when the jurisdiction is smaller than the domain of the environmental problem.

This crucial point is really also evident in the paper by Professor Hansmeyer and Dr. Ewringmann, but I would now like to get to the *opposite* problem. This is a problem I have been much less successful in getting agreement on, but I'm convinced it is no less important. Let us take the case of a jurisdiction that *more than* encompasses the environmental problem at issue. Consider a highly centralized government, say France, and think of the problem that arises when that government has to deal with water pollution in a particular city or valley. The usual assumption—and indeed this seems implicit in the paper under discussion—is that the national government will be able to deal satisfactorily with this problem. This conventional view seems to me to be utterly incorrect.

Let us stop and think. Suppose that the costs of providing the clean water are less than the benefits, i.e., that this ought to get government attention. Note, however, that the water pollution by stipulation affects only a small subset of the citizens of the national government. We are considering an environmental problem, the amelioration of which would bring *more gains than the costs*, but there are *more losers than gainers* from solving the problem. If national taxes pay for the solution of the local environmental problem, then even if the benefits from dealing with the local problem greatly exceed the costs, the number of losers will normally greatly exceed the number of gainers. Thus we cannot expect a national jurisdiction—at least if it operates in a plebiscitary way—to deal adequately with local problems. Though the plebiscitary method is not the normal technique for descision-making in most jurisdictions, actual methods of decision-making often resemble those that would occur in plebiscites. There will sometimes be bargaining in a national legislature or parliament that will provide for local problems, and sometimes there will not be. Logrolling, to use another word, may or may not take place. The result is, on average, a tendency for underprovision of environmental quality.

I conclude that if we have either the familiar "externality" problem or the "internality" problem that I am trying to argue is significant, we tend to get an underprovision of environmental quality—a biased and inefficient outcome. The two systematic forces I have described will be at work in every country and period, though they may of course be countervailed, or even more than offset, by still other forces.

What is the necessary condition for a jurisdiction to deal optimally with an environmental problem? The necessary condition is that the domain of the environmental problem must match the boundaries of the political jurisdiction. There must be what I like to call "fiscal equivalence." The taxing or regulating area must match the benefit area.

If the argument that I have made here is correct, we should see in the world about us various developments that would suggest a tendency, however faint, in the direction of fiscal equivalence. I believe there is some such faint tendency. Let me start with the United States, where the conventional wisdom is that there are too many local governments. By various counts there are around 100,000 local governments in the United States, and almost everyone says that's far too many. But even though the consensus is that there are too many governments, the number increases as time goes on. Why?

I hypothesize that the number of governments increases because there are new pollution problems, and new needs for publicly provided airports, and new neighborhoods whose residents share some common interest. So new governments are presumably set up because the need for them grows more rapidly than old governments can be gotten rid of, even when people believe there should be an overall cut in the number of governments.

Let's turn next to the jurisdictional pattern in Western Europe. This pattern is complex and a thousand and one forces are at work. Yet is it not striking that at the very same time that the Common Market, NATO, the United Nations, and other supra-national jurisdictions have been created, there have also been demands for more sub-national governments—varying from the demands for autonomy or independence among the Basques, Bretons, Catalonians, Crosicans, Flemings, Scots, and Welsh, to a concern for decentralization in many ethnically homogeneous societies. Some of these demands for new jurisdictions have their sources in cultural groups with demands for distinctive and identifiable public goods, some in unsatisfied communal needs of small neighborhoods, some in new patterns or perceptions of pollution, and some in opportunities arising from new and large-scale technologies, and some in military insecurity. Some of the new jurisdictions arise not so much out of the demand for classic public goods, as out of the perception of gains from trade over a large free trade area. In any case, a multi-level complex of jurisdictions, some of which are smaller and some of which are larger than the existing national governments, is what the theory of fiscal equivalence says is needed. And Europe does seem to have been moving, albeit slowly, toward such a complex.

To the extent that the world is relatively peaceful and military means of settling disputes are of lesser importance, this trend may well continue. The national government is after all the level of government that has the guns.

The local jurisdictions and the international organizations are given altogether subordinate roles and have to accept these lesser roles because they usually do not have independent military power. In a world where military force is virtually the only source of authority, the level of government that has the army is the level of government that decides everything.

I sense that there is some attenuation of that inefficient and rudimentary structure of government in the post-war period. Environmental problems are essentially prototypical in that they illustrate the problems for which we most need separate jurisdictions, if we are to handle them effectively. A lot of *ad hoc* governments at many levels seem to me to be a necessary condition for optimality.

Of course, one could push the argument that I have made much too far even if one generally accepts what I have said (and many people do not). I certainly wouldn't want to push the argument to the extreme of saying that for every environmental or other public problem with a unique catchment area we should have a separate jurisdiction with a boundary that matches the problem. Just as there would be gains from such a lattice of governments, so there would be a cost of keeping track of the jurisdictions, and sometimes the costs could exceed the gains. What I suggest is that, for various minor environmental problems, there is no need to have a separate jurisdiction. But for more important ones it makes a lot of sense. If you take an area like the Rhine and the public problems common to this river valley—which involve *parts* of several nations and many states and municipalities—you have common problems significant enough to raise the question whether there is a need for some kind of separate jurisdiction.

In general, one good way of dealing with some of the needed jurisdictions is for higher-level governments to allow groups of citizens or groups of subordinate jurisdictions to petition for taxing and spending authority within whatever boundaries the petitioners specify. The higher level jurisdiction could then conduct elections and authorize the new jurisdiction if it had carried the relevant electorates or local governments by a "constitutional" margin. There would also need to be provisions under which otiose or archaic governments could be eliminated, since the officials of organizations may have a vested interest in their survival even if they are no longer necessary.

However great or small the steps that we should take toward fiscal equivalence, and by whatever method choices about jurisdictions and boundaries should be made, it seems clear that the conception of government structure of Victorian and Edwardian times—the period of unalloyed nationalism—was far, far too simple. It was not of course an accident that this period of intense and simple-mined nationalism led to so much trouble. The mosaic of public goods that needs to be provided, requires at the least some important sub-national and supra-national jurisdictions, and surely a corresponding reduction in the domination of and reverence for the "national" government. Perhaps the growth of pollution and other environmental problems, serious as they sometimes are, brings one blessing. The collage of environmental problems we face has such spatial complexity that the simple nineteenth century vision of the optimal governmental structure may not survive it.

CHAPTER 7

Environmental Aspects of Resources Policy in a Regional Setting

The Case of Air Quality Policy in the Southwestern United States

ALLEN V. KNEESE and MICHAEL WILLIAMS

The natural resources of the southwestern United States, and the Rocky Mountain region more generally, are an actual and potential source of national wealth. Coal, uranium, and oil shale appear to be the next generation of basic energy resources, and they are found in great abundance in this region. It is generally the most mineralized area of the United States, and most of the nation's remaining stores of hard-rock minerals such as copper and molybdenum are also located there. Economic growth and efforts to reduce foreign dependency could lead to the development of these resources on an enormous scale. Because the nation must call upon natural resources that are progressively more difficult to exploit, the potential environmental implications are extreme. Going from a 1 percent copper ore to 0.5 percent ore requires the processing of twice as much material with proportionally larger landscape disruption and application of energy. Moreover, future energy sources for this purpose are more environmentally destructive than current ones. At present, natural gas is used as a fuel; in the future coal is the likely energy source. Similarly, electric utility boilers now fired by gas will soon have to be converted to coal, and the production of synthetic gas and oil threatens to be much more costly in both monetary and environmental terms than the earlier production of petroleum gases and liquids.

Superimposed on the natural resources picture is an evident shift of the United States population to the south and west. The region as a whole, but particularly Colorado and Arizona, has experienced rapid population growth for reasons other than the development of extractive resource industries. Metropolitan centers such as Denver and Phoenix have multiplied in size in recent decades.

Of all the environmental impacts of these developments degradation of air quality is coming to be understood as probably the most severe. The atmosphere of this region of deserts and mountains is especially delicate. As a result, even cities of modest size and great charm and beauty, such as Santa Fe and Aspen, occasionally have air pollution episodes. The largest cities have persistent and sometimes severe air quality degradation.

The rate and level of future development of the region is very uncertain. It depends upon the extent to which efforts to conserve energy succeed, the degree to which less dependence on foreign sources of minerals is accomplished, and the extent to which the Sunbelt phenomenon continues to induce a southerly and westward migration of population and industry. These uncertainties create difficulties in the crafting of environmental policy, since it must be prepared to cope with a variety of possible circumstances and stand ready to be flexible in response. But the development of an effective and efficient environmental policy, and especially an air quality policy, is imperative. The alternative is aggravation of the existing poor air quality situation where it already exists, if development proceeds at a measured pace, or disastrous conditions over enormous areas if development occurs at a brute-force pace.

The air quality problem in the Southwest region has two major sources. The first is emissions from giant heavy industry sources, power plants, copper smelters, and potentially, synfuel plants and oil-shale facilities. The second is a very large number of small sources—automotive vehicles.

In this paper we will consider the potential impacts of the former, and various policy issues surrounding them. The paper is based on some research results obtained by the Southwest Region Under Stress Study Team. This study is a multi-institution interdisciplinary study directed by Allen V. Kneese.

THE 1970 AMENDMENTS TO THE CLEAN AIR ACT

By the end of the 1960s it was generally conceded by most observers that the national air quality legislation then in place was ineffective in protecting the nation's air quality resource. In 1970, Congress amended the Clean Air Act to produce the basic law that still governs today. Prior to these amendments the national policy had depended primarily upon national directives to the state to set ambient air quality standards and enforce them and on a conference procedure analogous to that initiated in the Water Pollution Control Act Amendments of 1965.

The 1970 Clean Air Act Amendments sharply expanded the federal role in setting and enforcing standards for ambient air quality. The act embodies the concept of a "threshold value"—a level of ambient concentration below which it is assumed that no damage occurs to health. Materials subsequently designated to have threshold values include the main pollutants by mass, sulfur dioxide, carbon monoxide, nitrogen oxides, particulates, and oxidants. The notion of threshold value can be regarded as a politically convenient fiction that permits the law to appear to require pollution damage to health to be reduced to zero—an absolutely unambiguous number.

Congress directed the Environmental Protection Agency to use scientific evidence to determine threshold values for pollutants assumed to have them and then to set those values minus an adequate margin of safety as primary standards. These standards, which relate to injury to human health, are to be met first. More rigorous standards to be met later relate to public welfare and aim to protect property, crops, public transportation, and aesthetics from pollutants. The states were to prepare implementation plans assuring that the primary standards would not be violated anywhere in the state after mid-1975. This requirement is even today far from being met, and in many areas air quality continues to decline. This may be especially true in the Southwest. The act also expressed the intent that the quality of the air be maintained or enhanced. This has since been interpreted by the courts to mean that no new source is permitted to significantly degrade air quality anywhere.

Congress did not rely solely upon the established standards for ambient air quality to control stationary-source pollution. It also gave the Environmental Protection Agency power to set specific limits on emissions of certain kinds of pollutants. It recognized a category of substances called "hazardous pollutants," which are considered to have especially serious health implications (some of the heavy metals are examples). The EPA was directed to prepare a list of such substances and to issue regulations limiting their emissions, by both new and existing sources, which were to be enforced at the federal level. Very little progress has been made in implementing this part of the act.

The act also directed the administrator to set new source performance standards that would limit the emissions of pollutants from new industrial plants to an amount no greater than that obtainable with "the best adequately demonstrated control technology."

Implementation and enforcement of national clean air policy, with the exception of automotive emissions control, is primarily the responsibility of the states. Their performance in carrying out this mandate has been variable but generally weak judged in terms of the objectives of the Clean Air Act, and none of the goals of the act has been fully met.

STATIONARY SOURCE REGULATIONS IN THE SOUTHWEST

Introduction. As indicated, national law endeavors to lay two types of restrictions on the discharge of residuals to the atmosphere: (1) emission regulations and (2) ambient standards. Emission regulations prescribe the allowable emission rate from the source, usually as a function of the amount of input material used by the source. Thus, a power plant may emit some number of pounds of sulfur dioxide for each million Btu's of heat input. Examples of emission regulations are the Federal New Source Performance Standards. States also have NSPS's, which in many but not all cases are equal to the federal standards, and as indicated, enforcement of the standards falls primarily upon the states.

Under federal law states are required to establish compliance plans pertaining also to existing sources, and these involve emissions regulations that in some instances are more restrictive than federal emissions standards or apply to existing sources not covered by these standards. In the Southwest, for example, New Mexico's new source standards are far more restrictive than the federal standards or those of other states.

Ambient standards, as contrasted with emissions standards, specify the allowable concentrations of pollutants at ground level for various time periods. The major goal of the federal Clean Air Act is to achieve ambient air standards and to prevent deterioration of air quality. Related to the ambient standards are "non-deterioration increments." These are defined permissible increases in the ambient air concentrations associated with new industrial sources that are taken to be consistent with nondeterioration. The increments are different for each geographical area classification.

Under present interpretation of the law a geographical area may be classified in categories I, II, or III (*Federal Register* [1974b, pp. 42510-42517]). All areas are initially classified class II, which is presumed to permit moderate growth of polluting industries. Class I areas are places such as national parks where small changes in air quality may be detrimental (*Federal Register* [1973, p. 18993; 1974a, p. 31004]). These are areas where industrial facilities are presumed to be inconsistent with current land use. The most recent amendments (1977) *require* that such areas be designated class one.

The regulatory program which is designed to achieve ambient standards is then based on two components: (1) emission restrictions under state law for old plants in addition to an across-the-board restriction on new plants under federal law; and (2) construction permits under state law for new plants. In the case of the latter, in principle no new plant may be constructed if its operation will result in a violation of ambient standards or if its emissions will aggravate an existing violation of ambient standards. In theory, emissions regulations for existing sources in addition to emissions control and siting considerations for new sources are designed to meet ambient standards.

In practice, both technical and legal difficulties have limited effective implementation of this principle. There is also an important question about whether state agencies may control existing sources to levels below ambient standards in order to permit location of other sources in the interest of resources and economic development. In New Mexico an appelate court struck down regulations applicable to existing coat-fired power plants because the regulations were designed to provide room for new sources. The State Supreme Court upheld the appellate court decision. A proposed amendment to the state Clean Air Act to deal with the question was defeated in the last session of the state legislature. This in effect allows one large established source to "use up" the "assimilative capacity" of an entire region.

For new sources emissions regulations at the federal level (New Source Performance Standards) are supposed to represent the best available control technology for the type of source in question. However, NSPS have rarely been revised, and since they are usually set for the worst combination of plant type and coal, frequently they do not represent the best available control technology at a given time for a source with anything but the worst of conditions.[1] These emissions regulations are set without regard to plant size (the larger the plant the greater the permissible emissions), meteorology, existing ambient air quality, or terrain. Thus, compliance with New Source Performance Standards does not guarantee compliance with ambient standards; indeed there is no logical connection between them. Efforts to implement NSPS with respect to sulfur compounds has resulted in a standoff between industry and the regulators about what devices are "technically feasible."

For a source where nondeterioration is pertinent, the existing air quality is not a consideration as long as the air quality is better than the standards minus the allowable increment. In this case, the relevant question is whether or not the proposed new source plus all other new sources that were not under construction by 1975 will produce increases of the pollutant in question by more than the permissible increment (U.S. EPA [1975]). In this context any point, no matter where located, which may reasonably be expected to receive significant pollution from this source must be considered. In some cases, the source may be in an area classified in one fashion, while associated degraded air may be in an area classified in another fashion. In this case, the source is still required to meet the increment appropriate to the point where the in-

---

1. The Environmental Protection Agency has implicitly admitted that a higher degree of control is achievable in the case of Western low sulfur coals. Materials provided by EPA to the Congress during deliberations on the nondetermination clause of the rejected 1976 Clean Air Act Amendments used the assumptions of 90 percent SO_2 removal. The EPA is currently holding hearings on a reconsideration of the current NSPS. For EPA 90 percent feasibility see U.S. EPA and Federal Energy Administration (1975a, 1975b).

creased concentrations are expected. Thus, if Bryce Canyon were classified class I and a plant were to be located on the Kaiparowits Plateau, which was classified class II, the plant would in principle not be permitted to produce concentrations beyond the class I increment at Bryce Canyon.

For any new source the effective criterion is whether or not a computer model of the distribution through space of the emission from the proposed source (called an air dispersion model) predicts a violation of the ambient standards of the nondeterioration increments. In the case of the ambient standards, actual measurements may be used to confirm the modeling predictions, but there are few locations where monitoring networks are adequate for this purpose. If the standards are predicted to be exceeded, further control may be required.

Even with existing sources, air dispersion modeling plays an important role in relating emission regulations to ambient standards. For point sources whose emissions are expelled far above the land surface and therefore spread out over large areas, it is costly to put enough monitors in the field and operate for long enough periods of time to determine the actual highest short-term concentrations that may occur. Thus, modeling is frequently used to extend monitoring results in both space and time.

Air dispersion modeling is at best a rather imprecise science. This is especially so in the mountainous West where high terrain may be impacted by emissions. Taking account of other than flat terrain greatly complicates air dispersion models, but predictions that don't consider high terrain may be greatly in error. Recent experiments by the Southwest Region Under Stress Study Team have shown that flat terrain models may dramatically underestimate actual concentration (Rockwell International [1975] and Williams and Cudney [1976]). For this reason we developed a high terrain dispersion model to analyze regulatory alternatives. As well as being complex, such models have difficult data input problems. A discussion of how these were handled is found elsewhere (Kneese and Williams [1977]).

The San Juan Basin example. In order to examine some of the implications of various regulatory options, we have taken the San Juan Basin in northwestern New Mexico as one of our case studies. This area has large coal resources and available water. Currently there is one 2,175 megawatt (Mw) coal-fired plant (Four Corners Power Plant) and a 660 Mw coal-fired plant (New Mexico Public Service Company's San Juan Power Plant). The San Juan plant will have another 1,000 Mw added to its capacity. Construction permits have been obtained for the new units. In addition, four coal gasification plants with a total output of 1,750 million cubic feet of syngas have been proposed (U.S. Department of Interior [1974a, 1974b]). The first plant, owned by WESCO (Western Coal Gasification Company), if constructed, will be composed of two 250 mcf/day units located south and slightly west of the

Four Corners plant. The regulations for WESCO I has lapsed and must be re-considered from scratch. The San Juan permits are active; however, they were granted under the assumptions that high-level SO_2 control was required at Four Corners (the regulations struck down by the appellate court), and thus their status is not clear. A second plant consisting of two 250 mcf/day units is planned about five kilometers to the northeast. The second plant does not have a new source construction permit. There are two plant sites proposed by El Paso Natural Gas Company located east of the WESCO sites. There are no construction permits granted for these sites except for small pilot units.

Prominent high terrain features virtually surround the area. The Chuska and Carizo mountains form a barrier on the western side of the basin that is broken only at the northern end where the San Juan River flows out. To the north, the foothills of the San Juan Mountains include the Mesa Verde Plateau. On the southern and eastern borders there is also high terrain, although it is not as steeply rising nor as high as that which forms the western and northern boundaries.

The actual and projected situation with respect to the regulation of emissions and plant siting in the San Juan Basin is rather intricate. We therefore do not include in this paper detailed discussion of the regulatory assumptions underlying the modeling of various alternatives. (A detailed discussion can be found in Kneese and Williams [1977]). In general, the initial modeling assumes that state and federal emissions standards are met by all new sources, that the sites of such sources can be effectively controlled, and that retrofitting at all existing sources can be instituted flexibly—a *strong* set of assumptions indeed in view of the historical record of regulation.

Figure 7-1 sketches the range of physical and legal assumptions currently tenable and their range of implications. Under these assumptions we explore how much development could occur in the basin without violating existing standards and what other environmental consequences related to emissions might be associated with such development. Later we explore the situation that might prevail if existing regulations are violated.

When ambient standards are met. It appears that the San Juan and Four Corners power plants, four coal gasification plants, plus an additional seven new 2,000 Mw plants could be accommodated without violating primary ambient standards in the region. The proposed WESCO II facility would have to be resited because of contributions to excessive NO_2 levels on the Mesa Verde Plateau. Furthermore, NO_2 standards would be exceeded on the Hogback, a promontory in the region, and on the Mesa Verde Plateau. However, the new sources would make no significant contribution to the excessive levels. This analysis assumes that Four Corners' SO_2 would be cleaned up enough to meet standards at all points. If existing emissions at this plant were permitted to continue, an effective block on development within ten miles of the plant

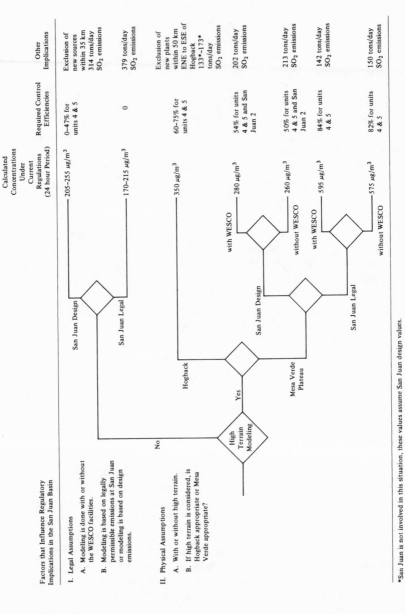

Figure 7-1. Implication tree for restrictions on SO₂ emissions posed by ambient standards.

*San Juan is not involved in this situation, these values assume San Juan design values.

194

would be occasioned because any new source might aggravate an existing violation.

There is one circumstance that has not been modeled that may prove very important—air stagnation. In this case a high-pressure system is stationary over an area and one or more day's emissions may be trapped within a confined area. Light and variable winds slosh the pollutants around, but they are not carried out of the basin. Unfortunately, there are no generally accepted models to deal with this circumstance. But stagnation does occur and could result in severe standards violations.[2]

Other possible implications of development include acid rain, elevated sulfate concentrations, elevated nitrate concentrations, and visibility reductions. In addition, trace element deposition and contribution to downwind ozone production are also potential areas of concern. All this while ambient standards are being met.

There are no adequate models yet developed to address the acid rain question. It is clear that coal-fired power plants will raise the sulfate concentrations in rainfall and lower the pH (Hales et al. [1971]). Furthermore, it seems evident that in one case emissions of approximately 410 tons/day of SO_2 contributed to widespread damage of Christmas tree plantations in mountainous West Virginia (U.S. EPA [1971] and Gordon [1972]). The damage was related to direct acid attack on the plant surfaces and thus did not involve a change in soil characteristics. Thus, this damage would not be confined to acid soils, which are not common in the Southwest. The expected emissions after control in the San Juan Basin would be 300–485 tons/day of SO_2. In addition, the NO_x emissions would be 350 tons/day.

With respect to visibility, the principal effects within the basin would be expected during low wind-speed stable conditions. Under these circumstances a significant plume would probably be visible as one looked across the basin. Specifically with low wind-speed conditions and winds out of the west, an observer looking to the north-northeast from the southwestern corner of the basin would be unable to see beyond the plumes. With higher wind speeds and winds out of the east with the observer near the southeastern corner and looking north-northwest, the observer would be able to see only about 60 kilometers (about 35 miles) as opposed to a normal pre-power-plant background range of 160 kilometers (around 100 miles). The result will be a striking brown plume as seen against a blue sky. Such plumes have been observed to

---

2. It should also be noted that the modeling assumes normal plant operation, whereas during a cold start-up of operations, emissions are many times higher than during normal operation. Thus, the model does not capture the extreme events that could occur. Cold starts occur eighteen–twenty times per year and last eight–ten hours.

be associated with the Navajo plant. During start-up when the particulate emissions are greatly increased the adverse effects would occur under a greater variety of conditions. Visibility is an important issue in the Southwest, whose crystalline skies and large, colorful landscapes are among its finest features.

It is also possible that significant effects on visibility and elevated nitrate and sulfate levels may occur outside the basin. For example, with winds out of the west in the early evening the pollutants could probably be transported to the Rio Grande valley with little loss of pollutants to ground uptake. Visibilities would be significantly reduced; probably to 50 to 60 kilometers or less in the valley. Modeling of visibility reduction continues, and results reinforce the conclusion that visibility effects may be the most destructive effects of further energy development and the tightest constraint on energy development if environmental quality is to be protected. Present standards, as has been pointed out, do not protect against visibility reductions, but the most recent amendments to the Air Quality Act (1977) do contain some language about protecting visibility.

When ambient standards are relaxed.   So far we have been considering the case where ambient standards have been essentially met. Now suppose we consider what happens if ambient standards are relaxed and emissions regulations are also relaxed, or equivalently, if the administrative legal process is not successful in implementing the standards. Under these conditions the SO_2 from Four Corners would probably remain at its present 328 tons/day. If the Public Service Company of New Mexico stopped its control, the level of SO_2 emissions would probably reach 330 tons/day from the San Juan units. The coal gasification units would also have increased SO_2 emissions of perhaps 200 tons/day. In addition, another new 2,000 Mw plant would probably produce emissions of 400 tons/day of SO_2. These levels would total over 1,200 tons/day of SO_2 emissions. Maximum SO_2 concentrations would reach approximately 1,100 micrograms per cubic meter for a twenty-four-hour average on the Mesa Verde Plateau. This is approximately *five times* the New Mexico standard and about *three times* the federal standard. Near a promontory called Hogback the values would be 550–750 micrograms per cubic meter for a twenty-four-hour average. In addition, on flat terrain values of 335–420 micrograms per cubic meter of SO_2 would be expected.

Total NO_x emissions would probably also increase as measures required to reduce NO_x formation were dropped or not successfully implemented. This would probably mean increases in the order of 30 percent in the NO_x emissions. Nitrate levels would increase correspondingly.

Particulate emissions would also be increased. The exact level is difficult to specify, but current particulate emissions from Four Corners are about 90 tons/day as opposed to the 5 tons/day assumed in this analysis. In the case of

San Juan, since the equipment is already in or under construction and there is little energy penalty associated with it, the values would probably only increase to 5 or 6 tons/day. It is also possible that Four Corners would decide to quit using the existing scrubbers on units 1–3, with consequent large increases in particulate emissions. Under currently existing conditions, total suspended particulates probably approach the standards at Hogback. Visibility effects would extend to a greater variety of circumstances, and effects on distant locations would be severe.

Thus, large-scale energy development in the San Juan will have catastrophically adverse effects on the environment unless both emissions and site locations are carefully and successfully controlled. Even with such controls, development keyed to existing ambient standards could cause serious environmental deterioration, especially in terms of visibility deterioration, acid rain, and deposition of hazardous materials. Studies we have conducted in other areas in the Southwest (e.g., the Price–Green River corridor and the Kaiparowits region) tend to confirm these general conclusions (Kneese and Williams [1977]).

AN ALTERNATIVE TO REGULATIONS

As we have just seen, even meeting the federal primary ambient standards in the region, much less protecting against visibility and other ill effects, would place heavy demands on the regulation process. Careful location of activities with implied land-use planning and precise programs of control, including successful and timely retrofitting of existing facilities, would be required to do the job. In practice, the regulatory process has been cumbersome, slow, litigation-ridden, and has spawned endless arguments about the availability of control technologies rather than induced technological innovation. In light of this, it is hard to be optimistic about how successful and efficient the regulatory process can be in the region, even for the conventional goals of high-level control of sulfur oxides and particulates, especially if pressure to develop energy resources is strong. It is therefore worthwhile to examine whether there may be another approach that would be more effective and efficient in meeting at least the elementary goals of air quality protection.

Many students of environmental policy have concluded that the system of economic incentives must be changed if we are to have a more successful environmental policy (see Kneese and Schultze [1975]). The suggested way of doing this is to levy a regulatory fee on polluting residuals that are released to the environment. The idea is to make it in the economic interest of the industrial enterprise, whether it is an old or a new plant, to control the discharge of pollutants to the environment rather than to discharge freely, as is now the case. Such a fee also has the effect of inducing the highest degree of control at those sources where control costs are lowest. At those facilities where control costs are low, it will pay to control to a high degree and avoid having to pay a fee on those units not discharging. Where control costs are high, it will pay to control emissions to a lesser extent. A number of studies have shown that when such a pattern of control occurs, a given ambient condition can be obtained at a much lower cost to society than when uniform requirements are laid on all dischargers to the environment. With the large scale regional effects we have projected, it is clear that control must be exercised at all sources, and especially at the largest sources, normally the ones least costly to control. Moreover, and perhaps more important, the profit will be taken out of polluting the environment, and the powerful system of economic incentives will work for the environment rather than against it, as is now the case when the valuable environmental resources of the region are used at zero price.

This being the case, the states of the Southwest region might well consider implementing a system of emissions fees for polluting substances that are discharged into their environment in order to: (1) supplement efforts to enforce regulations already in effect; (2) compensate for social costs imposed upon their citizens; (3) provide a continuing incentive to the industries of the region to use clean technologies and to control the discharge of polluting substances that are nevertheless generated; and (4) provide an economic incentive to develop more cost-effective control technologies.

A sulfur emissions fee. The best place to start is to establish emissions fees for the discharge of sulfur compounds. There are two reasons for this. (1) Sulfur compounds are discharged to the Southwest's atmosphere in very large amounts by industries whose products most often are almost entirely exported. The uncompensated social costs are therefore, under the present system, imposed on southwesterners, while beneficial products are in most cases consumed by others. (2) The monitoring that would need to be done to effectively implement a discharge fee is considerably simpler for sulfur compounds than for most other polluting substances discharged to the environment.

The proper level of a sulfur charge. How high would a charge have to be to provide a genuine incentive to control emissions? We use some examples from New Mexico to estimate the needed level of the charge.

During August 1974, the New Mexico Environmental Improvement Board held a hearing on SO_2 regulations for coal-fired power plants. An expert, Milton Beychok, who is frequently employed by industry, testified that 90 percent control of SO_2 at Four Corners would cost 2.4 to 3.7 mills/kwhr;[3] this number includes capital costs. The higher figure amounts to $34 million a year for units 4 and 5 while the lower amounts to $23 million a year. Arizona

---

3. This value is taken from the transcript of the EIB hearings (New Mexico Environmental Improvement Board [1974a, p. 616]).

Public Service Company estimates of operating costs were apparently about the same,[4] as the upper value used by Beychok and their estimates of capital costs were perhaps slightly lower. With a 70 percent load-factor total, Four Corners emissions would be about 84,000 tons per year. These values could be increased slightly with higher sulfur coals as exist in the field being mined for the plant or decreased with the lower sulfur coals in the field. The emission of units 4 and 5 comprise 82 percent of this total, or 68,800 tons per year. Thus, a charge of 350 to 550 dollars per ton of SO_2 or 18 to 28 cents per pound of SO_2 would probably induce cleanup of units 4 and 5. Significant cleanup of units 1–3 would probably occur at a lower value.

Arizona Public Service (APS), which holds the chief interest in the Four Corners plant, has fought two major court actions to prevent any cleanup. Currently they are required to clean up about 35 percent of their potential emissions from units 4 and 5 and 65 percent of the emissions from units 1–3. They currently remove about 40 percent of the SO_2 emissions from units 1–3 as a by-product to particulate control. Thus, under current regulations they would emit 44,720 tons per year from units 4 and 5 and 8,866 from units 1–3. At 25 cents per pound, this would produce revenues of $26.8 million per year from Four Corners. The EPA has ruled that 35 percent control on units 4 and 5 is inadequate to achieve ambient air standards. Thus, further regulations can be expected; however, based on past history it is likely that APS will attempt to delay enforcement of any new regulations. It should be underlined that while at present levels of emissions a regulatory fee would yield substantial revenues, the primary purpose of the fee is not to yield revenues but to induce abatement action. Thus, the revenues from a well-designed fee system should drop drastically as companies like Arizona Public Service find it in their economic interest to stop fighting regulation and get on with the job of emission control.

The other major coal-fired power plant in the San Juan region is Public Service Company of New Mexico's (PSCNM) San Juan plant. Apparently the sulfur content of its coal is slightly higher than that of APS, so that total emissions from a 1,660 Mw plant (to be completed in 1983) would be about 84,300 tons per year at 70 percent load factor. However, PSCNM is committed to control 90 percent of its SO_2 emissions.[5] Thus, PSCNM would emit only 8,400 tons per year, while under current regulations APS would

---

4. This value is from the transcript of the EIB hearings of the New Mexico Environmental Improvement Board (1974b, p. 775).

5. The sulfur value is reported in a booklet, *San Juan Generating Station PSCNM*, which also gives 180 tons per hour coal consumption for a 330 Mw unit out of a total of 1660 Mw. The booklet also describes 90 percent control of SO_2.

have emissions of 53,600 tons per year; thus, PSCNM's emissions would be
only 16 percent of APS's emissions. A fee of 25 cents per pound on PSCNM's
San Juan plant would net only $4.2 million per year. Furthermore, PSCNM
is in the process of installing equipment on its units, while APS continues to
stall. The much lower payments PSCNM would have to make would be an
economic reward for its much stronger commitment to control, while the fact
that it would still have to pay for all units discharged would provide a continuing incentive to do better and some compensation for the external costs
associated with even the controlled level of emissions.

The other major set of sources of sulfur emissions in the Southwest is the
large copper smelters scattered through the region. In a percentage sense,
high-level control of sulfur emissions from smelters can be achieved much
more cheaply (on a per pound basis) than is the case for power plant emissions. Mead and Bonem (1976) in a Southwest Region Under Stress project,
have done some estimates of copper-smelter emission fees that would produce
high percentage control. At charges of 0.6 cents (6 mills) per pound of SO_2,
smelter emissions would be reduced by about 60 percent (as compared with
an uncontrolled situation). Charges of 0.8 cents (8 mills) per pound of SO_2
would result in reduction of emissions by about 95 percent. These estimates
are in 1975 dollars. It should be pointed out that there are reasons to believe
that these estimates are somewhat low; in fact, an emission charge of $1\frac{1}{2}$ to
2 cents per pound of SO_2 might be required to reduce smelter emissions by
90 percent. Even if the actual charge needed were double, this amount would
still be small when compared with that needed for power plants.

The large discrepancy between required emission charges for smelters as
opposed to power plants is the result of copper smelters having very large sulfur emissions, most of which can be controlled by process changes involving
the recovery of sulfuric acid. But uncontrolled emissions from a large smelter
are perhaps six to eight times as large as those of a 400–500 Mw power station, and this seems that a high level of control in percentage terms still leaves
a large amount of emissions in absolute terms.

Furthermore, to achieve sulfur emission reductions above 90 to 95 percent
appears to be extremely costly. For copper smelters, very high sulfur reduction levels can be achieved only by such methods as installing a two-stage sulfuric acid plant instead of a one-stage plant or by scrubbing tail gases from an
acid plant with limestone. Kellogg and Henderson (1976) estimate that the
removal efficiency of a single-stage acid plant on a converter might be 97.3
percent, and for a two-stage acid plant 99.3 percent. But the two-stage acid
plant uses 40 percent more power (electric requirements in acid plants are
quite high) and requires a capital outlay at least 15 percent high than a
single-stage plant. Putting limestone scrubbing on the tail gas from an acid
plant would probably involve even larger costs. Consequently, at high re-

moval levels, costs of treatment are high, probably comparable to those from a power plant.

In summary, it appears that a regulatory fee of about 25 cents per pound of SO_2 would provide a strong incentive to both power plants and copper smelters in the Southwest to clean up to a high degree.[6]

Monitoring emissions. A prerequisite for any sort of reasonably accurate emissions control system, whether it be based upon standards or charges, is a suitable means of monitoring emissions. There are two major questions in this respect: (1) Who will do the monitoring? (2) Is an acceptable technology available for making the measurements?

One of the first questions that must be answered in designing a monitoring scheme is whether the initial burden of making the quantitative and qualitative measurements on which the charges are to be based will lie on the discharger or on the charging authority. When one considers the expense and the practical difficulties of allocating the entire measurement task to the government, the answer comes rather easily. The bureaucratic burden that would result from exclusive reliance on monitoring carried out by the regulators would be enormous, but fortunately this is a problem that is easily avoided by requiring each major pollution source to monitor and report its own discharges. Moreover, equity and economic efficiency suggest that the costs of monitoring be imposed on the sources of the problem rather than on the public at large.

But would not self-reporting provide too great a temptation for under-reporting? Is it realistic to expect discharges to be completely honest in their measurements? What happens when the measurement device breaks down (either accidentally or with assistance) and produces no data about pollutants? The answers to these questions are not so difficult as they may seem. To begin with, there is a precedent for the viability of a self-reporting approach in the income tax system. While it cannot be denied that there is some income tax cheating, the majority of business tax returns are entirely honest; the amount of false reporting is not nearly great enough to threaten the viability of the system. The application of a self-reporting system to charges would require occasional verification by the authorities (analogous to income tax audits) and penalties for intentional misreporting, but such provisions are hardly novel to our legal system. They might be supplemented in the environmental field by provisions for "bounties" to private citizens who developed evidence leading to the exposure of a polluter for false reporting.

Nevertheless, no matter who does the monitoring, the government agency

---

6. It would of course be necessary to index this number to an inflation indicator if its incentive effect is not to be eroded by inflation.

or the discharger, someone must produce acceptable estimates of emissions. In general, the measurement of gaseous discharges from large stacks is rather tricky, but instrumentation does exist and for large sources, such as would be involved in sulfur emissions fees in the Southwest, the cost is relatively small.

But one of the reasons for starting with sulfur components in the development of a regulatory fee approach is that a very simple method can be used for monitoring emissions. It is a simple matter to determine by chemical analysis the sulfur content of a fuel and the sulfur content of the ash material, and therefore the proportion going up the stack. If a plant installs abatement equipment to remove sulfur from the stack gases, it is again a relatively simple matter to determine the amount removed and deduct that from the total sulfur burned to arrive at the amount that goes up the stack.

The Navajo fee. It is interesting that the Navajo Indian tribe has been the innovator in establishing a sulfur emissions fee. The Appendix to this study contains a resolution of the Navajo Tribal Council, which enacted a sulfur emissions fee for sources of sulfur emissions located on the Navajo reservation. This includes the Four Corners plant. It is the first example in the world of a sulfur regulatory emissions fee to be enacted by any unit of government anywhere. The resolution is currently in litigation.

CONCLUDING COMMENTS

Some of the conclusions of this paper are quite depressing. Particularly it was found that if the regulatory approach under present law, including the regulation of siting were to work perfectly, further large-scale development of the electric power and synfuels industries would be possible without violating air quality standards. However, the studies we have done make it almost impossible to imagine that such development could occur without extremely destructive effects on visibility in a region noted for its expansive vistas, blue skies, brilliant colors, and the abundance of national parks, national monuments, and wilderness areas.

There is nothing in the history of regulation in the environmental quality area to suggest that it will be perfect or even acceptably effective. Thus, in exploring large-scale development without highly effective emissions control, we found that such development could be described only as a massive disaster for air quality in the Southwest.

To help afford, at least, effective control of major emissions, and to help reimburse the region for the damage that would nevertheless occur, we have explored the use of state-level emissions fees as an incentive for control.

The visibility issue appears to be much larger than just the question of emissions control at particular sites or site selection in a limited regional sense. Large questions of strategy appear to be involved here. If visibility is to be protected in the Southwest and the coal resource is to be used, it may well be necessary to mine the coal where it is found (there being no alternative to that) and ship it out of the region for combustion or conversion. There are bits of evidence that this may be the direction things are taking.

REFERENCES

Federal Register 138, no. 135, Monday, July 16, 1973.

Federal Register 139, no. 107, Tuesday, August 27, 1974a.

Federal Register 139, no. 235, Thursday, December 5, 1974b.

Gordon, C. C. "Plantations vs. Power Plants." *American Christmas Tree Journal* 16 (August 1972).

Hales, J. M., et al. "Final Report on Field Investigations of Sulfur Dioxide Washout from the Plume of a Large Coal-Fired Power Plant by Natural Precipitation." Battelle Memorial Institute (March 1971).

Kellogg, H., and J. Henderson. "Energy Use in Sulfide Smelting of Copper." In J. Yannapoulos and J. Agarwal, ed., *Extractive Metallurgy of Copper*. Baltimore: American Institute of Mining Engineers, 1976.

Kneese, Allen V., and Charles L. Schultze. *Pollution, Prices, and Public Policy*. Washington, D.C.: The Brookings Institution, 1975.

——— and Michael D. Williams. "Air Quality Issues and Approaches in the Southwest." A Report of the Southwest Region Under Stress Policy Project. Xerox (May 1977).

Mead, Richard, and Gilbert Bonem. "Residuals Management in the Copper Industry." University of New Mexico. Working paper. Xerox (June 1976).

New Mexico Environmental Improvement Board hearings on regulations 602 and 504 held at Farmington, New Mexico (August 1974a).

New Mexico Environmental Improvement Board, supplement to the testimony of Tom Woods of the Arizona Public Service Company (1974b).

Rockwell International, Air Monitoring Center, Meteorology Research Inc., Systems Applications, Inc. "Navajo Generating Station Sulfur Dioxide Field Monitoring Program." Vol. 1. Final Program Report (September 1975).

U.S. Department of Interior. "Draft—Environmental Impact Statement El Paso Coal Gasification Project, New Mexico" (July 1974a).

———. "Draft—Environmental Impact Statement WESCO Gasification Project and Expansion of Navajo Mine by Utah International Inc., San Juan Basin, New Mexico" (December 1974b).

U.S. EPA, "Mt. Storm, West Virginia—Gormann, Maryland, and Luke, Maryland—Keyser, West Virginia Air Pollution Abatement Activity—Pre-Conference Investigations" (April 1971).

———. Office of Transportation and Land Use Policy. "Guidelines on Re-

classification of Areas Under EPA Regulations to Prevent Significant Deterioration of Air Quality" (June 1975).

_____ and Federal Energy Administration. "An Analysis of the Impact on the
Electric Utility Industry of Alternative Approaches to Significant Determination." Vols. 1 and 2 (October 1975a).

_____ and Federal Energy Administration. "Analysis of House Discussion
Draft Ruled October 16, 1975." Supplement Report 2. General Edi-
tion (1975b).

Williams, Michael D., and Robert Cudney. "Predictions and Measurements of
Power Plant Plume Visibility Reductions and Terrain Interactions."
Presented at the Third Symposium on Atmospheric Turbulance, Diffu-
sion, and Air Quality. American Meteorological Society. Raleigh, North
Carolina, October 19–22, 1976.

APPENDIX

CJN-45-77

Class "C" Resolution
No BIA Action Required

RESOLUTION
OF THE NAVAJO
TRIBAL COUNCIL

Requiring a Permit for the Discharge of Sulfur or Its
Compounds into the Atmosphere from Within
the Navajo Nation

WHEREAS:

1. The preservation of the natural environment and the health and
well-being of its people is a responsibility of any sovereign government;
and

2. The discharge of sulfur and sulfur compound into the atmosphere

of the Navajo Nation from sources within the Navajo Nation may impair the health and safety of residents of the Navajo Nation; and

3. It is the responsibility of the Navajo Tribal Council, as the governing body of the Navajo Nation to take every action which will encourage those presently discharging sulfur and its compounds into the atmosphere from points within the Navajo Nation to cease or curtail such discharges; and

4. The Navajo Environmental Protection Commission has endorsed this effort and has agreed to work jointly with the Navajo Tax Commission in implementing this charge.

NOW THEREFORE BE IT RESOLVED THAT:

1. From and after the effective date of this resolution, no person, corporation, partnership, government, syndicate, or other form of organization shall discharge sulfur or compounds of sulfur into the atmosphere without first obtaining a permit from the Navajo Environmental Protection Commission.

2. This resolution shall become effective after ninety (90) days has elapsed after approval of this proposed resolution by the Navajo Tribal Council.

3. The Courts of the Navajo Nation are vested with full authority, pursuant to their own rules, and the rules and regulations of the Navajo Environmental Protection Commission and the Navajo Tax Commission to hear and determine any and all matters arising out of the imposition, administration or collection of this permit fee. This authority includes the right to hear and determine any and all matters without regard to the status (Indian or non-Indian; natural person or partnership, government, corporation or association, etc.) of the parties to any action. The Courts of the Navajo Nation are further specifically empowered to enjoin the operation of any facility discharging sulfur or its compounds into the atmosphere from within the Navajo Nation in violation of this resolution or the rules and regulations promulgated in accordance therewith by the Navajo Environmental Protection Commission and the Navajo Tax Commission.

4. No permit shall be required for any person who discharges less than 100 lbs. of sulfur into the atmosphere annually.

5. Every permit holder shall report to the Navajo Tax Commission the quantity of sulfur discharged into the atmosphere during each calendar quarter, commencing with the quarter beginning after the effective date of this resolution. Together, with such report, the permit holder shall remit a sulfur discharge fee according to the following schedule:

Calendar Quarters *Beginning On:*	*Fee (per lb.)*
July 1, 1977	$.10
July 1, 1978	.20
July 1, 1979	.30
July 1, 1980	.40
July 1, 1981	.50

The report and payment to the Navajo Nation required by this section shall be made on or before the forty-fifth (45th) day after the end of the quarter for which the report is made.

6. The Navajo Environmental Protection Commission and the Navajo Tax Commission are vested with the authority to enforce this permit system by appropriate rules and regulations. The Commissions may divide this authority as they deem fit and mutually agree.

7. All resolutions or parts of resolutions (including any attachments thereto) which are inconsistent with the provisions of this Resolution are hereby repealed, including without limitation, any resolution or resolutions which purport to waive or limit the right of the Navajo Nation to regulate the operation of any business activity within the Navajo Nation.

8. If any provision of this resolution or its application to any person or circumstances is held invalid by a final judgment of a court of competent jurisdiction, the invalidity shall not affect other provisions or applications of the proposed resolution which can be given effect without the invalid provision or application, and to this end the provisions of this resolution are severable.

CERTIFICATION

I hereby certify that the foregoing resolution was duly considered by the Navajo Tribal Council at a duly called meeting at Window Rock, Navajo Nation (Arizona), at which a quorum was present and that same was passed by a vote of 50 in favor of 0 opposed, this 8th day of June, 1977.

Peter MacDonald
Chairman
Navajo Tribal Council

DISCUSSION

Integrating Resources Policy in a Regional Environmental Framework

ANTHONY SCOTT

Allen Kneese's and Michael Williams's paper on the threat posed by coal exploitation on the New Mexico environment is a very neat contribution, authoritatively dealing with four elements that come into conflict in the awe-inspiring desert with its crystalline skies and colored landscapes, which he evokes so effectively. These elements are the exploitation of *resources;* the *national policies* that govern their utilization; the consequent damage of the *environment;* and the essentially local or *regional* nature of the damage. This fine account can be read as a fairly straightforward sorting out of a threat that, he suggests, could be mitigated by economic-incentive measures that he has so well refined in earlier writings. But his analysis provokes reactions that go well beyond his treatment of the particular situation he discusses, and I must apologize in advance that my comments devote so much space to ruminations on the state and direction of environmental economics.

In these comments I will deal successively with the changing significance in environmental economics of the authors' phrase "regional setting"; with the implications for policy of the different structures of "resource economics" and "environmental economics"; and with two minor aspects of the analysis presented in the chapter.

"REGIONAL" ANALYSIS OF ENVIRONMENTAL PROBLEMS

Because dealing with nature inevitably brings spatial relationships into the otherwise dimensionless body of neoclassical positive welfare economics, it is not surprising that in environmental analyses the word "region" recurs repeatedly. Allen Kneese has been in the forefront of those who have reminded policymakers of the importance of regional concepts, and his reputation was rightly enhanced by the publication, in 1964, of the pathbreaking *The Economics of Regional Water Quality Management.*

My first point in this section is that the significance of the word "region" in 1964 was different from its significance today. Let us recall the situation then. Water (and air) pollution themselves were not new subjects. Every economist's graduate training had touched on the difference between social and private benefits, and between internal and external economies. The incapacity of the market system to deal with air pollution, of which smoke was taken to be a representative and familiar example, was recognized. Lawyers, of course, were even better informed on regulatory (and damage) procedures compelling certain types or groups of polluters to undertake abatement activities. And sanitary engineers and public health doctors had already had more than a century of experience in planning, construction, or commanding facilities for dealing with wastes, chiefly organic and chiefly urban.

Consequently, although sewage treatment was not a popular subject for applied economists, they (and public administration experts) were roughly in agreement with the doctrine that waste management units should be geographically coterminous with the resource to be "managed" (in this case, a watershed). Where the economic contribution of Allen Kneese diverged from current policy thinking and common practice was in being "utilitarian" rather than "regulatory." By this I mean that the recommended approach would require some agency to examine *all* alternative abatement procedures. To compare and combine these alternatives, it would be necessary to refer their respective benefits to some goal or maximand. Herein lay the real innovation. Existing policy was oriented toward forcing polluters to take prescribed actions. Like other regulatory policies, it was administered by concentrating on preventing wrongdoing.

The new approach would force administrators to broaden their vision. A moralistic search for miscreants doing wrong things was to be replaced by a rational search for the best way of attaining a set of social objectives. The strong arguments in favor of this "utilitarian," goal-oriented, internalizing, rational approach had three corollaries. One was that preventive policy toward individuals could not be "uniform" and so could not be enforced mechanistically, as with the earlier public health standards about sewers and chimneys. The second was that, in order to achieve a social rationality in discriminating between sources and between victims of pollution, "planning" would be necessary. This corollary was also justified by the realization that, contrary to the earlier literature, quality management involved, not only private externalities and spillovers, but also public goods. The third corollary, almost incidental, was that the internalizing management agency would need powers to control or coordinate actions over a wide area; hence the name "regional" policy.[1]

---

1. Being coterminous prevents there being externalities, by definition. Kneese and Bower advocate "internalizing" all effects as a criterion for the size of regional unit. Another teminology refers to the process of making a resource more "specific" (Scott [1955, pp. ix, 184]).

In contrast, today's use of the word "regional," as illustrated by the chapter under consideration, is much closer to the common usage of "regional scientists." This treats the general welfare of a region as a miniature replica of national or social welfare analysis. Pollution becomes only one of many regional choice problems. The region is not defined by the watershed but by a complex of common problems and common ends and by inward-moving and inward-looking activities.

The main point is that, whereas in earlier work "regional environmental quality management" was a rallying call for rationality in achieving national social goals, today it is a cry of despair that externally oriented activities place an unduly heavy burden on residents of particular regions.

Many economists will say, "Welcome to the club." Development economists in particular will point out that Kneese's theme is identical to their lifetime concern that in interregional and international trade in raw materials, the tail wags the dog: small changes in demand in the OECD nations, for example, cause greatly magnified welfare, social, developmental, employment, and environmental effects in Asia, Africa, and Latin America. The pollution threat in New Mexico is analytically the same as the despoliation and ruin of islands, lakelands, pastoral countrysides, and deserts all over the world.

What can these small countries do? Obviously, they must implement local environmental policies. In this connection it is interesting that the authors still hesitate to recommend that "regional policy" be the responsibility of region-conscious states and local governments. Perhaps, having once urged planners to broaden their horizons, Kneese is naturally unwilling now to recommend that their powers be confined within regional or political borders. Thus, we are given the impression by the paper under consideration and its title that the authors are searching for *national* policies that will be able to discriminate sympathetically between impacts on different regions. Among independent materials-producing countries there is no such hope. External policies, in the absence of a world society and an international law, cannot be relied on to protect local environments. Local and regional policies administered by local governments are the only feasible response. It seems to me that by choosing in the title to deal with problems "in a regional setting," the authors evade an implication of the subject: regions in a federation, no less than regions that are nation-states, must face up to balancing the benefits and costs inherent in making their own differing environmental policies.

THE MARRIAGE OF RESOURCES POLICIES AND ENVIRONMENTAL POLICIES

In the opening pages, the authors refer briefly to the conflict that is also succinctly described in the prospectus for the conference. Both agree in suggesting that resources policies are inherently "national," while environmental policies are regional or local.

This observation about institutional realities, at least in the United States, is mirrored by a schizophrenia in economic analysis, which I will attempt to define and explain. I refer first to economic theory, later to applied economics.

The economic theory of resource utilization starts with consumer sovereignty in demand for final products and works back to the plan of the firm in producing the necessary raw materials. This can be seen in the contributions of, say, Hotelling and Herfindahl. Krutilla, in his concern that certain other consumer benefits of wilderness and resource availability may be sacrificed by final-market-oriented production planning for energy, lumber and minerals, merely confirms my generalization. There is no need for "the region" in this concept; markets call everywhere for material supplies (and their substitutes) as price increases. There is a need for distinguishing between stocks and flows; expected future consumer demands dictate the rate of exhaustion and replacement of reserves and biological populations. In summary, one might say that the economic theory of resource supply and demand is "vertical" in its structure.

In contrast, we may describe the economic theory applying to environmental quality as "horizontal." It is concerned chiefly with competing uses of given locations or environments. Transactions and decisions do not pass up and down between successive production stages of given products, but sideways between successive stages in the movement of water or wind in given watersheds and airsheds. There are some problems of stocks, for some pollutants are cumulative and some absorptive capacities are limited. But economic theory typically deals with alternative techniques for allocating the services of a given flowing resource among competing disposers who are, implicitly, each assumed to be at roughly the same intermediate production stage in supplying its own final product to consumers elsewhere. Even at the most abstract level, such theory cannot deal with such problems without concepts of space and region.

This difference in theoretical approach is also to be found in applications to actual problems and policies. As the "energy crisis" reveals, economists all over the world are led to analyze the policies to be followed by *consuming* regions and countries. Economics' neglect of producing-region considerations makes the discipline unprepared to cope with problems on the supply side, such as the mobility and adaptability in social and economic structure dictated by frequent depletion, redevelopment, and relocation of industrial and social activity; the preoccupation of regional governments with exploration, investment, royalties, and time rates of production (exhaustion); and the anxieties stemming from many types of uncertainties about local physical stocks and about external markets. Local policies that deal in these problems are assimilated into economics as brands of local parochial nationalism, obstacles to be overcome by resource policies perceived as solutions to national procurement problems. Even this regional paper views the demand for coal and energy as given, the fruit of national analyses of scarcities experienced in consuming regions. In one place the authors do refer to varying the pace of coal and energy development in the interest of regional environmental quality, but the important implication that such variation would mean that the nation would then have to change its energy import, or consumption, policy is nowhere mentioned.

By contrast, the applied economics of pollution problems is led to study ever more intensively the actual policy choices within particular regions. This neglect of final markets and alternative techniques or production makes the environmental specialist indifferent to the potentialities of substitution of different goods to final demand, or different inputs to production. This was well illustrated a few years ago when the "polluter pays policy" (PPP) was urged on all nations as preferable to governmental subsidies to finance pollution cleanups. Although it had an obvious symmetry with the textbook question about whether polluters should be controlled by payments or charges, most environmental economists did not participate in the PPP debate. This was because, I submit, environmental economics is not structured to examine the vertical dimensions of the industries that cause pollution and consequently are ill-equipped to know whether alternative regional strategies have their ultimate impact primarily on employees, local and national tax revenues, owners, or consumers, and whether they are experienced at home or overseas.

Environmental economists, in other words, are often led to take national or external resource policies as given. They accept the handmaiden role of working on the "environmental and social aspects" of predetermined national resource policies.

Of course, there are some important contributions to developing analytical linkages between resource policy and regional environmental policy. I have already referred to one of these. The work of John Krutilla with several colleagues on the environmental cost of energy policies sometimes is stated as a criticism of the energy policy itself: its preoccupation with the present demands of energy consumers inefficiently neglects the present and future demands of the same consumers for direct environmental services. Thus, Krutilla sometimes escapes from the tryanny of the split between the two theoretical approaches, although he rarely considers alternative energy suppliers overseas.

And Allen Kneese has cooperated with others in working out some aspects of a materials-balance approach, in which both the state of resource and environmental stocks and the supply of raw materials can play an equal role. This approach is so comprehensive that it could serve as the theoretical structure for both resource policy and regional policy. But in fact, it seems to me, it is being utilized merely as a pedagogic device for the understanding of the role of recycling.

This section amounts to a mild criticism of Kneese's and Williams's paper and of all environmental economics. We have allowed resource economics and policies to maintain their vertical structure, and their consequent indifference to the "horizontal" concerns of the supplying regions. The paper brings out well the frustration felt by the market-conditioned economist when he sees the powerlessness of regional residents to control their own ambience. The solution, it seems to me, is for the economist with regional concerns also to adopt the vertical approach. However, instead of working backward from the derived demands of consumers, he should work forward from the given preferences, time preferences, stocks, and environmental potentialities of the supplying regions to derive the amounts to be offered, over time, to the consuming regions (plus or minus exports and imports).

TWO SIDE ISSUES

This paper left me wondering about two aspects of the New Mexico problem that were not explored.

First, timing. The paper does mention alternative paces of development; and, of course, it deals by implication with the environmental consequences of various combinations of mineral activity in the region. These references whet the appetite for more on the same question. Why does each unit have to be so large and short-lived? What would be the financial and present-value cost of proceeding to mine coal and generate electricity with a lower annual output? Presumably capital costs demand and economies of scale in generation are part of the explanation, but these are not *imperatives*. All of the United States is connected on an electrical grid, and this could be strengthened. When this is done, no region need be the sole source of a large fraction of the national load at one time. Exhaustion of some sources could be attenuated over many decades, and other sources could be brought into production earlier. Of course, this strategy would have a cost, compared with the savings obtained by lurching indivisibly from one huge coal project to another. But the cost is that of obtaining the benefits of smaller and steadier regional environmental impacts.[2]

Second, emission fees. As is well known, transferable property rights to

---

2. Harry Campbell and I have looked into this in a recent paper dealing with the rate of production and of opening up three uranium mines. See Campbell and Scott (1978).

emit are, theoretically, a complete institutional substitute for fees or charges. In the context described by the authors, they might help to deal with administrative problem better than fees (plus interregional coordination agreements), where there is no clear boundary to the region. Assume that the original distribution of rights to emit pollutants has been somehow settled; that they add up to a rate of emissions that conforms to present legal standards; and that everyone affected has "standing" in that he is represented by a state, municipal, or district government, by an industrial corporation or by a native organization. Then the rights can not only do the job that the authors assign to fees but can be used to: (a) change the ambient standard easily, and (b) take account of remote persons and firms. Function (a) simply calls for states or municipalities to buy some emission rights from industrial holders and to retire them. Function (b) allows people in the same airspace, but outside the region, to participate. Persons who wish to pollute New Mexico from sites in other regions would have to buy a right from its original New Mexico owner. And victims resident in other regions can (through their governments) buy New Mexico pollution rights to reduce the spillovers across regional boundaries. Furthermore, (c) residents of other regions or countries who wish to obtain more coal or electricity can buy emission rights from smelters and assign them to new energy installations to transmit energy to remote regions.[3] There are many pros and cons of rights systems; in this case, two important advantages would seem to be that there is little need to obtain information about the costs of abatement; and there is an easy way to deal with persons outside the region.

REFERENCES

Bramsen, Christopher Bo, and Anthony Scott. "Draft Guiding Principles Concerning Transfrontier Pollution." In *Problems in Transfrontier Pollution* (Paris: OECD, 1973). See Appendix B, pp. 300–345.

Campbell, Harry, and Anthony Scott. "Postponement vs. Attenuation: An Analysis of Two Strategies for Predicting and Mitigating the Environmental Damage of Large-Scale Uranium Mining Projects." Resources paper no. 26. Programme in Natural Resource Economics. University of British Columbia, Vancouver, 1978.

Scott, Anthony. *Natural Resources: The Economics of Conservation. Canadian Studies in Economics* no. 3, V. W. Bladen, ed. Toronto: University of Toronto Press, 1955.

---

3. For a discussion of an international rather than an interregional, context, see Bramsen and Scott (1973).

DISCUSSION

An Outside Perspective on the Issues Raised in the New Mexico Case

DAVID W. PEARCE

In their paper, Kneese and Williams (subsequently referred to as KW) have focused on some of the problems of what we might call "unachieved environmental legislation" laid down in federal and state laws in a context of a specific region of the United States that is clearly environmentally "sensitive." It may seem inappropriate to solicit comment on a paper that is set in a federal/state context from a European who is, ostensibly, unused to such a political system. On the other hand, the United Kingdom effectively has a national/regional context for much of its environmental policy in that, for example, water quality control rests largely with water authorities whose regional boundaries do not coincide with any local political boundaries. Moreover, the United Kingdom will have to get used, even if it has successfully resisted in many respects so far, to compliance at a national level with environmental standards and recommendations laid down in mandatory form by the European Economic Community. Finally, there was every prospect of establishing a quasi-state/federal system in the United Kingdom in 1979, when we voted on limited political devolution for Scotland and Wales. I rely on at least these factors in common to overcome my initial hesitancy in commenting on a paper that seemed to me to cry out for expert testimony from someone closer to the residents of New Mexico.

To press the matter further, I have never been to New Mexico and therefore have little impression of its evident natural beauty, so frequently mentioned in the paper. I am therefore at a disadvantage in not perhaps being able to appreciate the authors' obviously heartfelt concern over its invasion by the American upper middle classes in search of sun and environmental benefit. On the other hand, I am perhaps at an advantage in therefore being able to approach the matter a little more dispassionately than the authors do, since my first overriding impression is that KW have unashamedly superimposed their own subjective assessment of the environmental damage function they regard as being implicit in the compliance with even the *existing* federal and state air emission and ambient concentration levels, let alone the more likely scenario in which those standards are not met. Having said that, there is a reason for not dissenting from the implied valuation that KW place on environmental damage in New Mexico and in the specific subregion of San Juan they present to us. This is that, if the truth be known, we have no reason in economic science to regard valuations based on "passion'" as being inferior to those based on "impassion," the positivist empirical tradition of British and American philosophers notwithstanding. In the event, I do not dissent at all from seeing KW exhibit their own personalized concern in a paper that is otherwise set in a cost-effectiveness framework, if only because I too inhabit a part of the world already partly disfigured by the exploitation of a resource that will bring much-needed if transitory benefits to the United Kingdom's economy.

Indeed, this comparison elicits a further comment in that the technologies that most threaten the American Southwest seem to me to belong to an awkward transitional stage in which coal oil shale and perhaps uranium will figure prominently. The term "transitional" is deliberate but encompasses periods that may last 50 or 150 years. In the United Kingdom we have a very short-lived resource in North Sea oil, and the search for its substitute is already on. In the U.S. Southwest case, one imagines that shales could considerably extend the transition period between conventionally exploited resources and the twin prospects of a renewable-resource-based economy or one based on plutonium. In both cases, however, there are prospects for long-term recovery of the environment if suitable care is taken. It is, however, not altogether clear that we can discount *irreversible* environmental effects in the KW paper, especially as one notes the use of the term "catastrophic" for the outcome on noncompliance with even existing ambient standards. Moreover, oil-shale development is well known for its disfiguring impact on a natural environment. If irreversibilities exist, or if terms like "catastrophic" are actually justified, then one would want to suggest a quite different approach to the problem, namely outright prohibition of development of any kind, as might be dictated by the algorithms developed by Krutilla and his associates (Krutilla and Fisher [1975]) or, on a more humble level, by myself (Pearce [1976]).

My subsequent comments follow the sequence of the KW paper. The early part of the paper is devoted to a brief exposition of the Clean Air Act standards as laid down for the United States by the amendments to the 1970 act. Two features struck me in this early section, one relatively minor and one of more substantive interest. The first point concerns KW's remark that the concept of a threshold value for sets of air pollutants is a "politically convenient fiction." In terms of Figure 7-2, they imply that the damage function (expressible in physical terms, since they, rightly in my view, do not espouse monetary damage cost functions) lies above that of the "official"

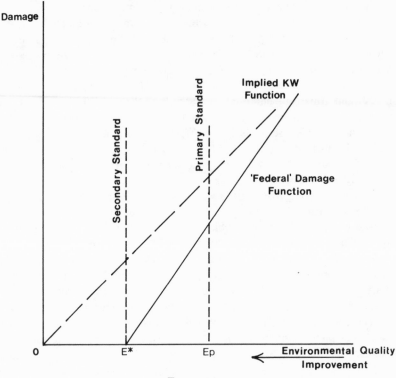

Figure 7-2

implied function. In short, whereas the central government view embraces the idea that damage can be reduced to *zero* by setting and achieving standards of E^*, KW imply that some damage will always prevail within the Clean Air Act standards. Certainly, their view is consistent with all that seems to be known about toxic materials and radiation where the dose-response relationship at least goes through the origin even if its exact shape thereafter is not agreed. Although this point is, of itself, minor, it links into KW's concern, expressed later, that *even if* all standards were observed, some very undesirable environmental impacts would remain. In short, if the dose-response function implicit in the federal rules is a "fiction," the way is open to challenging those standards as being themselves too lax, depending, of course, on one's valuation of the physical damage done.

Interestingly, but I suggest not surprisingly, KW point to the fact that standards in the region of E^* in Figure 7-2 have not been met. Indeed, many primary standards based on observable health impacts and implying minimum acceptable standards have not been met. The "gap" between standard and achievement is significant. In terms of KW's implied damage function, the gap is even larger. This raises the second issue that seems to me to be extremely important. Why have standards not been achieved? The fundamental situation is of course one of conflict. The polluter does not wish to comply with a standard that increases cost or administrative complexity. The enforcement agency is charged with achieving the standards laid down. Noncompliance with standards is more the norm than the exception, and the United States is not unique in this matter. Nonetheless, one could argue that there is a feature of the U.S. legislation that is absent in a country such as the United Kingdom. For want of a better term, one could suggest that "haste" characterizes not so much the legislation itself but, more importantly, the time horizon over which standards are to be achieved. By contrast, the United Kingdom's situation is one in which British pragmatism (mistakenly identified by ex-colonials as the "British disease") permits a fairly steady transition to the desired aim. It could, unquestionably, be faster, especially in the case of air pollution, but the United Kingdom's achievements in smoke and SO_2 control have been very significant over the last twenty years with, for example, emissions of smoke being reduced from some 2.3 metric tons in 1958 to about 0.5 metric tons in 1972. Of course, our Scandinavian friends will be quick to point out that our SO_2 reductions have perhaps been secured through their export to other countries, but that is another matter![1]

The suggestion is that haste in environmental legislation can be counterproductive. The very suddenness of legislation, especially legislation as comprehensive as many of the U.S. environmental acts, and its explicitly short time horizons can quickly cause polluters to close ranks and coalesce in an effort to defeat, modify, and postpone standards. Moreover, short time horizons must inevitably lead to disputes about what is "technologically possible," and one notes that KW themselves point to a "standoff" situation between polluters and legislators about what "the best adequately demonstrated control technology" is in respect of sulfur emission control. Exactly the same disputes exist within, say, the United Kingdom's situation, but they are hardly as "polarized." Of course, there are costs to the pragmatic approach in that one bears damage costs longer than perhaps need be the case. But given that short time horizons for achievement levels can generate the

---

1. The "export" of SO_2 now seems to be accepted, in part, by the United Kingdom's Government. The damage done is disputed. A simple observation of the emissions curve compared with the ground-level concentration curve for SO_2 for 1958–72 shows a widening gap, with the former being fairly constant and the latter falling. The first law of thermodynamics would suggest that the emissions must be being "immitted" somewhere.

conflict context in the United States, it is quite possible that total damage, cumulated over a time period, *can* be higher the shorter the time period for compliance if polluters have access to obstructing tactics. The "optimum" achievement period may therefore be more than that laid down in the U.S. acts and possibly less than that implicit in the U.K. legislation.[2]

KW go on to illustrate the use of an air dispersion model to predict the effects of development within the San Juan subregion. Clearly, in a short paper, they are summarizing the results of an extensive study, which one looks forward to seeing in all its comprehensive detail. In using the model their own implied damage function emerges again, for they observe that, even if all standards are complied with, the developments they outline would nonetheless cause at least some episodes of acid rain with consequent damage to trees and reductions in visibility, thus causing aesthetic damage, which they clearly regard as important. They also posit other effects, including those that might be transmitted outside the San Juan Basin region. If their own valuations are anywhere echoed among the other residents of the region, then it is clear that the emission and ambient standards are, in some sense, "inadequate." We are denied full knowledge of what the trade-off is, however, since KW do not speak of the incidence or magnitude of the abatement costs relating to observation of these standards. No doubt this is covered in the full study.

Of more significance, since regulation has failed in the past, by its own measuring rod, KW's second scenario in which the development is associated with noncompliance with the laid-down standards is more relevant. Here they find that, on likely degrees of noncompliance, the SO_2 levels alone will be three times the federal standards and five times the New Mexico State standards. These, they state, would be "catastrophically adverse effects." Since regulation has failed, and is likely to fail, they search for an alternative policy instrument. Given Allen Kneese's long-standing advocacy of pollution charges, it is no surprise to find that a pollution charge is the sought-after instrument. Leaving aside the issue of whether regulation really has failed because of some intrinsic feature or because it has simply been attempted too hastily, one or two points on the use of charges at the regional level seem worth making.

---

2. The issue is of course complicated by the American preoccupation with the use of courts of law on almost any environmental matter. While the courts are used in the United Kingdom in some environmental issues, the vast majority of "disputes" are settled outside the court system. As an obvious extreme example, the United Kingdom has no case of court action being taken against the nuclear industry.

This is not the place to rehearse the many and varied arguments for and against standards or charges in the field of environmental policy. What KW advocate is a charge on sulfur emissions, in the first instance (a) because it is relatively easy to monitor (the sulfur content of fuels and their sulfur emissions being fairly established relationships), and second (b) because the sulfur-generating products are exported from the region. The second point is interesting, since it implies that a pollutant should somehow be treated as a "priority" if its costs are borne in the producer's locality and its benefits are borne elsewhere. This introduction of an "equity" argument for selecting cases is welcome in one sense—namely, that it does not elevate economic efficiency alone to a misplaced status—but in another sense could imply something about loss of comparative advantage if industries have located in the polluted region for other least-cost reasons.

KW compute a tax based on 90 percent sulfur removal and arrive at figures of between $350 and $550 per ton of SO_2. What they recognize is that the superiority of a tax over regulation rests very much with the efficiency of a monitoring system. Here, however, they seem to exhibit a surprising faith in their own proposals. Essentially, they accept that a monitoring system would be too expensive and administratively complex to be handled by a regional authority. They therefore advocate "self-reporting"—that is, the polluter should actually report *his own* discharges of SO_2 and be charged accordingly. They counter the obvious challenge that there will be underreporting by saying that the same incentive exists in the income tax system where, in practice, little underreporting takes place. Of course, the penalties for noncompliance with accurate reporting on an income tax can be severe, especially in the United States. KW seem to envisage the same effect in a self-reporting context combined with "occasional verification by authorities" for air pollution. This view has been echoed elsewhere (Anderson et al. [1977]), and it seems widely accepted that polluters regard noncompliance with regulations easier than noncompliance with charges.

One wonders, however, just how far the case for self-reporting rests on an empirically tested view. As KW admit, there are precious few examples of charging mechanisms in existence for us to use in evidence. Moreover, it is difficult to see why there should be any difference in noncompliance in the regulation and self-reporting cases. Both rely on inspection by some authority, and the latter would seem, in the KW view, actually to impose less of a demand for inspection. If the United Kingdom's experience is anything to go by, there is little difficulty in "bending the rules" when necessary (Royal Commission on Environmental Pollution [1976]). It is least easy for such toxic chemicals as cyanide, where a nighttime release would still, for example, result in fish kills and subsequent investigation. With SO_2 it would seem comparatively easy not to comply unless the number of installations in question is small and the ambient monitoring equipment detects excesses over the standard. Possibly this fits the San Juan subregional model that KW present in this paper. It would, however, seem at least questionable as to how far the example can be generalized. The fact that there is sample monitoring plus a "materials-balance" relationship between fuel use and emissions provides a check of some sort, of course, but one wonders then about the efficiency of self-reporting compared with a system of charges based on the checking mechanisms themselves. There may be little to choose.

The above is not an argument *against* charges. They still have many features that make them superior to standards, and the fact that they can generate revenues that, on equity grounds, can be used for compensation is important, even if not strictly in compliance with the dictates of Pareto efficiency. Nonetheless, one wonders if the confident advocacy of charges by KW is likely to be fulfilled. One can but hope so. For combined with an entirely predictable rigor and thoroughness of approach and analysis in the KW paper is an express and personal concern for an area of natural beauty close to the authors' hearts. It is both pleasant and reassuring to find this kind of view in a science that is all too often soulless and more than occasionally devoid of relevance to anyone.

REFERENCES

Anderson, F. J., et al. *Environmental Improvement Through Economic Incentives*. Baltimore: The Johns Hopkins University Press, 1977.

Krutilla, J., and A. C. Fisher. *The Economics of Natural Environments*. Baltimore: The Johns Hopkins University Press, 1975.

Pearce, D. W. "The Limits of Cost-Benefit Analysis as a Guide to Environmental Policy." *Kyklos* 1 (1976).

Royal Commission on Environmental Pollution. *Fifth Report: Air Pollution Control—An Integrated Approach*. Cmnd. 6371. London: HMSO 1976.

CHAPTER 8

Environmental Aspects of Industrial Policies in a Regional Setting

MICHEL POTIER

During the 1960s, the industrialized countries experienced a period of high economic growth to which highly polluting industries such as the iron and steel, chemicals, pulp and paper, nonferrous metals and electrical power industries contributed largely. The development of such industries, while providing for economic benefits to those countries as a whole by increasing the national income, led to the deterioration of the state of the environment of the regions where high-polluting industries were located.

In response to this deterioration, industrialized countries introduced, progressively, environmental concern as a constraint for industrial policy. It was done in different ways, which can be characterized broadly as follows.

On the one hand, a few countries decided to concentrate areas of industrialization in part of their territory; this option consists of indentifying a limited number of areas where the installation of additional polluting activities would not seriously aggravate local conditions, which had already suffered from existing industrial plants. This solution, from the economic viewpoint, presents obvious advantages in the sense that there may be benefits from economies of scale in pollution control measures (sharing of investment and operating costs, including energy production; combined treatment processes; better opportunities for recycling and for use of excess heat). In addition, such a policy may help to maintain a high level of the quality of the environment over the greater portion of the territory to the benefit of the largest portion of the population without jeopardizing the economic growth of the country. There are, of

221

course, limitations to such a black-spot policy, to the extent that an extreme concentration of industrial activities may give rise to irreversible effects in terms of deterioration of the environment while being the source of severe equity problems for those who have to bear the social costs of such a policy.

On the other hand, other countries decided to spread individual industrial plants over the whole national territory, thus calling for maximum geographical dispersion. This option, in principle, endeavors to balance the advantages of assimilative capacity of the environment spread over the whole territory of the country, against the at-source control measures aimed at limiting the detrimental effects on the environment associated with the location of industrial plants.

Such a solution presents advantages as well as drawbacks. It presents the advantage of using the overall assimilative capacity of the national territory to the maximum possible extent while, at the same time, avoiding excessive pollution loads likely to cause irreversible effects and reducing the exposure of the population to smaller groups of people. However, such a policy may give rise to much higher pollution loads than anticipated while presenting difficulties for the implementation of effective pollution control due to the large number of individual plants to be supervised.

In spite of the efforts made in a large number of countries to reconcile, through the above-described options, environmental policy objectives and industrial policy objectives, more and more industrial policy objectives developed at national level are challenged at the regional level through the growing opposition to the siting of high-polluting industries. There are more and more examples now where the growing opposition at the regional level to the location of high-polluting industries is leading to deadlocked situations. This is the reason there is a more and more urgent need, on the one hand, to develop mechanisms that could be used for compensating the affected regions and their inhabitants for the inconveniences suffered due to industrialization and from which no benefits are derived, and, on the other hand, to develop anticipatory policies that could insure better coordination between industrial policy and environmental policy.

In the light of the above remarks we will examine first, based on the experience of some OECD countries, the extent to which OECD countries endeavor in various ways to integrate their environmental concern as a constraint of industrial policy in a regional setting. We will then turn to the case where industrial policies are challenged more and more at the regional level for environmental reasons, before considering the need for developing new mechanisms to reconcile environmental policies and industrial policies.

Based on the experience of OECD member countries, we may distinguish two main categories of countries. One is a group of countries, representing a minority, where efforts have been made to mitigate the adverse environmental effects resulting from the development of industrial activities by selecting particular areas for industrial purposes—for example, by developing physical-planning policies. Another group comprises the majority of countries, where the prevailing feeling is that industrial location should not be geographically limited but that limitations and controls should be imposed in order to insure an acceptable state of the environment everywhere.

LAND-USE PLANNING

Among OECD countries, the Netherlands and Sweden certainly belong to the first category of countries. We are going to examine in detail the case of Sweden; it is possible to draw preliminary lessons from the Swedish experience in the use of national physical planning to control the expansion of industries likely to damage the state of the environment (OECD [1977c, pp. 74-87]).

The need for national physical planning came in Sweden from numerous conflicts related to industrial location in the middle of the 1960s. During that period, open-air recreation, holiday homes, as well as certain types of industry were the three main protagonists in conflicts over native natural resources. Claims were often directed at areas—mostly coastal ones—which while offering favorable locations for certain industrial installations also included assets particular value for different leisure activities and for nature and cultural conservancy.

The planning procedure has been going on in stages since 1967. It has included comprehensive investigations in order to obtain a complete picture of the claims likely to be made over the next few decades on land and water, and also of the resources available for satisfying these claims. The possible effects of these activities on an environment were also investigated.

Particular emphasis in the investigation was placed on open-air recreation sites, tourist facilities, scientific nature conservation and industrial activities. These industrial activities include steelworks, petrochemical industries, pulp and paper industries, oil refineries, and power stations. The role of agriculture and forestry was investigated as well. The aim has been to isolate the claims made by each of these sectors and also to illustrate the environmental disturbances and other consequences that may be associated with the development trends studied. A consistent effort has been made in the course of the investigation to elucidate development both during the 1970s and during the ensuing decades up to the year 2000. The investigations were carried out by the responsible national or regional authorities, by the appropriate industrial organizations, and by other organizations, on the basis of instructions and programs worked out by the Ministry of Physical Planning.

Finally in 1972 the Swedish Parliament adopted national guidelines for land use. These national guidelines are of two different kinds: (1) there are general guidelines indicating how certain types of activities should be handled by means of physical planning at the regional and local levels (activity guidelines), and (2) there are guidelines for the management of certain natural resources, in certain parts of the country (geographical guidelines).

The basic principle that has guided the Swedish Parliament is inspired by the philosophy of the black-spot policy. In other words, it was thought that it was desirable to concentrate new industrial units in those places where industry was already established in order to leave as many areas as possible untouched elsewhere.

Guidelines for the location of certain industries were consequently proposed. The areas that have been considered most suitable for location of industries are those that:

(i) offer a good combination of natural assets and transport facilities that are needed by the industries concerned;

(ii) are situated in the vicinity of areas where these types of industry have already affected the environment; or

(iii) are situated within commuting distance of urban areas earmarked as regional centers in the regional development program.

These guidelines have been implemented by geographical guidelines that mainly cover the coastline but also cover the mountain area and certain river valleys. A distinction is made between areas where the value for scientific and recreational purposes on a national scale is so great that the establishment of polluting industries must not be permitted, and areas where, under certain conditions, industries will be allowed to locate. Whereas the guidelines concerning the first category of areas are considered to be of a long-term nature and unlikely to be changed, those in the second category are considered to be of a less long-term nature owing to the fact that they are dependent on a number of rapidly changing factors (technical progress) and, consequently, are likely to be subject to revisions.

These geographical guidelines concern the coastline, mountain areas, and rivers and their tributaries. The coastline has been divided into three different categories: (a) the continuous, unexploited archipelago coasts where location of heavy-polluting industry will not be permitted; (b) the heavily exploited coastal areas, where new establishment of industry is likely even to damage the environment will be allowed adjacent to areas only where such industry already exists, the main parts of the western and southern coasts, the Stockholm region; and (c) the remaining coastline, where the relatively small num-. ber of highly attractive areas for recreation and conservation must be protected.

As a result of the implementation of the industrial and geographical guidelines, the following communities were chosen for new industry and industry likely to cause detrimental effects to the environment: Lysekil, Stenungsund, Värö, Karlshamn, Norrköping, Nyköping, Oxelösend, and Nynäshamn. However, it must be stressed that such guidelines had no immediate legal effects. Their implementation was connected with further refinement or amplification in the context of more detailed location decisions.

The results. How has national physical planning been working in Sweden? Three main lessons can be drawn from the Swedish experience: (a) numerous sites that were put aside for industrial development have not been used;(b) the derogations have been quite limited; and (c) comparison between the existing industrial sites has produced interesting results from the viewpoint of the environmental policies.

First, at the time national physical planning was initiated late in the 1960s, the prospect for industrial development was very optimistic. But Sweden, like other countries, has been affected by the economic recession. Consequently, the areas of the southern part of Sweden that had been set aside for resource-demanding industries and industries likely to cause detrimental effects to the environment proved not to be used, as had been expected.

Second, the national or geographical guidelines do not appear to have been seriously challenged when the stage of implementation came. In one case, the case of a Göteborg refinery, the prime minister intervened to allow the refinery to be built, whereas the municipality opposed the project. This is really the exception. In spite of pressures to revise the guidelines that insure the protection of the rivers of the northern part of Sweden, preventing any dams from being constructed in these rivers, there has so far been no sign that the Swedish government will sacrifice the rivers to the new energy policy requirements.

Third, a study that has recently been completed points out interesting results from a comparison drawn from the seven sites chosen for industrial development. This study, which focused on the effects of the conventional pollutants, shows in particular that the open west coast offers better natural conditions for diluting and dispersal. There is only one case where the location of a petrochemical plant in the archipelago led to such a strain on the environment that any further expansion had to be very strictly restricted. The western parts of southern Sweden are receiving a fair amount of airborne sulfur from Great Britain and the Continent that contributes to the acidification of the soil and water. Since the soil itself is also susceptible to acidification, it follows that any further siting of sulfur-emitting industries has to be forbidden.

The prerequisites for location along the seashores of the Baltic are somewhat more varied. In some places the coast is relatively open, in others there are more archipelagoes. The climatic conditions here are more favorable, making the acidification problem less acute. However, there is a need for duly examining the vulnerability of the area to some types of contaminants.

On the whole, the Swedish experience appears to be unique in the sense

that Sweden is one of the first countries where the decision was taken to concentrate the resource-demanding and the polluting industries in a limited
number of places. The development of such a black-spot policy does not
mean that Swedish industry has not been subject to control through regulatory
measures, but it implies that the situation as regards environmental quality
has been or will be different in those areas set aside for further industrial
development.

GEOGRAPHICAL DIFFERENTIATION

The majority of OECD countries endeavor to integrate environmental and
industrial policies through a geographical differentiation in setting standards
or effluent charges. We will distinguish between those that rely primarily on
effluent charges and those that mainly use the regulatory approach.

In the field of water management (OECD [1977d, p. 157]), a system based
on economic instruments has been adopted by both France and the Netherlands.

In France, charges are levied and redistributed under River Basin Agency
programs. The basis of these charges is the weight of raw pollution discharged
(not the volume of discharges and the proportion of polluting matter in
them). The chemical, physical, and microbiological elements included in the
calculations are: (a) suspended solids (SS); (b) oxidizable matter (OM), expressed as a weighted average of the chemical oxygen demand (COD) and the
biological oxygen demand (BOD):

$$OM = \frac{COD + 2(BOD_5)}{3}$$

(c) soluble salts expressed in (ohm/cm) $\times$ M^3 (conductivity $\times$ volume of
water discharged); and (d) inhibiting matter expressed in toxic equivalent per
day. Later the heating of water will be taken into account.

Presently the rate is not an optimum one—it depends entirely on the expenditure forecasts of the River Basin Agencies as determined by their action
programs.

It is interesting to note that a zoning coefficient is applied to the basic rate
in order to make allowance for conditions at the place of discharge that may
influence water quality. This coefficient, however, will vary—strictly speaking—
in accordance, not with geographical differentiation, but in accordance with
the water uses assigned to rivers. Three kinds of action zones are distinguished, with correspondingly different rates: (a) highly-polluted zones,
where the action is focused on the most serious sources of pollution, the object being maximum treatment at minimum cost; (b) upstream zones, where
the aim is to abate all the sources of pollution as quickly as possible and keep

away highly polluting and toxic industrial plants; and (c) intermediate zones, in which the overall objective is the medium-term restoration of rivers at present containing average pollution by giving priority to the protection of abstraction for potable water.

The rate of charge will vary not only according to a zoning coefficient within a river basin but also among river basins. For instance, the rate of charge (in francs per year per population equivalent) was 7.10 frs in the Seine/ Normandy River Basin for the highly polluted zones and only 5.70 frs in the Loire/Bretagne River Basin for corresponding zones. Every discharger is treated in the same way, whatever kind of pollution he causes, as the rules apply to the different types of pollution and the new polluters are bound by the same rules. Flat-rate charges have been worked out for various industrial activities and relate pollution to quantity of output or other quantitative measurements of activity. These flat-rate charges are thus affected by a zoning coefficient, depending upon the water use.

The charges, which are levied as described above, are collected by the River Basin Agencies and redistributed among users who require action by these agencies. Such redistribution implies that some redistribution can take place between industrial activities. In other words, levies collected from the chemical industry or the pulp and paper industry can be used, for example, to help the metal-plating industry comply with the action program of the River Basin Agencies.

In the Netherlands, raw (untreated) pollution is assessed on the basis of chemical oxygen demand and the Kjeldahl index for nitrogenous substances (N) divided by 180 grams, representing the pollution produced by one person per day:

$$\frac{COD(grams/day) + 4.57\ N(Kjeldahl)(grams/day)}{180}$$

Pollution after treatment is assessed similarly by putting biological oxygen demand in place of chemical demand:

$$\frac{2.5\ BOD + 4.57\ N}{180}$$

Thus, the *Waterschappen* take into account only the discharge of oxidizable and nitrogenous substances in assessing pollution, but there is a plan to include salinity. In 1976 some Waterschappen established a levy on heavy metals discharged into surface waters. These levies are charged per pollution unit and were intended, in principle, to meet the cost of purification of the effluent water insofar as this is carried out by public bodies. The amount of the levy is calculated by means of an estimate of the number of pollution units and a cost estimate of the treatment. If the levy per pollution unit is equal for residential and industrial polluters within the catchment board, this amount will vary among the various catchment boards to the extent that the polluter-pays principle is respected.[1]   Thus, the relatively high charges of some catchment boards result from the recent construction of sewage purification installations or from a structure of purification installations where small purification plants prevail.

To be complete, one has to distinguish two kinds of charges in the Netherlands. The first one is paid directly or by means of the Waterschappen to the Ministry of Transport and Waterways. These charges are levied on discharges into state waters[2] and are redistributed in the form of grants toward the investment costs of treatment plants to improve the quality of these waters (the maximum grant according 60 percent of the investment costs involved). The second kind of charge is paid to the Waterschappen to enable them to balance the budget covering the operation, use, and depreciation of the facilities they own and manage.

The experience.   A distinction must be drawn between two categories of countries: (1) countries in which the legislation aims at laying down uniform quality objectives for the whole country (Canada, the United States, Japan, Germany) but where, particularly for federal state countries, the states may enforce stricter legislation; and (2) countries where pollution control is exercised by local authorities.

In the United States ambient quality standards and emission standards are set at the federal level. They are defined to be applied across states and across industries. They are considered to represent a limit below which the various states cannot set emissions standards. However, it is still possible for more environmentally conscious states to set stricter standards (e.g. California and Orgeon).

It may be argued that from the economic viewpoint such a policy is likely to give rise to misallocation of resources to the extent that no provision is made for the varying assimilative capacities of the environment in every state. On the other hand, it must also be pointed out that it is not certain that the advantages derived from taking more account of the assimilative capacity of every state and of every region or subregion in every state will equal or exceed the advantages derived from economies of scale or of construction in series of the manufacturing of pollution control technology to comply with the "best practicable control technology currently available" or "the best available technology economically achievable."

It must also be stressed that corrections can be made to this system, al-

---

1. For example, the amount of charges per population equivalent varied from 22 florins to 51 florins among the *Waterschappen* in 1978.

2. They include the river Rhine and the river Meuse, the river Ijselmeer, and estuaries.

though through a costly and complex judicial mechanism, whenever industries or firms prosecute the EPA at court and challenge the proposed requirements.

In Japan, ambient quality standards are also set at the national level, which means that the same minimum standards apply to the country as a whole (OECD [1977b, p. 24]). However, local authorities are able to fix stricter environmental standards. Just as in the case of quality standards, the executive plays an important role in setting the standards. In the field of water management, the 1970 Water Pollution Control Law, for instance, deals only with broad principles and states that "the standards of an effluent shall be provided for in the Prime Minister's Office Order" (article 3). The emission standards were in fact issued in the 1971 and 1974 ordinances of the prime minister's office. In the field of air management, the 1968 Air Pollution Control Law prescribes that "emission standards with respect to soot and smoke generated from soot and smoke emitting facilities shall be established by Order of the Prime Minister's Office" (article 3). Consequently, the central government established many emission standards in various fields (air, water, noise, automobile exhaust gas standards). These standards have often been complemented by standards set up by local governments (prefectures and cities). In numerous cases the prefectures issued ordinances of a stricter nature for soot, dust, and for toxic components found in soot and in dust. Furthermore, local governments enter into detailed negotiations with some major plants for setting specific standards and even for the manner in which they could comply with them.

In the Federal Republic of Germany, in the field of air pollution, national standards were set up in the Federal Immission Control Act that was passed in 1974. However, the responsible enforcement authorities are allowed to set stricter standards on the basis of local conditions. In this sense, the situation in Germany is similar to that of the United States or Japan. In the field of water pollution, the federal government also attempts to introduce minimum effluent standards. Water emission guide values for effluent treatment are also laid down, but these have no legal status. They are applied on general approval by the *Länder* authorities when issuing license conditions.

On the contrary, *in the United Kingdom* there is no such thing as national ambient quality standards or a regional ambient quality standard; instead there are emission limits for particular plants that are set by the Alkali Inspectorate. In particular, these emission limits, in the case of air pollution, are set with reference to the "best practicable means." Flexibility is the key concept in this approach. The Inspectorate works closely with industry, and attempts are made to find acceptable solutions. Acceptable emission levels are set that are considered to be currently achievable in the light of the available technology, the nature and effects of the pollutants concerned, the costs to industry, and the assimilative capacity of the local environment. In other words, the emission limits set are likely to vary widely over the territory.

LOCATIONAL SHIFTING

Do pollution control costs cause location of industries? The answer depends to a large extent upon the weight that pollution control costs represent in production when the standards are met or when the charges are paid. We will address this issue before examining actual cases of relocation of firms for environmental reasons.

The share of pollution control costs in production costs. There are relatively few date available on an industrial basis on pollution control costs for OECD member countries. Detailed figures are available for the United States and Japan. In 1976 the burden of pollution control costs was relatively heavy for industries, if expressed in terms of percentage of total plant and equipment investment, as is shown in the accompanying table.

	U.S. (%)	Japan (%)
Iron and Steel Industry	15.1	22.3
Nonferrous metals	18.9	15.0
Primary metals	15.7	
Pulp and paper	14.7	17.6
Chemicals	11.4	17.6
Petroleum	10.9	31.4*
Electric utilities (thermal power stations)	10.5	44.0*

*The high figures are explained by the massive investment put up for abating nitrogen oxide emissions.

Source: For the U.S., Council on Environmental Quality; for Japan, (Ministry of International Trade and Industry).

It is therefore fair to say that these industries may have to overcome some temporary cash problems to insure the financing of such antipollution investments. However, to assess the extent to which the impact of pollution control measures can, in the long term, influence industry to change location, it is important to have some idea of annualized pollution control costs related to production costs: little data are available. However, it emerges from studies carried out in the OECD that annualized pollution control costs do represent a small fraction of total production costs. For example, we have considered the case of the iron and steel industry in two countries, Sweden and the United States (OECD [1977a, p. 186]). It emerges from the study of the Swedish iron and steel industry that annual costs incurred by existing factories during the period 1970–73 in order to meet given emission standards were of the order of 1.3 percent of total production costs in 1973, including tax.[3] During the same period some 8.5 percent of total capital expenditure by the iron and steel industry was allocated to pollution control.

In the United States it was estimated that meeting the emission standards proposed for 1983 would require capital expenditure on pollution control in the region of 14 to 17 percent of the industry's total capital expenditure, while the annual cost would probably be approximately 4.5 percent of total production costs for 1973. On the whole it may be argued that this additional burden to the borne by industry seems fairly reasonable, particularly when this additional burden is compared with that borne by industry as a result of annual changes in the level of wages, raw material prices, and so on. Furthermore, what matters is in fact the *net* additional burden to industry. There are cases where this burden has been lower owing to financial assistance granted by governments to industries. In the case of Sweden, for the iron and steel industry government subsidies relating to capital expenditure on pollution control reduced the costs to approximately 1 percent of the total production costs in 1973. The results of the OECD procedure of notification of financial-assistance schemes indicate that the amount of aid expressed in percentage of total industrial investment varied between 4.5 and 14.2 percent in 1975.

With respect to the burden of pollution charges data available in the case of France, these indicate that the charges borne by industry vary from 0.2 to 0.5 percent of value added. Even if the net burden on industry appears to be small, the critical question is whether, at the margin, environmental factors are sufficiently important to induce industries and firms to take decisions to shift locations away from domestic toward foreign alternatives.

All studies available and conducted so far lead to inconclusive results (Pearson [1977] ; Gladwin and Welles [1976] ; Walter [1977, p. 49]).

Ingo Walter carried out an analysis of aggregate foreign investment patterns. U.S. investment flows were examined in terms of their destination and industry mix, both for developed and developing countries. Similarly, investments by foreign firms in the United States were examined in terms of the environmental characteristics of the corporate home countries and the regions in which the projects were sited. He underlines the fact that they reveal a great deal of overseas production by pollution-intensive firms based in Western Europe, Japan, and the United States, but points out that there is very little evidence so far that such investment is seriously influenced by environmental considerations.

At the firm level, the available evidence seems to suggest a certain amount

---

3. The annualized costs were calculated on the assumption of a depreciation period of ten years and an interest rate of 10 percent.

of geographic mobility, not to be attributed to interregional or intercountry differences in environmental standards, but to delays involved in obtaining authorization that result in possible cost overruns and problems of adequate capacity. In particular, a number of petrochemical complexes and chemical plants originally planned to be located in West Germany and the Netherlands have been resited in Belgium, France, and Spain. For example, a carbon disulfide plant of Progil was built in Belgium instead of Holland for environmental reasons. Dow, which has thirteen plants in Europe, is reportedly contemplating new ventures in the Middle East as a means of overcoming the growing opposition to the siting of large industrial polluting plants in Europe. Recently, however, Japanese firms, because of a severe shortage of industrial land as well as severe environmental constraints, have been looking for alternative sites in the less developed countries of the Pacific basin (South Korea, Philippines, Indonesia). It has also been reported that metal ores mined in Australia have been shipped to countries such as India or the Philippines for processing, particularly for the extraction of the arsenic content in copper ores, and afterward, are shipped to Japan.

However, a recent study carried out by Barry Castleman on the export of hazardous factories to developing nations, and released in June 1978 by Congressman David R. Obey (Wis.), points out patterns of relocation for a number of potentially hazardous industries, including the production of asbestos textiles, asbestos friction products, arsenic, zinc, mercury, benzidine dyes, and pesticides. The strongest pattern of flight of U.S. firms appears in the asbestos textile industry in response to U.S. control on worker exposure in asbestos production, where there is evidence that new plants have not been set up in the United States but in Mexico, Brazil, and Taiwan. The interesting issue is that the major determinant in this relocation trend has not been pollution control measures or external environment measures but measures aimed at the protection of workers.

To conclude on this point, it may be argued that environmental constraints have so far played a small role in inducing enterprises to take locational decisions to shift away from domestic toward foreign alternatives.

However, there are recent indications showing that there is perhaps a flight of hazardous industries from some industrialized countries to developing countries. This is an area we have to monitor closely. The implementation of the various new laws for the control of chemicals that have been adopted recently may accentuate this trend.

INDUSTRIAL POLICY VERSUS ENVIRONMENTAL POLICY

As has already been suggested, there is growing opposition at the regional level against the location of highly polluting plants that expresses the dissatisfaction of the local population at having to bear the social costs of industrial development without benefiting completely from it. In other words, as soon as costs and benefits of a policy are not felt to be borne in an equitable way, the basis of such a policy is challenged: opposition to the siting of new polluting industrial plants is growing, leading to deadlock situations. This is particularly evident in the case of the development of an energy policy, the benefits of which will accrue to the population of a country as a whole but the cost of which will be borne only in some parts of the territory. We will first examine the reasons for this growing antagonism; pointing out some concrete examples, we will then examine the need for developing new principles of reconciliation between the objectives of an industrial policy and the objectives of an environmental policy by examining in what sense compensation mechanisms may help and in which way a better integration of industrial policies and environmental policies may lead to positive results.

The opposition to the siting of polluting industrial plants. Iron and steel plants, pulp and paper plants, nonferrous metals plants, primary metals plants, and energy facilities are generally large installations that are considered to be among the most polluting of industrial plants. They are generally located along coastlines or the banks of major rivers or on the shores of lakes, mainly in areas where there is already a major industrial or urban development and transport infrastructures. But opposition is also still strong in areas that have not yet been touched by industrial development. We will examine a few concrete examples in some OECD countries before reviewing the major causes of the opposition against the siting of polluting industrial plants.

Obstacles to the siting of nuclear power stations have been met in Belgium, France, the Federal Republic of Germany, the Netherlands, Sweden, Switzerland, the United States, and other OECD countries. An oil refinery at Nigg Point in Scotland has been delayed largely owing to environmental and land acquisition difficulties. Planning permission was subsequently granted, and a master plan for the refinery agreed on. A 700 Mw bituminous coal-fired power station in Duisburg (Federal Republic of Germany), one of a planned series aiming at a total of 6,000 Mw by 1980, has been objected to on environmental grounds, and work has been suspended pending further appeals in the Federal Administration Court. A large coal-fired power station (about 4,000 Mw capacity) in the state of Utah in the United States has been canceled, at least partially owing to objections on environmental grounds. The construction of the Naussac Dam on the upper reaches of the river Loire catchment area in France has been delayed owing to the opposition of the local population living in the upper reaches of the Loire and their unwillingness to bear the social costs of supplying water to those living in the lower reaches and benefiting from the construction of such a dam. In Japan projects for steel mills have been postponed or scaled down (at Shibushi in Kagoshima prefecture, at Oga in Aikita perfecture, and at Tomakomai in Hokkaido). The construction of petrochemical complexes met strong opposition at Shibushi in Kagoshima prefecture. These are a few examples of a phenomenon that is to be found in most OECD countries with respect to the siting of major energy facilities and other large polluting industrial installations.

The main reasons. The opposition to the siting of industrial installations did not appear suddenly overnight; it is the result of a sequence of events that developed slowly in the 1950s and that accelerated during the 1960s. There are of course many factors that played a role: among those that played a predominant role, one may cite (a) the high rates of industrialization that reached record levels during the 1950s, and particularly during the 1960s, benefiting from cheap energy and from an expansion of world trade; and (b) the increasing trend for industrial plants to locate, for technical and economic reasons, along the seacoast or along major waterways in areas, which in many instances are heavily industrialized and populated.

Countries with little or no seacoast, appear to face more difficulties than others. However, siting along the seacoast can create resistance because large percentages of the population live along the coast and because of potential conflicts with other valuable uses, such as recreation and fishing. Similar conflicts may also occur along river courses in localized instances, particularly where water use is a major concern (e.g., in the Western United States and along the river Rhine):

1. The gigantism that characterized industrial plants in the 1960s owing to economies of scales. For example, power plants grew from typical sizes of 100-250 Mw to 500-1,300 Mw, and refineries increased from 10,000 to 50,000 barrels per day to new plants that can process 100,000 to 300,000 barrels per day.

2. The growing dissatisfaction of communities resulting from an uneven distribution among the populations of the costs and benefits associated with the siting of industrial plants.

3. The objections of a community to dramatic changes in the character of their social and cultural environment.

4. The increasing concern of citizens and governments with the pollution of the environment and the improvement in the quality of life. The use of technical and economic criteria alone for choosing the sites leading to the neglect of social values and to the deterioration of the environment provoked a reaction on the part of the public. The public did not object only to emissions exceeding ambient concentrations or emission standards but also to changes of the environment, whether social, economic, or physical.

5. The demand of citizens to participate in decisions that are likely to affect their lives or their way of living. Until recently the siting of most indus-

trial plants was largely decided between the developer and the local authority having the major responsibility for drawing up and implementing land-use plans. It was very much an administrative procedure, with little if any public participation. An industrial plant was a source of taxation income for the local authority, of jobs for the local labor force, of increased business for the local community, and of possible further industrial development.

The first indication of the concern of citizens demanding to participate in decisions likely to affect their well-being appeared with the advent of nuclear energy as early as the late 1950s in the United States. During the 1960s and 1970s opposition became more institutionalized, with the involvement not only of interested individuals but of national environmental groups, and became more politicized with the involvement of local and national politicians and political parties.

All these factors have played a more or less prevailing role in the opposition in OECD countries to the siting of industrial plants and have contributed to the creation of an attitude of confrontation. This attitude of confrontation has helped to aggravate many of the problems associated with the siting of industrial plants and has led to deadlock situations.

In the light of these developments, it became of paramount importance to suggest the development of new mechanisms likely to be of use in an effort to reconcile the legitimate concern of the communities affected by industrial development and the interests of the country as a whole. In particular we may single out two needs: (a) the need, in the short term, for compensating mechanisms; and (b) the need, in the long term, for a better integration of environmental policy and industrial policy.

The need for compensating mechanisms. Although preventive and control measures are taken to limit industrial pollution or disamenities to the level that public authorities believe to constitute an acceptable one, this "acceptable level" inevitably implies a residual damage or a loss of amenity to be borne by the people of the community affected by the industrial development. First, we will examine the possibilities of compensation to be envisaged for restoring the well-being of the people in the community affected by the industrial development. Second, we will refer to concrete examples borrowed from the experience of some OECD member countries.

The possible forms of compensation. Two forms of compensation may be distinguished: compensation in kind and compensation in cash.

Compensation in kind implies a direct supply of goods or services either as a payment or as a measure of protection (e.g., soundproofing). It is intended either to restore directly an actual damage such as the replacement of property damaged by corrosion; or to restock a river, the fish resources of which have been destroyed by pollution; or to restore indirectly by providing the victims or the community with resources identical in terms of services rendered to those resources of which the community would have been deprived as a result of the industrial development.

Compensation in cash may be defined as the least amount necessary to compensate those who would suffer from a change of environmental quality (see OECD [1976]). Monetary compensation may serve the purpose of financing the cost of the repair of the damage caused or of providing the victim with a sum of money in order to compensate him for all or part of the damage suffered.

Compensation may be paid direct by the polluter to the victim. However, within the same region it is possible also to envisage transfer of money from one region to another, particularly to compensate the region bearing the environmental and social costs of an industrial development benefiting another region.

Furthermore, an additional distinction must be drawn between predamage and afterdamage compensation. Predamage compensation implies negotiation between private or public bodies planning to site industrial plants and local residents or communities likely to be affected by the locations. The damage to be compensated is usually economic damage, not health damage. Afterdamage compensation is meant to compensate health damage as well as economic damage. As a means of overcoming the opposition to the siting of industrial plants, it is clear that we are referring here only to predamage compensation.

Examples of predamage compensation in some OECD member countries. With respect to *compensation in cash*, many examples can be found in Japan (OECD [1977b, p. 38]). In June 1974, two fishermen's cooperatives agreed to let the Tokyo Power Company build eight nuclear reactors (8,000 Mw) and discharge hot water into the sea against a 4,000 million yen compensation. In November 1975, the 175 members of the Tomakomai Fishermen's Cooperative decided to give up their fishing rights in favor of the building of a giant industrial port for 5,356 million yen compensation. There is no clear-cut way of calculating the amount of compensation that is the result of a negotiation process. For example, in one instance compensation associated with the building of a steel plant was calculated by multiplying the surface of the fishing area by a fraction of the market price of onshore cultivated land. In another case of a steel plant, compensation was determined by calculating the sum of annualized yearly income losses related to the pollution.

In France, compensation in cash for industrial development is not the result of negotiations between the public or private planners and the local residents, but consists of tax revenues that will benefit the local community. This compensation is somewhat different in the sense that is not really earmarked for economic or health damage. However, it does represent a fiscal counterpart to the disadvantage to a local community that is situated close to an industrial plant. Up to January 1, 1976, the local taxes paid by industrial establishments included a land tax and a business activity tax known as the *patente*, which represented nearly four-fifths of the total taxes paid. Under this system the commune in which the plant had to be located very often benefited from substantial revenues (e.g., the amounts paid by Electricity of France for nuclear power corresponded to 6,480 francs per head of population for St. Laurent des Eaux in 1975), whereas the neighboring communes did not benefit at all from such revenue, while bearing, to some degree, the disadvantages of the siting of the industrial plant. A new regime was set up from January 1, 1976, replacing the *patente* by a *tax professionnelle*. According to this new regime there is a ceiling on the amount of tax revenue that can go to the commune in which the plant is located, the balance being paid to a departmental fund for distribution by the Conseil Général. The communes adjacent to that in which the plant is located receive some share of the tax, calculated according to the number of wage earners living in each commune.

With respect to *compensation in kind*, it is worthwhile underlining that there are, in a few countries, recent developments leading in this direction. In the recent French act on nature conservation July 10, 1976, article 2 stipulates that impact studies must include at least an analysis of the site's initial state and its environment, a study of the changes the project would bring about, and the measures proposed in order to eliminate, reduce, and if possible compensate for any harmful effects on the environment. Another case of compensation is related to a contract between the Electricity of France and the French government according to which whenever Electricity of France has an authorization to build an electric power station, it will make a financial contribution to the Conservatoire du littoral, which in turn will create positive environmental goods on the coastline.

Similarly, in Germany the destruction of any wooded area by a major infrastructure, such as a motorway, is accompanied in certain areas by its replacement elsewhere so that the same amount of forestland will be at the disposal of the local population.

In spite of the recent development of compensation plans in some OECD member countries, it is nevertheless clear that the development of such mechanisms does not constitute the solution to all problems of opposition concerning the siting of industrial plants. In the short term it may constitute a good basis for unlocking difficult situations. Meanwhile efforts should be devoted to integrate better, in a long-term perspective, industrial policies with environmental policies.

The need for a better integration of industrial policies and environmental policies in a long-term perspective. The development of low-waste technologies or of clean technologies will undoubtedly, in a long-term perspective, provide for greater flexibility for the siting of industrial plants. However, if this condition appears to be a necessary one, it is not sufficient. In addition to this, there is a need to propose a new framework for the siting of industrial plants in order to further improve the efficiency of the process. It is proposed that four basic principles be adopted for the siting of industrial plants:

1. *The planning for industrial plants should be based on long-term environmental policies and integrated with industrial policies.* Given the long lead times required for building industrial plants and the increasing opposition of the public to accommodate them, it has become clear that the availability of sites will be a real constraint to the implementation of industrial policies, and as such it has to be taken into account earlier in the planning process. Such long lead times provide for carrying out comprehensive assessments of environmental, social, and economic impacts, while permitting the local public to be prepared for accommodating these impacts.

Furthermore, the integration of environmental and industrial policies calls for a coordination far beyond the consultation level of industrial and economic policy departments; of environment and land-use planning departments on one hand, and of the regional authorities on the other. It is essential that the time horizon for industrial policy and land-use planning be similar.

2. *The siting of industrial plants and the assessment of their environmental impacts should be carried out within long-term land-use planning.* A few OECD member countries are implementing environmental impact assessments and land-use planning procedures. Experience shows that land-use planning is carried out with little assessment of environmental impacts of either the plan as a whole or of individual developments within the plan, whereas the environmental impact assessment procedures that have been prepared on an ad hoc basis bear little relation to long-term social, economic, and land-use plans. A better integration of these two procedures would permit, in particular, alternative sites to be considered for industrial plants within the concept of a plan that has established where land can be used for industrial development without meeting unacceptable distortions of land values.

3. *Regional authorities should undertake the major responsibility in siting procedures.* Whereas the national or federal government is thought to be best suited to undertake the formulation of long-term industrial siting policies, regional governments seem to be better placed to identify, assess, and secure sites for industrial plants on a long-term basis through regional land-use plans. It is clear that the concept of region will vary largely from one country to another because of differences in size, population, and population density. However, regional authorities seem to be better placed to take a major part of the responsibility for land-use planning and for siting industrial plants. This is because, unlike local authorities, they can offer alternative sites to developers

that will suit local preferences and needs for economic development of the region as a whole.

4. *Public participation should be encouraged and incorporated in all stages of the siting process.* In recent years it has been recognized in most OECD countries that the persons or bodies affected by a proposed development, either directly or indirectly, should be directly consulted. Therefore, there are now more and more legal requirements for advertising industrial projects, and for obtaining the views and comments of local residents before the final decision is taken. However, in most of the public participation methods tried so far, the local public was brought in when the plans for the proposed activities were nearly completed. Experience indicates also that the opposition of the public is not confined only to local problems; sometimes a problem is of national scope, as is obvious in the case of nuclear energy. Consequently it seems that public participation should be integrated in the decision-making process for the siting of industrial plants at all levels of government, and not only at the local level. Developments along these lines took place in some instances with respect to nuclear power plants when referenda were organized on a regional basis (in six states of the United States and in Austria).

CONCLUSIONS

The survey we made of the environmental aspects of industrial policies in a regional setting has enabled us to highlight two main conclusions.

1. On the one hand, although OECD member countries have reacted in different ways, the constraint that environmental concern has represented in industrial development does not seem to have constituted a factor important enough to induce intensive-polluting industries to benefit from interregional differences caused by differences in environmental constraints. If there is, so far, little evidence of shifts of locations of industrial plants for environmental reasons, there is, however, a potential that is mainly associated with the constraints of new legislation that some OECD countries are adopting and implementing to insure better protection of workmen's safety, particularly in the field of chemicals.

2. On the other hand, siting of industrial plants has become an important issue in many OECD countries. The opposition that has appeared during the last few years has to be considered as the result of high rates of industrialization, an increase in the size of installations, the environmental protection movement, and the unbalanced distribution of environmental social and economic costs and benefits among groups of citizens. If compensation mechanisms can be considered for solving short-term problems, there is clearly a need for developing more integrated environmental, industrial, and land-

use planning policies in order to reconcile the interests of the region concerned and those of a country as a whole.

REFERENCES

Gladwin, T. N., and J. G. Welles. "Environmental Policy and Multinational Corporate Strategy." In Ingo Walter (Ed.), *Studies in International Environmental Economics*. New York: Wiley, 1976.

OECD. *Economic Measurement of Environmental Damage*. Paris, 1976.

_____. *Emission Control Costs in the Iron and Steel Industry*. Paris, 1977a.

_____. *Environmental Policies in Japan*. Paris, 1977b.

_____. "National Physical Planning in Sweden." (Chap. 3.) *Environmental Policy in Sweden*. Paris, 1977c.

_____. *Water Management Policies and Instruments*. Paris, 1977d.

Pearson, C. "Trade and Investment Impact." (Chap. 3). *Environment: North and South*. New York: Wiley, 1977.

Walter, I. "Environmentally-Induced Industrial Relocation to Developing Countries." Mimeograph (1977).

DISCUSSION

On Problems of Growth, Pollution, and Industrial Policy

KLAUS-WERNER SCHATZ

In his paper, a report on policy aims and policy instruments, Michel Potier starts with two aspects of pollution on which indeed many current environmental policies have been based. The first aspect concerns the relation between economic growth and environment; and the second aspect is that pollution, while bringing benefits for some persons or regions, causes losses for others, and that hence an equity problem arises. However, in my opinion, both these aspects mostly have little to do with the specific economic problems that the usage of the environment and its pollution pose.

To begin with, from two properties of the environment, namely constituting both a means of production and a means of consumption, it follows that there are conflicting interests for the use of the environment if either production or consumption is accompanied by pollution. Since in the process of economic growth, material goods, produced with the aid of the environment, become more abundant, environment, relative to these material goods, becomes scarce. So one should expect that from these changes in relative availabilities of goods changes in prices would emerge that bring about structural changes. Changes like these are quite normal within the process of economic growth, and I do not see a specific requirement for environmental policies that could be based on changing relative scarcities between environment and other goods. In this respect, orthodox policies that generally try to strengthen competition and to abolish barriers to changes in relative prices in order to allow for structural changes could do very well in the fields of environment and pollution, too.

The second aspect mentioned by Potier deals, as noted above, with equity problems. Equity may be a high-ranking policy aim. However, first, and again, I do not see why inequities arising from the usage of the environment should be treated differently from, for instance, inequities arising from structural changes that harm some persons or regions while others benefit from them. Second, equity policies should not be mixed up with allocation policies in general and industrial or regional policies in particular in the way they are—as Michel Potier's report shows. Whenever there is a conflict between equity and efficiency, and whenever equity is introduced as a constraint for allocation policies, actual social welfare will fall behind potential social welfare. Allocation policies should aim at bringing about an optimal allocation and use of resources in order to reach the potential social welfare maximum—disregarding whether equity aims are hurt or not, since higher welfare would allow compensation of victims of environmental usage or structural change without worsening the absolute welfare position of others.[1]

While efficiency is the aim of allocation policies, obstacles to an efficient allocation of resources is the topic economists are interested in when dealing with environmental usage. However, environmental pollution diminishes social welfare and is an obstacle to an efficient allocation of resources only insofar as the benefits for polluters or for polluting regions are smaller than the losses the victims of pollution have to bear.

Unfortunately, there is scope for reasoning a priori (and empirical evidence exists in addition) that pollution exceeds its social optimum. This reasoning

---

1. Throughout this paper a policy is labeled "efficient" or "welfare maximizing" if it brings about an optimal allocation of resources and, with this allocation of resources, a maximum of production.

stems from the observation that very often there exist no markets on which the victims of pollution can trade with the polluters in order to reduce pollution to an amount optimal for both groups of economic agents and, hence, for society. In effect, the price of the environment is often even zero, leading to overuse of this resource. Nevertheless, there should be incentives to avoid pollution exceeding the social optimum, since, in the case of excessive pollution, the gains for polluters from pollution are less than the losses for the victims of pollution. Thus, there is scope for negotiation.

However, negotiations of this sort usually do not take place because of high transaction costs, and thus pollution may exceed its social optimum. As it becomes quite obvious from Michel Potier's report, in this situation governments are inclined to directly control pollution by levying charges or by introducing differentiated regulations, both of which may differ from region to region. What becomes obvious from the report, too, is that apparently many of these government pollution control measures are intended to avoid from the very beginning that pollution either emerges or exceeds certain limits, or to concentrate polluting industries in regions where the pollution control costs are assumed to be lowest or to repair damages that may have occurred. This more or less total prohibition of pollution takes account of neither the fact that from a welfare point of view pollution should be prevented only up to the point at which marginal social losses exceed the marginal social gains, nor that marginal gains and losses from pollution differ among activities and places of production.

The tendency to prohibit pollution whenever it occurs partly seems to reflect the helplessness of the authorities involved. Since the allocation of resources that is associated with a welfare maximum cannot be known *ex ante* but only *ex post*, authorities being forced to act *ex ante* are inclined to take care of apparently revealed pollution and pollution damages. To another part, however, actual policies are not governed by efficiency targets but by equity arguments. This, again, becomes very clear from Michel Potier's paper. Since pollution by its very nature is always connected with damages for others, be it persons, industries, or regions, it is quite near at hand to prohibit any pollution when introducing equity issues. However, as mentioned above, to make equity a topic of pollution control policies means to miss the task of allocation policy by substituting equity for efficiency or by inconsistently mixing both.

The fact that equity arguments do play a strong role in pollution abatement may partly be due to the view, at least the view of politicians and of lawyers, that environment is too high ranking a good to let profit-oriented market agents decide on its use and the degree of its pollution. This view may strongly support the need for direct and detailed government pollution controls. On the other hand, however, the nonexistence of markets on which the losers and the winners from pollution could negotiate supports the need for government pollution abatement policies for economic reasons. Nevertheless, it should be kept in mind that from the fact that markets do not yet exist, it does not follow that markets could not exist. So it seems that to an important extent markets do not exist because the care of the environment is taken of by public authorities and through public control. Where marginal transaction costs required for negotiations are now higher than marginal damages or gains by pollution and where in this way they prevent the difference between losses and gains from pollution from diminishing, it can be assumed that in the course of time, with the establishment of markets, transaction costs will decline.[2]

Market solutions for the pollution problem lead to an efficient allocation of resources if other solutions do not exist by which social (net) losses from pollution can be reduced at lower costs. However, in many cases, given the marginal transaction costs (including the costs of preventing free riding), government standards would presumably be a cheaper way of solving the pollution problem. In contrast to Michel Potier, I would argue that central governments should not be involved too much in detailed planning and regulation on the regional or on the industry or even on the plant level. Instead I would prefer a modified version of the pollution rights proposal that Dales has put forward (Dales [1968]). According to the Dales proposal, the federal government should fix the physical amount of pollution for individual pollutants based on best estimates for marginal gains and losses for the whole economy. For this amount of pollution, government could issue certificates, and these certificates could be sold at auctions. The certificates, which should be tradable, would allow their owner the emission of a definite amount of a certain pollutant within a given period of time. The pollution maximum fixed in this way should be revised periodically, and new certificates, either for a larger or a smaller amount of pollution, should then be sold at auction again. The regional or the industry allocation of certificates and thereby the decision in what regions and in what industries pollution will emerge would in this way be brought about by market forces.

It has been objected that under such a regime of pollution rights, since

---

2. Transaction costs are an obstacle to an efficient allocation of resources when means of reducing them could be introduced at marginal costs (in terms of welfare) that are lower than the marginal (welfare) gains from a reallocation of resources induced by lowering the transaction costs. From this it follows that transaction costs, which hinder the exercise of usage rights, prohibit efficient market solutions for the pollution problem only if the opportunity costs involved in the reduction of transaction costs are smaller than the marginal (net) welfare gains from the reduction of pollution.

there are no interregional price differences for the certificates issued, polluting activities would be allocated over regions irrespective of intraregional
differences between marginal gains and marginal losses from pollution and of
interregional differences in the ratio between marginal losses and marginal
gains from pollution. Therefore, interregional reallocation of polluting activities could bring about a higher level of national welfare. However, one
has to be careful with this argument. If interregional differences in marginal
gains and losses from pollution exist, there are incentives for the losers from
pollution to move to regions where the absolute damages are smaller; hence,
differences in marginal gains and losses from pollution would be reduced,
although interregional price differences for pollution certificates do not exist.
However, given the opportunity costs for movements to other regions (including, for instance, transportation costs or lower wages than those which have
to be paid in polluted regions in order to keep people working there), interregional differences in marginal gains and losses from pollution may exist,
and they may be optimal. Thus, issuing central government certificates by
which pollution is limited is an efficient solution for the pollution problem
only if other solutions do not promise a same reduction of pollution at lower
costs. In this context, Tom Tietenberg's proposal on the interregional allocation of pollution rights seems to be of great value (see Tietenberg's paper in
this volume). In contrast to Dales, he proposes to issue certificates on a regional, not on a national level. Tietenberg starts from the assumption that
very often the optimal level of pollution for a region is better known or can
be found out more easily by regional authorities than by central governments.
In this case, the creation and sale of pollution rights by regional authorities to
each polluter who contributes to the pollution of a given region could be an
efficient solution for the pollution problem, if no cheaper solutions exist.
Pollution from polluters within the region as well as across the border could
be priced according to some individual regional pollution standards. No central government intervention would be necessary; all trading of pollution
rights could occur at the local level. In this way, by taking into account both
possible net welfare losses from pollution and positive welfare effects from
employment or income in the polluting activities, the interregional allocation
of polluting activities would be determined in a competitive process.

As compared with Dales's approach (central government's certificates),
Tietenberg's proposal has the advantage of possibly bringing about a level
and structure of pollution that is closer to optimal levels and structures,
and as compared with the usage rights approach (usage rights to be exercised
by individuals), the advantage is that transaction costs seem to be lower. The
final outcome in terms of welfare gains from reducing pollution largely depends on the actual pollution cases at hand. In the cases in point it may also
be cheaper, if, in contrast to the Tietenberg's proposal, regions do not claim

property rights against (and sell pollution rights to) polluters, but against other regions, for in the case of across-the-border pollution, it may be a less costly solution to claim rights against regions from which the pollution stems instead of trying to identify individual polluting firms and to force them to pay for their damages on a region.

REFERENCE

Dales, J. H.   *Pollution, Property and Prices: An Essay in Policy-Making and Economics.*   Toronto, 1968.

DISCUSSION

Reconciling Theory and Policy in a Regional Setting

LAWRENCE J. WHITE[1]

Michel Potier's paper is different from most of the other papers presented in this volume. Rather than providing an abstract model, he has tried to describe briefly what is currently happening with respect to environmental policies among the OECD countries.

I learned a number of things from the paper: about Sweden's "black-spot" philosophy; that Holland and France have effluent fees on water discharges; that Great Britain has virtually no national pollution control requirements but rather has a pragmatic, localized approach to pollution problems; and that various kinds of compensation programs (for those who bear the costs of pollution) are being tried. (Parenthetically, I should add that the French and Dutch effluent fees are among the best-kept secrets in the environmental literature. I consider myself reasonably well informed on environmental matters, and though I knew about the German experience with

---

1. The views expressed in this discussion are purely those of the author and do not necessarily reflect the views of the Council of Economic Advisers.

effluent fees, this is the first time that I have heard of the French and Dutch fees.)

I would like to offer a few specific comments on Potier's paper. First, his discussion of the French effluent fees makes it appear suspiciously as if the fees are based on assumed fixed coefficients between output (or employment) and effluent. To the extent that this is actually the case, the most important aspect of effluent fees—providing the incentive for firms to find ways to reduce their effluent other than by reducing their output—is lost. This must clearly be considered an unfortunate aspect of the system.

Second, in the discussion of compensation programs, it is important to make clear that current U.S. efforts in the air pollution area are really not compensation programs. Rather, in areas that are "dirtier" than the ambient air standards established by the Environmental Protection Agency (EPA), firms that will add a significant amount of new emissions must induce some other firm to reduce its emissions by a greater amount ("offsets"). In effect, rudimentary property rights in existing emissions are being established, and a rudimentary market may develop. For completeness, it is worth mentioning that in areas that are "cleaner" than the ambient air standards, the EPA has set limits on the amount of additional emissions that will be permitted. Again, in effect, property rights in emissions are being established. In these latter areas, the EPA is currently giving away these rights for free, on a first-come, first-served basis. Some thought is currently being given to the possibility of auctioning these rights. Thus, though the United States is far from the futures market in emissions rights that Edwin von Böventer has mentioned in his comments, we may be on our way to developing spot markets.

At the end of his paper, Potier offers four recommendations to OECD governments with respect to the siting of industrial plants that are likely to have a significant environmental impact on their surroundings. I cannot take exception with these recommendations, but neither will anyone else (except for those who insist that market solutions for environmental problems be installed immediately). But that, I fear, is the problem. These recommendations are so noncontroversial that they are unlikely to be of practical use in solving the difficult problems of plant siting and pollution control.

Finally, I would like to raise the question of whether competition among regions (sacrificing environmental amenities in return for attracting industrial growth) is or is not desirable. This point is not specifically raised in Potier's paper, but it is raised in a number of the other papers. The argument that regional competition is undesirable is the usual justification for the setting of national ambient standards or national emissions standards (or both) from which local areas may be allowed to deviate in a more stringent direction but not in a more lenient direction. This is the case, for example, in the U.S. Clean Air Act Amendments of 1970.

I suspect (though I have not proved) that in the neoclassical microeconomic model that serves as the starting point for much of our thinking about pollution control problems, there would be nothing wrong with regional competition (as long as there are no environmental spillovers *between* regions; if there are these spillovers, then unfettered competition is no longer guaranteed to provide optimal outcomes). It is thus worth asking ourselves which of the neoclassical model's assumptions fail to hold (or, perhaps, whether regional competition may not be such a bad thing after all).

Let me first describe an analogy which I think might mistakenly be used but which should be avoided. Developing countries have frequently argued that if they were to band together and agree on common terms with respect to foreign investment, they would compete away less of the gains from foreign investment and thus keep more of the gains for themselves. It might be tempting to use this analogy for the case of regional competition. But in the case of developing countries, the argument is a monopoly cartel argument; it is an "us-against-them" argument. But in the regional competition case, the investment is usually domestic (national) in origin. There is no "them" and no monopoly advantage to be gained.

So, if this analogy fails, we must examine the neoclassical model and the real world. Are actual wages too sticky downward? Is actual capital too long-lived? Are the regions too shortsighted? Do they lack complete information as to the consequences of environmental damage compared with the views at the national level? These are possibilities. But I am not sure they provide any stronger argument for preventing competition in this particular case than for preventing competition generally—and most of the authors of the papers in this volume would be extremely reluctant to abandon pro-competitive policies for private industry on the basis of these possible real-world failings. Or is there a "them" after all? Perhaps the argument that regional competition should be prevented is based on income distribution considerations; that is, that preventing regional competition will capture environmental amenities for the general public that would otherwise go to firms' stockholders in the form of the higher profits. For this income distribution effect actually to occur, however, either there must be large monopoly profits to be captured (and which will not be recouped through higher prices on the relevant products), or the general competitive level of profits that is acceptable to investors must decline, which is unlikely if only a handful of industries are affected. Even if the income redistribution cannot (and does not) occur, policymakers may nevertheless have fond hopes that it might occur and structure their policies accordingly.

I am not sure that I know the answer to the question of whether regional competition is or is not desirable. I suggest that it deserves more thought than most of the authors represented in this volume have given it.

DISCUSSION

Efficiency versus Interregional Equity in Siting of Polluting Investment Projects

RÜDIGER PETHIG

In recent years we observed in many industrialized countries that almost every large-scale private and public investment program, such as the siting of (nuclear) power stations or even the construction of highways passing residential or recreational areas, is questioned, delayed, or eventually suspended because of violent opposition of regional environmental groups. In his paper, Michel Potier provides illustrative empirical evidence for this phenomenon. He also offers a convincing list of reasons for the growing opposition at the regional level against the location of polluting plants. The main point seems to be that residents demand to participate in location decisions that have a significant impact on their regional environmental quality or which bear environmental risks (such as nuclear power plants).

They are no longer willing to bear the bulk of the social costs of such a project while other regions are net benefiters. In fact, since modern technology, with its economies of scale, favors large projects for reasons of technological efficiency, one region typically carries the burden for the benefit of several others. For the same reason of gigantism, the increment of environmental impact on the region where the polluting plant is sited is far from being marginal and insignificant.

Industrial location decisions used to be administrative procedures involving only some local authority and the developer. But if one agrees to the proposition that "individuals' preferences are to count," a proposition that is fundamental to democracy as well as to welfare economics, it appears necessary to redesign the allocation process such that "regional preferences" are adequately considered in the public decision process.

At the first glance, the argument seems to be plausible that the regional right to veto the siting of a polluting plant is tantamount to an overall welfare or efficiency loss for the economy. More specifically, suppose regional environmental groups fight against an unduly heavy burden on their regions that will be imposed by siting a polluting plant. It is true that such groups make the case for interregional equity (or justice) at the cost of economic efficiency?

We start our analytical investigation of this "equity versus efficiency proposition"[1] by a brief reconsideration of the supposedly well established notion of economic efficiency. In Paretian welfare economics, an allocation is said to be inefficient (or Pareto suboptimal) if one can throw away a positive amount of at least one "scarce" resource while still permitting the achievement of the same individual satisfaction by a suitable reallocation of the remaining resources. In order to apply this concept to the problem at hand, we provide the regions of an economy with regional welfare functions.[2] Suppose now that an economy consists of two regions and that the economy's initial allocation is inefficient in the sense of Pareto, specified above. This can be illustrated by a point such as A in Figure 8-1, where w_1 and w_2 denote the welfare levels of the two regions and where the curve UV is the economy's welfare possibility frontier (presupposing a given endowment with resources). Since the Pareto rule is an incomplete ordering rejecting interpersonal utility comparisons, it cannot be decided by this rule whether the allocation represented by D in Figure 8-1 is more or less efficient than that of point A.

On the other hand, it seems natural to say that the allocation belonging to some utility distribution E is more efficient than that belonging to A whenever E is a point northeast of A below or on the welfare possibility frontier. This concept of efficiency comparisons encompasses, of course, substantial distributional constraints. Hence this notion of efficiency is not independent of that of equity or justice.

One may be in favor of a broader concept of efficiency comparisons, for example, the one professor Frey presumably has in mind when he speaks of a "strictly efficiency oriented environmental policy." Such a concept assumes that in addition to the points of the shaded area in Figure 8-1 all other points on the welfare possibility frontier are more efficient than A, since they are all (Pareto) efficient, whereas point A is not. Note, however, that the slightest failure to reach the frontier—if, for example, F' is attained

---

1. In section 4 of his paper, R. Frey discusses some aspects of equity versus efficiency trade-offs." Our subsequent comment partly aims at elaborating and, in our view, clarifying some of his arguments.

2. Although this concept is used today fairly frequently (see Scott's comment), it is highly questionable on the same grounds as the concept of an economy's social welfare function of the Bergsonian-Samuelsonian type. In addition the fact that citizens may fluctuate interregionally cannot be satisfactorily handled by regional welfare functions.

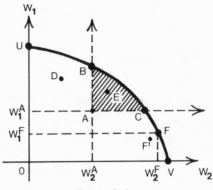

Figure 8-1

instead of F—destroys the efficiency comparability.[3]   Moreover, in the sequel we want to argue that for some basic informational reasons we are never certain whether we hit the frontier in a point like F outside the northeast region of point A. Hence if by some environmental policy strategy one region is made worse off, we are not able to decide whether this strategy implies an efficiency improvement. It then follows that efficiency gains relative to A can be assured only in the northeast region of point A in Figure 8-1, that is, by applying the narrow concept of efficiency comparisons.

In order to substantiate our claim with the help of a simple model, we assume that an industrial plant of given size is to be located in region 1. The production function[4] for this plant is

$$y_1 = Y^1(a_1 + a_2, e_1) \quad \text{with} \quad \frac{\partial Y^1}{\partial e_1} > 0 \quad \text{and} \quad \frac{\partial^2 Y^1}{\partial e_1^2} < 0, \qquad (1)$$

where a_1 and a_2 are the (fixed) resource inputs stemming from the regions 1 and 2, respectively; y_1 is the firm's output that is assumed to be distributed to the two regions according to their input shares:

$$x_i = \frac{a_i}{a_1 + a_2} y_1 \qquad (i = 1, 2) \qquad (2)$$

---

3. Efficiency comparisons between Pareto-suboptimal points like AD, AF' or DF' are not possible unless interregional welfare comparisons are admitted or some compensation criteria are applied. An interesting attempt to evaluate and compare the welfare losses of different misallocations can be found in Debrean (1954).

4. For more details of the economic interpretation of the subsequent functions (1) and (3), see (Pethig, 1976).

In the process of producing y_1, a useless by-product e_1 is generated and discharged into region 1's environment. The emission of e_1 causes environmental disruption according to the environmental impact function

$$s_1 = S^1(e_1) \quad \text{with} \quad \frac{dS^1}{de_1} > 0 \quad \text{and} \quad \frac{d^2S^1}{de_1^2} > 0, \tag{3}$$

where s_1 is an indicator of environmental degradation (pollution). Finally, regional welfare is determined by the welfare functions[5]

$$w_i = W^i(x_i, z_i, s_1) \qquad (i = 1, 2). \tag{4}$$

In (4) z_i is the output produced by regional resources. W^i increases with x_i and z_i but decreases (or remains constant) with increasing s_1; s_1 as an argument in the welfare function W^2 means that the pollution generated in region 1 spills over to region 2 and/or that the recreational value of region 1 decreases for region 2 with growing pollution in region 1.

Before the industrial plant is built, we suppose that the economy adopted the welfare distribution A in Figure 8-1. We may specify this allocation by $w_i^A = W^i(0, z_i^A, 0)$, where z_i^A is determined by the given regional resources. Then the amounts of resources a_1 and a_2 are drawn from the production of z_i to the operation of the plant, so that the production of z_i is reduced from z_i^A to z_i^1. Hence, after siting the plant the relevant welfare functions are $w_i = W^i(x_i, z_i^1, s_1)$ that can be completely described by their (strictly convex) indifference curves in the (x_i, s_1) plane.

In parts I and III of Figure 8-2 the straight lines KL and OM represent the linear functions (2) for $i = 2$ and for $i = 1$, respectively. Parts V and VI contain the graph of the functions (1) and (3). Under (1)–(3) we derive in part IV of Figure 8-2 the first region's (partial) transformation curve AB and in part II the second region's (partial) transformation curve GH. In this situation the welfare-maximizing pollution level is s_1^1 for region 1 and $s_1^2 > s_1^1$ for region 2.[6] Hence for given output share rules (2) and for given input $a_1 + a_2$ there exists no production $(\hat{y}_1, \hat{e}_1)$ satisfying $\hat{y}_1 = Y^1(a_1 + a_2, \hat{e}_1)$ that leads to a Pareto-efficient allocation. Note further that we (arbitrarily) depicted the indifference curves for w_1^A and w_2^A into parts II and IV of Figure 8-2 in such a way that for any feasible (y_1, e_1) under the above as-

---

5. The pollution generated in region 2 (s_2) as an additional argument in both welfare functions is suppressed here for simplicity.

6. The positive difference $s_1^2 - s_1^1$ is ceteris paribus the greater, the greater region 2's share of y_1 and the less concerned region 2 is about the pollution stemming from region 1 (i.e., the flatter region 2's indifference curves are in part II of Figure 8-2).

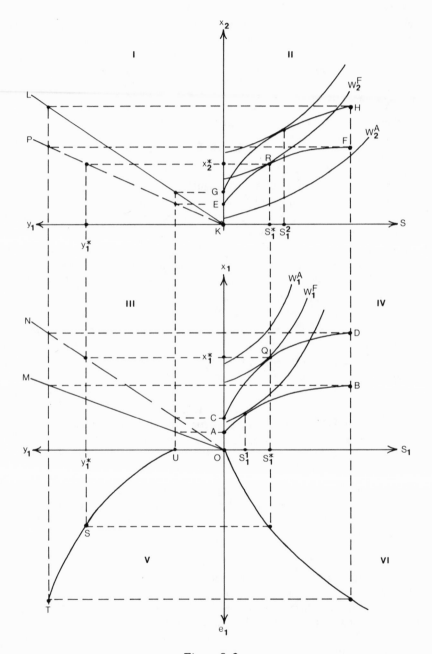

Figure 8-2

sumptions the regions end up with a welfare distribution, given by a point such as F' southwest of F in Figure 8-1.

This result raises the question of what can be done to achieve Pareto efficiency maintaining the given size of the plant (in terms of uneven resource inputs a_1 and a_2). One possibility is to change the output share in region 1's favor. For this reason we replace (2) by

$$x_1 = \lambda y_1 \quad \text{and} \quad x_2 = (1 - \lambda) y_1 \qquad (2')$$

and we claim that in the context of the situation described in Figure 8-2 there is λ^* satisfying

$$\frac{a_1}{a_1 + a_2} < \lambda^* < 1$$

such that with $\lambda = \lambda^*$ in $(2')$ a Pareto-efficient allocation

$$\alpha^* \equiv (z_1^1, z_2^1, y_1^*, e_1^*, S^1(e_1^*), x_1^* = \lambda^* y_1^*, x_2^* = \lambda^* y_2^*)$$

exists.

In order to give intuitive arguments for the validity of this claim, we represent the functions $(2')$ for $\lambda = \lambda^*$ by the straight lines PK and NO in parts I and III of Figure 8-2, respectively. The associated regional transformation curves are EF for region 2 and CD for region 1. In this situation the maximum regional welfare is w_i^F for $i = 1, 2$, and the corresponding indifference curves are tangent to the regional transformation curves at one and the same pollution level, s_1^*. It can be shown that the sum of the marginal rates of substitution in Q and R is equal to the marginal rate of transformation in point S of part V of Figure 8-2. This in turn is exactly Samuelson's well-known "summation-condition" for the Pareto-optimal allocation of public goods (cf. Samuelson [1954] and Pethig [1979]). This completes the sketch of a proof that α^* is a Pareto-efficient allocation, associated with the welfare distribution (w_1^F, w_2^F), as illustrated in Figure 8-1.

By now our former argument should have become substantiated: with imperfect information on the regional welfare function, a federal environmental agency has hardly any chance to find out the proper (and unique) transfer parameter λ^*. Even if the correct value of λ should be accidently hit, how should the agency then select the adequate production point S in part V of Figure 8-2 with insufficient knowledge about regional preferences? Moreover, it is also very difficult for a federal agency to improve its knowledge about regional preferences, since it is in the regions' self-interest not to reveal their true preference so that they can hope to gain from taking a free-rider position.

It may be helpful to repeat and summarize now our main line of arguments so far. We started with the observation that if a polluting investment project is sited in one of several regions and the location region carries a net burden while the other regions are net benefiters, then the residents of the losing region try to prevent this investment. Very often the siting and operation of such a project is defended by allocative efficiency arguments, and it is also maintained that giving in to equity-oriented regional opposition involves an efficiency loss. We tried to show that it is practically impossible to classify a reallocation (e.g., by siting a polluting plant in one region) as an efficiency improvement when the location region is losing while the rest of the economy is better off unless interregional welfare comparisons can be made.

Consequently, unambiguous efficiency comparisons can only be made between pairs of allocations that are ranked by the (incomplete) Pareto ordering. Hence if an inefficient initial interregional allocation is to be replaced by a more efficient one, the new allocation must be Pareto superior relative to the first one.[7] But in this case there is no longer any conflict between the efficiency objective and the equity requirement of regional environmental groups.

Our conclusion, then, is similar to Potier's advice for the short-term policy, namely to compensate the region affected by the industrial development so that it does not bear a net welfare loss. In the long run, Potier proposes a better integration of environmental policy and industrial policy. This may be interpreted in terms of our analysis as an attempt to balance intertemporally and interregionally the (environmental) net burdens of different polluting industrial or public investment projects. If, however, a black-spot policy is adopted, our efficiency concept requires compensations for the residents in the heavily industrialized and polluted areas.

REFERENCES

Debreu, G., "A Classical Tax-Subsidy Problem." *Economotrica* 22 (1954): 14–22.

Pethig, R. "Pollution, Welfare, and Environmental Quality in the Theory of Comparative Advantage." *Journal of Environmental Economics and Management* 2 (1976): 160–169.

_____. *Umweltökonomische Allokation mit Emissionssteuern.* Tübingen: Mohr, 1979.

Samuelson, P. A., "The Pure Theory of Public Expenditure." *Review of Economics and Statistics* 36 (1954): 387–389.

---

7. In our model of Figure 8-2 a necessary condition for such a policy is an even greater compensation payment (than represented by λ^*) for region 1.

CHAPTER 9

Interregional Pollution Spillovers and Consistency of Environmental Policy

JOHN H. CUMBERLAND[1]

INTRODUCTION

Opportunities for achieving significant gains in both efficiency and equity through the control of interregional environmental spillovers are widely recognized. The need for protecting downstream residents against excessive discharges by upstream emitters is obvious, but inadequate attention has been given to opportunities for improving welfare through consistency in policy and management across all environmental media, including air, water, and land. For example, in the United States, a reallocation of portions of the massive resources now spent on the construction of conventional sewage treatment plants toward improved control of carcinogens could result in net savings of human lives (National Academy of Sciences [1978a, pp. 227–250]).

This paper will argue that, in the absence of corrective effort, positive incentives exist for generating suboptimal outcomes with attendant welfare

1. The author is grateful to colleagues for comments on earlier versions of this paper. Robert A. Collinge provided material on dispersion and diffusion models. At the University of Maryland, Martin J. Bailey, Mancur Olson, Dennis J. Snower, Kwang Choi, James Kahn, Alan J. Krupnick, and W. Derek Updegraff were especially helpful. Additional valuable suggestions were received during the International Institute for Environment and Society Conference in Berlin, especially from Professors Ralph C. d'Arge, Manfred E. Streit, and Thomas H. Tietenberg. The author alone bears full responsibility for remaining shortcomings.

losses both from extensive interregional spillovers and from inconsistency in environmental policies. For example, pollution emitters in each region have strong incentives to import the gains from economic development while exporting the resulting waste residuals. This problem is exacerbated by the fragmentation of responsibility for environmental regulation among various agencies and levels of government, which invites inefficiency in environmental management. It will also be argued that both control of interregional spillovers and achievement of consistency among policies for different environmental media are conceptually related and can be modeled similarly, since both represent a failure to equate the benefits and costs of pollution control at the margin. Finally, the resulting implications for analysis and policy will be examined.

THE THEORY OF OPTIMAL ENVIRONMENTAL QUALITY: A BRIEF SUMMARY[2]

In order to achieve maximum human welfare, the level of environmental quality, like all other goods, public and private, should be optimized. The optimal level of environmental quality (EQ) in most cases is not pristine EQ, since this can be purchased only at the opportunity cost of giving up other goods and services in order to free resources for treating pollution or, more drastically, in order to reduce the production and consumption of goods and services that generate pollution-causing residuals.

Neither automatic market mechanisms nor natural treatment processes can be expected to insure an optimal level of environmental quality and pollution control, for two reasons. First, profit-maximizing firms and utility-maximizing consumers face positive economic incentives for overutilizing the unpriced waste-assimilating capacities of common property resources, thereby creating detrimental externalities. This excess pollution by firms and consumers will occur in uncontrolled markets. Second, since environmental quality is a public good from which no one can be easily excluded and for which full costs cannot be collected, it will normally be produced in inadequate amounts.

Figure 9-1A illustrates the case of detrimental externalities, such as pollution, which are caused by discrepancies between the private supply function, $s_p s_p$, which is priced below the actual social supply function, $s_s s_s$, by the amount of pollution damage per unit of output. The result is that the product is underpriced by $P'P''$ and therefore overproduced by $Q''Q'$, misallocating resources.

---

2. This section can be omitted by readers familiar with the standard marginal analysis of environmental economics.

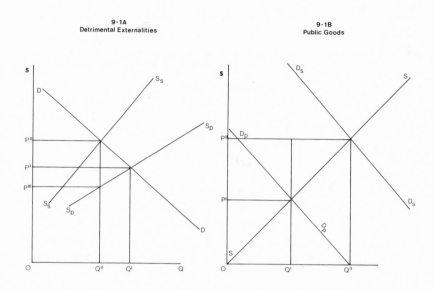

Figure 9-1. Detrimental externalities and public goods.

Figure 9-1B illustrates the case of inadequate provision of public goods, such as environmental protection. Public or private authorities have an incentive to produce only the amount Q', for example, of noise control, at a cost of P' per unit. However, the amount actually demanded would be Q'' at a higher price of P'', provided that the public revealed its true preferences, all beneficiaries contributed to meeting the costs, and all free riders were excluded. Consequently, the external diseconomies are created and opportunities for creating external economies are missed, thereby causing misallocation of economic resources and losses in human welfare. Baumol and Oates have pointed out that under restrictive conditions the resource misallocation associated with externaltities or public goods can be corrected by the imposition of positive or negative Pigouvian charges. The restrictions are severe, however, requiring, among other conditions, complete information and absence of nonconvexities in the production set (Baumol and Oates [1975, pp. 102–128]).

In such cases, the appropriate remedy is to eliminate differences between the private and social cost by adding a tax or subsidy to the good being produced in order to provide the correct signals and incentives for achieving the optimal level of prices and output. In the case of detrimental externalities, as shown in Figure 9-1A, the imposition of a tax of $P'''P''$ per unit of output, added to the price of OP' would reflect the added social cost of the externality, at the optimal level of output, and provide the signals in the marketplace needed to cut output back from Q' to Q'', the socially optimal level.

In the case of a public good like environmental quality, the market demand represented by demand curve D_pD_p (Figure 9-1B) fails to reflect the full social demand (D_sD_s), because the supplier cannot exlude anyone from enjoyment of the public good once it is provided. Therefore, the supplier cannot obtain payment from all those who enjoy environmental quality but who are not willing to reveal their true preferences for that public good. Since these free riders cannot be excluded from the enjoyment of a public good, the equilibrium amount provided by the market will be OQ' supplied at the price OP. Here again, in order to eliminate the discrepancy between the market equilibrium amount provided and the socially desirable amount provided, the traditional remedy is to impose a Pigouvian subsidy, or a negative Pigouvian charge, OP'', in order to elicit the socially desired amount of output of the good, OQ''.

Since emitters have generally appropriated the rights to environmental quality, and social action has been necessary in order to correct this imbalance, the most urgent social problem in environmental management is to insure adequate treatment of pollution in order to achieve a satisfactory level of environmental quality. However, it is theoretically quite possible for society to allocate a greater optimal amount of resources to the achievement of environmental quality. Indeed, accusations are beginning to emerge that antipollution activists are demanding and achieving excessively high levels of environmental quality (Denison [1978, p. 21]). Whatever the facts, it is simple to demonstrate that the achievement of either an excessively high or excessively low amount of environmental quality misallocates resources and reduces human welfare. It is therefore possible to improve welfare by reallocating those resources employed to achieve optimal environmental quality. This situation is demonstrated in Figure 9-2.

Point Q in Figure 9-2A illustrates the typical beginning point in the quest for environmental quality with no resources devoted to treating wastes and preventing pollution. Where competitive producers are not required to undertake any treatment of wastes, the amount of emissions generated could be as much as OQ, resulting in very high damages to society. Since the diagrams in Figure 9-2 contain marginal treatment cost (MTC) functions, and marginal damage cost functions (MDF), the amount of damage generated

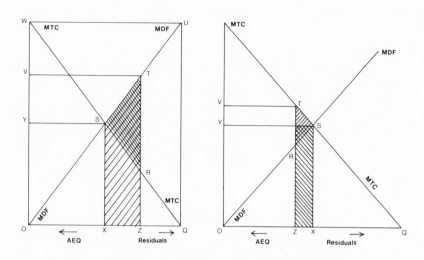

Figure 9-2. Optimal environmental quality.

with no treatment in Figure 9-2A would be the area under marginal damage function OQU. Clearly, this is excessive damage by the amount QSU, since the marginal damage function is higher than the marginal treatment cost function at all points to the right of OX. By requiring treatment to reduce the amount of residuals from OQ to OX, damage is reduced at a greater rate and at a lower cost than the expenses of treatment. Thus, society gains by pursuing treatment until emissions are reduced to X, at a cost of Y dollars, at which point marginal damage prevented is exactly equal to the marginal cost of treatment. This level of treatment can be achieved either by regulation or by Pigouvian charges equal to OY per unit of emission, the latter method being the more preferable from the efficiency point of view.

However, if an inadequate amount of treatment is undertaken, it can be shown that resources are misallocated and opportunities for improvement in social welfare exist. For example, if a standard requires that residuals are cut back only to the level of OZ, Figure 9-2A shows that an excessive amount of physical damages over the optimal amount OXS is generated. These excess damages are equivalent to the quantity of $XZTS$, as shown by the shaded area in Figure 9-2A. However, the true socially excessive damage is less than the amount $XZTS$, since social costs of treatment would have to be incurred to reduce this damage, these costs being the area under the marginal treatment cost function $XZRS$. The net amount of excessive social damage would be the difference between the marginal damages and marginal costs as shown by the crosshatched area SRT. Therefore, by raising environmental quality to the optimal level OX and thereby reallocating resources equivalent to $XZRS$, society could reduce the damages by the amount $XZTS$ for a net gain in welfare of the amount equal to SRT.

The opposite case is shown in Figure 9-2B. Society can misallocate resources by expending an excessive amount of resources on environmental treatment. This case is shown in Figure 9-2B. Here again, the specified level of environmental quality limits emissions to OZ, through regulation, by imposition of an optimal Pigouvian charge on residuals of OY dollars per unit of residual, or by other policies. Clearly, the optimal level of environmental quality would not be at zero emissions, since the marginal treatment cost necessary to achieve this level of quality is far higher than the marginal damage function, and remains so up to emissions levels of OX. If emissions are cut back to OZ, or an excessive emission charge of OV is imposed, the value of resources used in treatment is higher than the amount of damages prevented. Therefore, reducing residuals to a lower level than OX achieves higher levels of environmental quality than is warranted by their cost and results in a misallocation of resources. For example, as shown in Figure 9-2B, at emission levels of OZ an excessive physical amount of treatment has occurred as represented by the shaded area $ZXST$. However, this entire amount of excessive physical treatment is not socially wasteful, since some damage is prevented, as represented by the area $ZXSR$. Therefore, the socially excessive amount of treatment occurring is the crosshatched area RST. The resources represented by this area could be reallocated to another project, such as treating other, more harmful residuals, up to the point where marginal benefits equal marginal costs. This unnecessary expenditure represents an excessive allocation of resources to environmental quality improvements—resources that would increase welfare by being reallocated to other purposes.

We can therefore advance one definition of consistency in environmental policy as requiring treatment of each pollutant up to the point where the marginal cost of treatment equals the marginal damage created by that pollutant. This consistency condition should hold for each pollutant, across each location, and at each time period. Since environmental pollution usually results from externalities or public goods problems, the traditional corrective measure for achieving efficiency requires application of positive or negative Pigouvian charges under conditions described by Baumol and Oates.

Where incomplete information exists for meeting the Baumol and Oates conditions for effective use of a Pigouvian charge, which may be for the majority of cases in the real world, and where optimizing procedures are therefore impossible, these authors recommend a satisficing approach. Under these conditions, an environmental standard would be set and a Pigouvian charge established to create incentives for meeting the standard. Although this procedure would not permit optimizing, it would at least make environmental management possible in the absence of complete information, and it would utilize economic incentives to insure the achievement of any socially established standard at lowest cost.

SOME IMPLICATIONS OF ENVIRONMENTAL THEORY

Thus far, we have demonstrated that efficiency in resource allocation is essential in environmental management in order to maximize welfare, with efficiency defined as equalizing costs and benefits of environmental programs at the margin.

At this point, a distinction should be noted between optimality across public programs as compared with economywide optimality. First-best conditions would require that public budgets be large enough to permit public expenditures on environmental and all other public programs up to the point where marginal benefits equal marginal costs in each program. If constraints are imposed upon the size of the public budget, then a second-best solution requires expenditures in each program up to the point where marginal benefits per monetary unit are identical between environmental and all other public programs. (This condition would be met under first-best programs as well.)

After identifying the goal of equating marginal benefits per dollar spent between environmental and other programs, an obvious next step is to observe that economic efficiency requires equating the marginal benefits per monetary unit spent for abatement of each pollutant and across all environmental programs. The implication of this point is that misallocation of resources must result if inconsistencies are permitted to arise among programs for different pollutants and for different environmental media. Therefore, potential opportunities for improving human welfare exist by seeking consistent treatment across types of specific residuals, of waste-receiving media, and across space and time.[3] This is an obvious conclusion, but one whose practical implementation is subject to serious empirical, conceptual, and administrative dif-

---

3. The issue of consistency in environmental policy across time involves the major problem of intergenerational equity and efficiency, which, although similar to and inseparable from interspatial problems, is sufficiently different in concept that it will not be treated in detail here. (Cf. papers from the University of Maryland, Environmental Protection Agency Conference on Ozone Management by Bailey (1978a) and Mishan and Page (1978).

ficulties. Successful achievement of these potential improvements in welfare requires the collection of accurate data not only on cost of treatment but also upon the value of benefits, which is much more challenging, not only in a quantitative sense but even more in an economic sense.

The central problem of environmental analysis is that the conceptually convenient and well-behaved static benefit and cost functions shown in Figure 9-2 are actually dynamic, site-specific, time-specific functions, impacting upon specific individuals, and having quite limited aggregation characteristics. In reality, many synergistic pollutants are emitted into fluid currents of air and water that flow across the arbitrary political boundaries of regions populated by diverse and mobile groups. The adequacy of conventional static and mechanistic economic theory for dealing with these problems is further limited because of its exclusion of mass balance (Kneese et al. [1970]) and entropy (Georgescu-Roegen [1971]) phenomena, which lie at the heart of environmental problems.

Finally, in this complex and dynamic system of incomplete information and conceptual complexities, the fact that the groups who enjoy the benefits of economic activity will be separate in both time and space from those who bear environmental costs raises troublesome policy issues of equity as well as efficiency. Thus, although formidable problems stand in the way of achieving efficiency and equity in environmental policy, the possible gains to be achieved justify major efforts in this direction.

EFFICIENCY AND EQUITY ACROSS POLLUTANTS

Unlike the case of goods and services that are priced and traded in markets, inconsistency is to be expected a priori in the case of environmental services unless purposeful remedial action is taken. The reasons for this include information gaps, unequal zeal in enforcement programs, and divided responsibilities between environmental management agencies.

Since maximization of welfare requires environmental policy that equates the marginal cost of reducing damage with the marginal value of the damages, optimal implementation of this policy requires a knowledge of both of these functions for each pollutant at each location. It is generally conceded that although marginal treatment cost functions are derivable from engineering and related data, both the derivation and the very concept of damage functions present serious difficulties. Problems arise in the physical measurement of damages and, more seriously, in the assignment of economic values to environmental damage. It is the magnitude of these problems that has led senior investigators such as Baumol and Oates to the alternative strategy noted above of specifying arbitrary but reasonable environmental standards and then seeking to minimize the cost of their achievement, rather than pursuing the more difficult goal of optimization.

Despite the strength of the argument for this satisficing approach, an objection must be noted against it, in light of the preceding discussion of efficiency conditions. Abandonment of optimization efforts in favor of satisficing procedures in allocating scarce resources among environmental programs means abandonment of efforts to achieve economic efficiency and therefore perpetuates the risk of significant losses in welfare. If the probability of knowing enough about the environmental treatment and damage functions were close to `zero, then a reasonable case could be made that satisficing across all pollutants would provide the closest feasible approach to consistency and efficiency in resource allocation. While recognizing that in practice the magnitude and number of cases involved may favor satisficing as a practical pragmatic policy, the analytical goal of optimizing at the margin in environmental policy should not be abandoned. One justification for this position is that the derivation of damage functions, which has been the most intractable aspect of the environmental analysis, is beginning to yield some limited results that may point the way to a more satisfactory state of the art in the future.

Historical efforts to derive damage functions have foundered upon two formidable technical hazards. First, the identification of satisfactory dose-response relationships that could be extrapolated to human beings; second, the assignment of economic values to these damages and to nonmarket goods such as amenities. These technical problems in the study of damage functions have been compounded not only by the obvious knowledge gaps shared by economists and life scientists but also by disparities between their respective research methodologies and perceptions. However, fragmentary evidence suggests that the conceptual and data barriers to damage function analysis are beginning to yield so that benefit-cost studies of environmental problems can be made, and that decisions to abandon optimizing goals are therefore premature. The expansion of research efforts on the environmental damage and treatment cost functions that are necessary to achieve efficiency and consistency in pollutant abatement is particularly important in view of current pressures to delay and weaken environmental programs as an anti-inflation measure.

These advances in the understanding of damage functions have come on the biological side from expanded knowledge of dose-response relationships derived both from recent epidemiological investigations and from improvements in extrapolation of risk estimations from laboratory animal studies to human beings (Mough [1978, pp. 37-41]), and, on the economic side, from research on the value of life (Bailey [1978b]). Projections of risk estimates from dose-response experiments on laboratory animals to human beings is still speculative, and public health scientists engaged in this research work are cautious in developing risk functions. However, some tentative results have been reported. In the Kepone-Mirex study (National Academy of Sciences

[1978b, p. 44]), the number of human cancer cases associated with lifetime exposure of a cohort of ten million people to a dosage of one μg/day was estimated, using projections from laboratory animals, to range from a low of 510 to a high of 3,400 cases for Kepone and from 330 to 1,800 cases for Mirex at the same level of exposure.[4] However, no benefit-cost analysis was attempted.

Peter Behr has reported on an Occupational Safety and Health Administration study that does attempt to develop benefit-cost information on the control of exposure by workers to acrylonitrile. The number of incremental cancer cases among 5,130 workers exposed to levels of 2-20 ppm was estimated at 18 adults with 7 premature deaths. For an additional $126 million spent on treatment, exposure could be cut to 0-2 ppm with 2 additional cases of cancer and 1 additional death. No estimate was given for the value of life (Behr [1978, pp. 25-29]).

In a National Academy of Sciences study on chloroform in drinking water, damage functions, treatment cost functions, and value of life have all been estimated. Depending upon the initial concentrations of chloroform and the amount of intake, the estimated incremental U.S. annual cancer deaths ranged from less than 1 to 967, assuming most probable risk, and to 4,837 for upper-limit risks. The cost of complete removal of chloroform from drinking water was found to depend upon the scale of treatment plants and processes employed, ranging from about $3 per person per year in large cities to $8 in areas with small treatment plants.

The annual value of reducing the risks per capita with treatment depends upon the assumed value of life. Bailey's analysis in the National Academy of Sciences (NAS) study put the statistical value of life at approximately $300,000. The NAS study also examined the implications of individual life values ranging from $100,000 to $1,000,000 and concluded that the cost of treatment could not be justified on economic grounds alone for the concentration and exposure levels found in most communities, assuming the most probable risk. However, in areas of higher initial chloroform concentration and under the assumption of upper-limit risks, the cost of treatment was justified, even at low estimates of the value of life (National Academy of Sciences [1978a, pp. 227-250]).[5] Other toxins would also simultaneously be removed, adding to the value of benefits.

These advances are beginning to make possible the development of benefit-cost studies for treatment of individual pollutants, which, if systematically

---

4. National Academy of Sciences (1978b, p. 44). The economic evaluation of these damages was not attempted in this study, and treatment costs were not reported, so a benefit-cost analysis was not possible.

5. For a more extended version of the economic analysis see also Cumberland and Choi, (1978).

improved and implemented, should result in an approach to improved efficiency in treatment between pollutants. As indicated in Figure 9-2 and the accompanying discussion, failure to achieve this equivalence across residuals results in potentially large welfare losses, and these losses are inevitable in the absence of efforts to optimize treatment across pollutants. Welfare losses attributable to inconsistency between pollutants can be expected to be compounded by the inconsistencies in treatment of broad groups of pollutants. Wastes are usually classified as liquid, gaseous, or solid, according to their physical structure, or as waterborne, airborne, or land-dispersed, according to their receiving environmental medium. The fact that administration and enforcement of environmental regulations are typically divided by management agency along these lines is another barrier to efficiency in treatment. A strong argument can be made on efficiency grounds for centralizing the administration of all environmental services within a single agency charged with the responsibility for equating marginal damages and marginal treatment costs across all pollutants in the interest of achieving maximum environmental quality and welfare within the resources available.

The centralization of analysis and management for all pollutants is important, not only for efficiency reasons, but also for equity reasons, since otherwise population exposed to varying types of pollutants could be exposed to varying risk levels, depending upon the efficiency of the agency that happened to have responsibility for the pollutants peculiar to that region.

Another problem in achieving efficiency at the margin across environmental programs arises from inadequate attention to the mass balance concept with respect to the expanding problem of managing the vast amounts of waste emerging from waste treatment processes. Too often, primary waste treatment is viewed as the final solution to waste pollution problems without recognition of the obvious fact that treatment wastes do not disappear but must be managed according to the same efficiency standards as were the original pollutants (Cumberland and Stram [1977]). The Kepone case in Virginia, in which toxic wastes from the chemical industry were casually diverted through a municipal sewage plant with disastrous results, is an aggravated example of failure to deal competently with the mass balance -waste treatment problem. Since current research has, as yet, found no way of removing the Kepone now deposited in the sediments of the James River without generating greater damage than will be done by leaving these toxic substances in situ, the Kepone case may well become a classic case of environmental irreversibility (National Academy of Sciences [1978b]).

A less dramatic but more widespread example of failure to anticipate the full consequences of the mass balance and persistence-of-matter principles is the growing problem of dealing with sludge from municipal sewage plants and from stack-scrubbing processes. The magnitude of these secondary wastes generated in an industrial society and the need for efficiency in their treatment underlines the need for economic-environmental forecasting models capable of incorporating not only economic variables but also the accompanying flows of mass and energy (Thoss [1976, pp. 411–432] and Cumberland and Stram [1976, pp. 365–382]).

An important point to be noted is that comprehensive, consistent management of environmental problems and the achievement of efficiency across treatment processes for an entire national or regional economy requires not only microeconomic analysis at the margin but also the application of large-scale, disaggregated, macroeconomic-environmental models capable of forecasting total waste loadings based upon mass balance and entropy concepts. A second important point is that marginal treatment cost functions must be defined to include the cost not only of purchased inputs but also of any damages resulting from wastes emitted by treatment processes.

EFFICIENCY AND EQUITY ACROSS REGIONS

Definitions of environmental regions. Just as inefficiency should be anticipated in the treatment of different pollutants and environmental services, inconsistency and hence inefficiency can be anticipated, a priori, in the regional distribution of environmental quality. In fact, it will be argued that inconsistency and inefficiency in the pursuit of environmental quality across regions, just as in the case of inconsistency across pollutants and environmental media, results from failure to equate benefits and costs at the margin. However, the essence of efficiency in environmental management strategies is to define which margin is to be optimized, and thus to define the appropriate emissions, receiving medium, region, and population at risk.

The realities of physical location for population, pollution-emitting plants, and environmental receiving media raise perplexing problems in efficiency and equity for the appropriate definitions of regions. Kneese, Bower, and others have advanced convincing arguments for defining regions for environmental management in terms of the airshed, watershed, or other "problem shed" (Kneese and Bower [1968]). This course is appropriate where political, legal, and administrative conditions permit. In other cases having less flexibility, the region having the administrative and political decision-making authority becomes the second-best solution by default.

Diffusion, disperson, and transport of residuals. The interregional effects of interior as compared with downstream boundary locations for polluting activities depend upon the physical characteristics (diffusion, dispersion, and transportation characteristics) of the common property resources (air and water) into which the residuals are emitted. If all emissions were instantly dispersed with equal density around the surface of the earth, the consistency problem would be greatly simplified. However, since the density of pollution usually declines as some function of distance from the point of emission, and since air and water flows frequently exhibit consistent prevailing patterns, the probability is high that, in any pair of adjacent regions, an upstream-downstream relationship will exist (perhaps separately) for airborne and waterborne emissions, with options in effect for each region voluntarily to export its pollutant with concurrent damages and involuntarily to import pollution from other regions. These possibilities have significant implications for efficiency, consistency, and equity in interregional environmental management.

To bridge the gap between emissions of pollutants and ambient environmental quality, air or water diffusion modeling techniques must be employed. These techniques may be adapted to deal with either point- or area-source emissions. Though there is a large body of literature on diffusion models, particularly those dealing with atmospheric diffusion, estimates of ambient environmental quality are still characterized by wide margins of error owing to the large number of relevant factors, many of which are difficult to specify in a tractable model.

Atmospheric diffusion is highly dependent, directly or indirectly, on atmospheric temperature profiles and wind velocity. In modeling diffusion, the effect of turbulence is usually represented indirectly through specification of velocity and temperature profiles. A logarithmic, log linear, or power law functional form of the velocity equation is usually chosen (Stram [1976, pp. 401–413]). Some variation on the Gaussian (normal) probability function is generally taken as basic to predicting diffusion from point sources. Recently lognormal formulations have become popular. For instance, the International Institute for Applied Systems Analysis (IIASA) model for predicting sulfur dioxide (SO_2) emissions from coal-fired power plants employs a version of the Gaussian function in predicting diffusion. To relate average yearly SO_2 concentrations to average daily concentrations, a lognormal function is used (Buehring et al. [1976]).[6] In its simplest form, the Gaussian function is employed along with certain assumptions about atmospheric conditions. Modifications have been suggested to account for factors such as variable wind speed and direction, airflow blocked by buildings, airflow through urban "canyons," atmospheric variations associated with natural topography, and multiple stacks. Problems arise in adapting this model to account for spatial variability of meterological parameters or negligible winds. Furthermore, reactive or secondary pollutants cannot be included.

In modeling ambient environmental quality as a function of emissions from multiple sources, such as in urban areas, a more promising approach incorporates models based on the equation of mass balance.[7] Two main types of

---

6. Dennis (1978) exceeds this technique.

7. The discussion of Eulerian and Lagrangian models is based on Johnson (1976, pp. 503–563). For those interested in air quality modeling, this is an excellent reference survey.

models fall under this category: Eulerian (multibox) and Lagrangian (moving-cell) models. These approaches treat diffusion by K theory (concentration flux proportional to gradient). They avoid the problems mentioned in regard to Gaussian models. The Eulerian approach divides the atmosphere under consideration into a spatial grid. Pollutant flow among the boxes in this grid is predicted. Incremental effects on environmental quality accruing from a particular emitter cannot, however, be ascertained. This problem need not occur when the Lagrangian approach is used. The Lagrangian model involves tracking "cells" of air into which pollutants are emitted. The size of these cells will vary depending upon the application. Since the Lagrangian approach involves tracking trajectories, emitting sources may be uncovered. However, a number of approximations are necessary to arrive at a solution, and further problems arise in interpretation. Various authors have attempted to circumvent these problems by modifying or combining these models in various ways. No single method has as yet gained widespread acceptance.

To achieve reasonable empirical results in diffusion models, it is often necessary to incorporate an ad hoc element. Improvisation of this sort may be based on previously recorded observations or upon fluid scale models in which water currents are used to simulate airflow. Such models would be specific to a particular locale.

Though not as extensive as air diffusion models, a wide variety of water diffusion models is available. These range in complexity from The Massachusetts Institute of Technology's Transient Water Quality Network Model (47 computer routines with 4,445 source statements; see M.I.T. [1977]) to simple oxygen-sag models that predict biological oxygen demand downstream as a function of stream flow characteristics. Water diffusion models may be adapted to rivers, estuaries, lakes or oceans. As with atmospheric diffusion models, it is often useful to construct scale or computer models. For instance, a large number of computer simulations, for example, trajectories of possible oil-spill routes, can provide a frequency distribution similar to a more theoretical modeling effort.

The policy implications of these diffusion relationships is shown symbolically in Figure 9-3. The rate at which the emission of any residual affects welfare through the damage it generates depends upon local diffusion characteristics of air and water, as measured by the local environmental transformation function (ETF). Consequently, the ability of environmental authorities to optimize or to manage efficiently will depend upon their state of knowledge and upon the variables they control. If the environmental transformation function is known along with the damage and treatment cost function, the manager can optimize by specifying any one control variable, such as the ambient quality (Q) or the total amount of residual emissions (R) that will affect

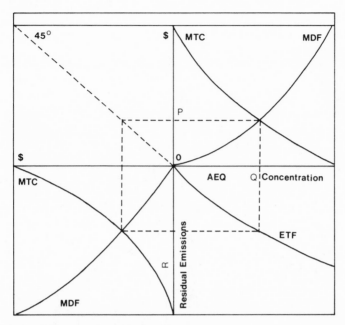

Figure 9-3. Diffusion of residuals. Environmental transformation between emissions and ambient quality. (From Cumberland [1975, p. 663]. Cf. also Freeman et al. [1973, p. 89].)

this quality, or preferably, the appropriate Pigouvian charge (*P*), which reflects the shadow price of the pollution.

T. H. Tietenberg has pointed out the efficiency gains from varying treatment practices and effluent charges as a function of local environmental assimilative capacity (Tietenberg [1973, pp. 503-522; 1974, pp. 462-466; 1978, pp. 265-277]). The authorities could also, if all these relationships were known, achieve efficiency by auctioning off emissions rights to the highest bidders to release the optimal level of residuals as suggested by Dales, (1968, pp. 791-804), provided that competitive bidding could be achieved.

Environmental location decisions within a region. Figure 9-4 indicates the environmental and welfare implications of locational choice for a region from the viewpoint solely of the welfare of its own citizens. This region can ignore the welfare of those in adjacent regions, when it has the option of locating a polluting activity in an interior location, or at a downwind (downwater) location such that most or all of the emissions flow into the adjacent region and all of the economic benefits of the activity are retained within the region.

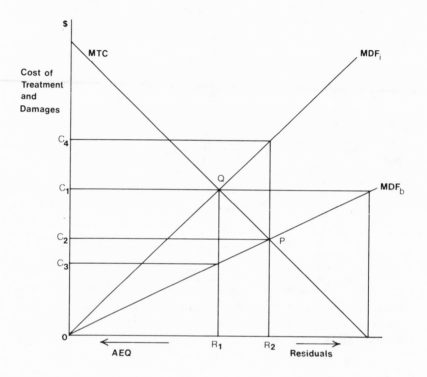

Figure 9-4. Effects in a region upon costs of treatment and damages resulting from upstream as compared with downstream plant sites.

The marginal treatment cost function (MTC) is a technical constant, regardless of location, since it measures the cost of achieving a given level of residual emissions (R) *at the plant site* (not necessarily a constant level of AEQ). Initially, we also assume that preference functions and damage functions for environmental quality are constant across regions.

From the viewpoint of region A, the upstream decision-making region, MDF_i measures the damage cost to region A as a function of the amount of residuals released at the internal plant site, and MDF_b represents the cost of damages to region A as a result of the amount of emissions for a downstream, or boundary site. These two damage functions indicate that for any given expenditure upon treatment of residuals, the boundary location results in less damages in region A than does an interior location. For example, expenditure of C_1 on treatment at the boundary location lowers residuals to R_3, whereas expenditures of C_1 on treatment at the interior location results in higher damages at R_1. Therefore, from the viewpoint of its residents, region A will prefer the downstream boundary location with equilibrium at P, rather than the interior or upstream location with equilibrium at Q.

Figure 9-4 can also be used to illustrate the effect of region A's decisions upon downstream region B. Let MDF_i now represent damage in region B from the upstream site as A picks a boundary location adjacent to region B. MDF_b now represents damage to B, had region A picked a site farther away from B, interior to A, which A normally would not do. Region B would prefer that A had picked an interior site, treating wastes and spending amount C_1 at this site resulting in low damages, C_3, to B. However, A picks a boundary site and spends only C_2 on treatment, emitting R_2 and causing high damage (C_4) to B. Given A's decision to select the boundary site upstream to B, region B would prefer to spend C_1 on treatment to limit residuals to R_1, but B has to accept A's decisions to spend only C_2 on treatment, inflicting R_2 residuals and C_4 damages on region B.

Therefore, region A's choice of a location downstream to its residents imposes detrimental externalities on the residents of region B. This choice is not Pareto optimal. Pareto optimality would require combining the damage functions and treatment cost functions for the two regions resulting in an intermediate selection of locations, treatment costs, and AEQ that would internalize the externalities. Therefore, some supraregional authority would be needed to achieve Pareto optimality from the standpoint of environmental analysis where upstream and downstream regions are involved.

Figure 9-5 represents the same phenomena but from the viewpoint of two different treatment cost functions. From the viewpoint of the upstream region A, in Figure 9-5, MTC_i represents the cost of achieving various levels of AEQ from an internal plant site, and MTC_b represents the cost of achieving the same levels of AEQ from a downstream or boundary location. The single marginal damage function represents the resulting cost of damages from each expenditure on treatment. Point Q is the equilibrium combination of treatment costs and damages for the interior location, and point P is the equilibrium point from A's point of view for a boundary location. This indicates that for any given treatment expenditure (C_2) region A gets higher environmental quality (R_2 vs. R_3) for a boundary location as compared with an interior location. Therefore, obtaining any level of AEQ (e.g., R_2) costs less (C_2 vs. C_3) at a boundary location rather than at an interior location.

Figure 9-5 can also be used to illustrate the effects of region A's choice of a downstream location on the downstream region B. From the standpoint of region B, MTC_i now equals the high treatment and damage costs imposed on region B of the boundary site chosen by region A. Marginal treatment cost B (MTC_b) now represents the low treatment costs and damages enjoyed by region B, had region A picked an interior site, which it would not nor-

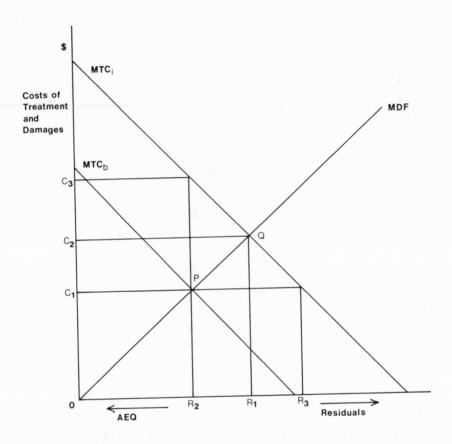

Figure 9-5. Effects in a region upon treatment costs required at upstream as compared with downstream plant sites in order to achieve specified levels of environmental quality.

mally have done. Therefore, B would prefer that region A chose a site interior to A, resulting in an equilibrium decision of Q (which would then have been optimal for region A, imposing low residuals, R_1, on B and bearing high treatment costs, C_1, in region A). However, region A, if concerned only with the welfare of its own residents, picks the boundary site, facing B with MTC_i. Given A's choice of the boundary site, region B would face MTC_i from its viewpoint, and prefer to incur treatment costs as high as C_1 in order to limit damages in B to C_1 and achieve AEQ at R_1. However, region B must accept A's decision to spend only C_2 on treatment, imposing higher residuals on region B (R_1) and lower AEQ. Therefore, from its point of view, region B receives deficient treatment cost expenditures $(C_2$ vs. $C_1)$ and deficient AEQ $(R_1$ vs. $R_2)$. We do not actually know how much emissions of residuals are associated with these levels of AEQ without knowing the environmental treatment function (ETF).

Therefore, the upstream region A's choice of the downstream or boundary plant site has imposed detrimental externalities upon B. From the viewpoint of the two regions taken together, a Pareto-optimal solution would require combining the marginal damage functions and marginal treatment cost functions with two regions, resulting in some intermediate combination of location, treatment costs, and AEQ. Again, we conclude that a supraregional authority is necessary to achieve the combined treatment and damage cost functions internalizing these externalities for the two regions involved.

Since the incentives and pressures to generate detrimental interregional environmental spillovers are implicit in the physical nature of the earth's surface, human welfare can potentially be increased by systematic policies and procedures for achieving consistency of environmental management of interregional flows. Federal or supraregional policy in general will be necessary for this purpose.

Disparities in environmental preferences across regions—without spillovers. We have seen above that even in the simple case where preferences for environmental quality can be assumed to be constant across regions, the fact that environmental media often transport pollutants unidirectionally in space can be expected to cause probable conflict of interest among regions in a hierarchical system, thus requiring the intervention of a supraregional authority. Where interregional disparities exist among environmental preference functions, another set of analytical and policy issues arises. One simple way of envisioning this problem is to refer again to Figure 9-4, letting MDF_b represent the national norm in perception of damage between regions, with MDF_i representing the perception of damage in a region whose residents have a higher-than-average preference for environmental quality with respect to all other goods, including economic growth.

The policy question is whether justification exists in terms of efficiency and equity for the residents of such a quality-preferring region to seek higher AEQ at higher treatment costs then the norm of the federal standards. Another way of putting this question is whether the federal standard should represent minimum or maximum environmental goals.

The case of inflexible federal standards or maximum emission and minimum quality standards is based upon equality in treatment of emitters across regions. The case for permitting local environmental standards to be raised above the federal norm can be based upon the welfare loss if local residents, preferring high environmental quality, as shown in Figure 9-4 by MDF_i, are forced to accept lower federal standards reflected in MDF_b, resulting in deficient environmental quality (R_2 vs. R_1) as perceived locally. If any weight can properly be attributed to local preferences and perceptions of environmental quality and damage, then refusal to permit local environmental standards to exceed federal standards results in failure to maximize local welfare.

Since an important element of environmental quality is perception and preference, a perceived or observed environmental impact represents a real welfare loss. Therefore, differing alternative local damage functions, as shown in Figure 9-4, even though based on preferences alone, can legitimately be regarded as the basis for permitting local standards to be established at levels higher than those of national standards. This principle is already embedded in U.S. environmental legislation as reflected in the federal Water Pollution Control Act, with amendments, and the federal Clean Air Act, both of which permit state standards to be higher but not lower than federal standards, subject to a few important areas preempted by the federal government such as standards for radioactive wastes, aircraft noise, and automobile emissions (Anderson [1977]). Adoption of local environmental standards higher than those of the federal norm may result in a local trading off of some employment and economic development for environmental quality, but this is a legitimate choice if it reflects the preference of local residents as arrived at through democratic procedures reflecting due process.

Permitting higher-than-federal standards in a region may indirectly impose some damage on other regions by excluding environmentally detrimental activity, but this is an argument not only for a well-structured federal minimum standard but also for allowing regions wide latitude in setting local environmental standards. If a sufficient number of regions begin excluding environmentally damaging activity, a strong incentive emerges for technological improvement in polluting activities. The establishment of higher-than-federal standards in a region is not inconsistent with allowance for bargaining and side payments along Coasian lines in order to internalize externalities and thus approach optimal location of pollutants across regions (Coase [1960, pp. 1-44]).

Thus, in the absence of interregional spillovers, we conclude that there are strong efficiency and equity reasons for the simultaneous existence of a carefully structured set of federal environmental standards with individual regions having the option of establishing and enforcing higher standards. The symmetry argument of permitting local regions to have standards lower than federal standards cannot be admitted, since the federal standards, if properly established, would be designed to protect local residents from lack of information on real but imperceived damages, excessive discounting of future damages, and other potential real costs impacting not only on the region but on the entire nation from excessive local relaxation of environmental standards.

The potential dangers of permitting local regions to establish minimum environmental standards without reference to a national standard can be illustrated by extension to growing problems of international global environmental management, especially in the area of nuclear energy. Many nuclear reactors are now being constructed in developing nations by governments that do not wish to pay for the nuclear safety features routinely added in industrial nations and that use labor forces that are largely illiterate. In these instances, lack of relevant information on prospective dangers, and a high discount rate applied to the future, may result in leakages and accidents that will increase global levels of radioactivity to hazardous levels.

The issue of setting standards is logically separable from the issue of how to implement these standards through policy instruments. Since emission charges are the preferred instrument from the viewpoint of efficiency, incentives, and technological change, a multitiered set of charges, with national minimums aimed at achieving the national AEQ goals and allowing optional state and local emission surcharges, would be an optimal envorcement instrument from the viewpoint of spatial optimization and least-cost achievement of national, state, and local environmental standards. Second-best instruments for achieving spatial environmental goals would be federal regulatory standards with optional state and local elevation of federal minimum standards if preferred locally.

Even if national policy rejects the use of emission charges, the logic applicable to the potential incentive and efficiency benefits of this approach argues strongly for experimentation with this instrument at the state and local levels.

Numerous questions are raised by the proposal for national emission charges with options for local surcharges, only a few of which can be raised here. One involves whether the national authority should establish regionally differentiated environmental quality goals. Another question raised is, if emission charges offer so many advantages, why have they not been more widely adopted? Answers to both of these questions require recourse to more general types of theory than the narrow resource allocation approach adopted here. The work of Mancur Olson, for example, on social choice and fiscal equivalence has pointed out the disparities between the location of those who bear the costs and of those who receive the gains, and has drawn attention to the social stress possibly resulting from arbitrary central decision-making on emission charges that may constitute formidable barriers to acceptance of emission charges strategies (Olson [1969, pp. 479–487]).

Disparities in environmental preferences across regions—with spillovers. While efficiency conditions argue for permitting high local environmental standards in the absence of spillovers, equity criteria would preclude permitting a local region from raising its environmental quality above the federal minimum through the device of a boundary location that damages an adjacent region if the resulting AEQ in the receiving region fell below the federal minimum. A region pursuing quality at the expense of its neighbors could reasonably, for equity reasons, be required either to desist or to compensate neighbors for imposing upon them lower quality than it sought internally.

Similarly, a quality-oriented region could be frustrated in its efforts by adjacent regions that barely met federal standards but not the standards of the environmentally sensitive region. Here, the environmentally sensitive region would not have a strong equity case, unless the high-emission regions had elected boundary locations and had generated higher emissions and lower AEQ than they tolerated internally. But even here, the high-emission regions would be technically within their rights if they were not violating federal emission or ambient standards and if the receptor region could not prove excess damages, negotiate higher federal standards, or offer payment in return for improved treatment.

Disparities between federal and state interests. Another possible form of interregional environmental conflict is a divergence between federal and state, or state and local interests. Recent proposals in the United States, since the energy emergency, have envisaged national powers to override local preferences in order to locate large energy facilities, such as refineries, presumably in the national interest. Similarly, some state programs, such as the Maryland Power Plant Siting Act, permit the state to override local interests. This type of proposal rests upon dubious federal constitutional grounds and upon dubious economic grounds from the viewpoint of welfare maximization. In conflicts between national and local goals, public interest requires avoiding both the damages attendant to a local region's frustration of legitimate national interests and the danger of regions having their legitimate interests sacrificed on the altar of national coercion. One recent effort to balance these goals can be found in the U.S. Coastal Zone Management Act of 1972 and its amendments. As is typical of new programs affecting federal-state interests, it applied the carrot-and-stick technique of providing federal funds for state coastal zone planning and then precluded federal government development of projects that are inconsistent with state plans (which state plans must be federally approved, however). Further interesting use of economic incentives under this act allows federal loans to states where construction of federal projects results in a lag in generation of revenues going to the state and of grants to reimburse states for irremediable environmental losses.

Both efficiency and equity goals could be well served in environmental management within a federal system by establishing federal minimum environmental standards for emissions and ambient quality, while letting state and local regions establish standards that are higher, but not lower, than federal standards. An efficient way of implementing this approach would be to set a schedule of federal emission charges designed to achieve federal environmental standards and to allow state and local agencies to live with these charges, or to add surcharges for achieving superior environmental quality if dictated by local preference functions. The role of economic incentives could be expanded by letting local regions bargain with the federal government over the size of subsidies required in order for the local region to accept a project that was locally unattractive but alleged to be in the national interest. Similar bargaining over emission charge levels could take place where private externality-generating firms wish to locate in a high amenity area. The use of a three-tiered federal, state, and local system of emission charges along with this type of bargaining safety valve could help avoid both federal coercion against local regions and frustration of national interests by local regions (Cumberland [forthcoming; and 1977, pp. 43–45]).

Disparities in efficiency and equity aspects of environmental policy among regions of varying population density, economic development, and political power. Another compelling reason for setting federal minimum standards for AEQ can be found in the possible conflict between efficiency and equity in the quest for consistency between regions of different population density. Consider the case of two adjacent regions, one densely populated, one sparsely populated, each having equivalent environmental transformation functions, and each being considered as the site for an environmentally offensive activity such as a fossil-fuel power plant. If marginal damage functions are defined in terms of incremental damage to the total population exposed, then efficiency considerations, *ceteris paribus*, would indicate location of the plant in the sparsely populated region. Note, however, that the marginal conditions defined in terms of equalizing marginal damage for the total population under the efficiency objective would permit much higher exposure per capita to those in the sparsely populated regions, thus permitting potentially unacceptable inconsistency in personal damage between regions in the pursuit of economic efficiency. For example, equating total marginal damage for the total regional population with marginal treatment costs for identical plants in regions with populations of one hundred thousand and one million persons, respectively, would permit exposure to those in the sparsely populated regions to be ten times the damage per person of that permitted in the densely populated area.[8] Movement of a damaging plant from the high-density region to the low-density region would be a potential Pareto

---

8. In this regard, it is interesting to note that U.S. regulations on nuclear power plant siting confine locations to those away from major population centers. By implication, this policy imposes future population growth constraints on any region that includes nuclear power plants.

improvement under certain conditions. If, out of their welfare gains, the residents of the high-density area compensated the victims in the low-density area or paid them to migrate from the polluted region, the potential Pareto improvement could become an actual Pareto improvement. However, since both compensation and migration of victims are uncertain, federal minimum environmental standards are essential in order to prevent gross inequities in per capita environmental damage.

The need for federal minimum standards for environmental quality across regions, including high- and low-density population regions, is aggravated by the danger that low-density regions may also be regions of lower-than-average levels of economic development and political power. Regions of less than average political power and sophistication may be especially vulnerable to the environmental aggression of more urban and populous states that seek to locate large-scale, detrimental, and hazardous activities at a distance from themselves in isolated rural areas. Trash dumps, gas storage dumps, nuclear waste storage, strip mines, power plants, and petroleum refineries are only a few examples of such phenomena. For reasons explored above with respect to downwind boundary locations, natural local pressures of self-interest will create strong incentives for powerful, affluent regional decision makers to engage in the ultimate form of downstream location, which is physical removal of the offending activities to other regions.

The temptation to engage in this form of pollution export while capturing the economic advantages of the activity can be visualized as efforts to reduce local marginal treatment cost functions and marginal damage functions to zero. Federal policy on minimum emission charges and/or standards, and on other aspects of environmental policy, are clearly desirable in order to prevent the inequity arising from this type of environmental imperialism.

Desirable as federal minimum environmental standards have been shown to be, one potential problem should be noted. Over long periods of economic growth and generation of wastes, federal minimum standards for air and water quality may tend to become maximum standards for environmental quality as development seeks out areas still having some remaining assimilative capacity. As economic development continues, even at low rates of growth, the time factor guarantees that the search for unexploited environmental assimilative capacity will become a dominating force in industrial location trends. Thus, over time, environmental quality could drop to minimum allowable levels everywhere, inexorably eliminating all areas of pristine or even attractive air and water quality. Therefore, additional specific programs are essential if the preservation of undamaged environments is a social objective. This is the rationale for special programs to protect wildernesses, oceans, and other unique regions whose preservation is a social goal in itself.

CONCLUSIONS AND POLICY RECOMMENDATIONS

We have arrived at a simple definition of consistency and optimal resource allocation in environmental policy that involves equating the marginal cost of treatment with the marginal cost or shadow price of damage for each pollutant discharged into each environmental medium at each location. Although problems of efficiency in environmental policy, both across pollutants and across regions, can be formally defined as problems of equating benefits and costs at the margin, the more difficult challenge arises in all cases in the specification of the appropriate margin to be optimized in terms of the pollutant, its receiving medium, the problem shed, the region, and the population at risk. Meeting the conditions for achieving optimal environmental quality and maximum welfare requires intensive research efforts to identify damage functions and treatment cost functions, rather than accepting satisficing procedures. Fragmentary evidence has been presented of useful results in this direction. Additional institutional and administrative requirements for welfare gains through consistency in environmental management include coordinated efforts to equalize marginal benefits and costs across all pollutants, environmental media, and locations. Achievement of efficiency in environmental management will require centralization of management authority, or at least standardization of analysis and enforcement across all pollutants and media. Since concepts of mass balance and entropy will be useful as guidelines in anticipating environmental problems resulting indirectly from harmful residuals from waste treatment processes, macroeconomic-environmental forecasting models as well as microeconomic models of marginal analysis will be useful in this task. We acknowledge this type of modeling as a challenging research frontier, which can be expected to yield only to massive research efforts, necessarily of a multidisciplinary nature.

In the pursuit of efficiency and equity in environmental management across regions, simple location analysis confirms what could be anticipated by a priori reasoning and empirical observations. In the absence of purposeful environmental policy, regional decision makers face powerful incentives to maximize the welfare of local residents by locating externality-generating activities in downstream locations, on boundaries, or, if possible, even in other locations altogether, in order to reduce internal costs of treatment, reduce emissions flow, and raise environmental quality locally. Depending upon actual spatial configurations and environmental transformation functions, some regions may suffer from serious environmental damage in the absence of corrective action, and there is no compelling reason to expect the outcome to be automatically corrected by bargaining policy or considerations of equity. Therefore, environmental spillovers can be expected, in the absence of correctional policy, to result in serious misallocation of resources and reductions in welfare because of inconsistencies in interregional environmental quality, residual generation, and treatment costs. As demonstrated above, these inefficiencies can be expected to emerge even in the case of equal interregional preferences for environmental quality and equal treatment costs, depending upon physical spatial configurations and environmental transformation functions; these problems will be aggravated in cases of interregional disparities in environmental preferences.

The obvious policy conclusion, where interregional spillovers are a serious problem, is that efficiency and equity in environmental management can be achieved only by the establishment of national standards, enforced by charges or regulations, both for emissions and ambient environmental quality by some supraregional level of authority. The simplest way to address this problem is to assign to the higher level of government the task of defining the marginal treatment cost and marginal damage functions as a summation of costs and damages for all small regions involved, so that the spillovers are internalized, and optimal levels of residual, treatment, and ambient quality are derived for the total region.

However, given information costs and possible conflicts of interest between national and local interests, a preferable approach in a federal system is to allow local regions extensive autonomy in establishing environmental goals and standards.

The major policy implication of this analysis is that total welfare can be maximized in a system of regions if a federal or other supraregional authority establishes a system of environmental standards that could not be relaxed by individual regions, but that could be raised by any region, depending upon local preferences. These federally established environmental standards could be achieved by any of a number of policy instruments, including regulations, pollution charges, subsidies, or combinations of these approaches. Under ideal circumstances, the establishment of optimal emission charges for each pollutant in each location would achieve the multiple objective of limiting pollutants and damages, providing incentives for eliciting beneficial technological improvements, and for achieving optimal environmental quality at lowest cost. The research effort needed to derive the necessary treatment cost and environmental damage functions would be demanding, but the potential benefits in health, longevity, and welfare from the resulting efficiency and consistency gains would probably justify the effort many times over.

Under this Pigouvian approach, the supraregional authority would establish a set of optimal emission charges for each serious pollutant at each location, as necessary to meet the federal environmental standards. Each state and local region could, if it desired, add a local environmental surcharge and seek higher- but not lower-than-federal minimum ambient quality.[9] Possible bargaining strategies between regions and firms could serve as an optimizing and allocating measure to achieve economic-environmental equilibrium across activities and locations. Thus, an appropriate set of federal emission charges with optimal local surcharges and with bargaining permitted could serve not only to reduce the bitterness and delays involved in such locational struggles as power plant siting but also make use of corrected market forces to arbitrate automatically the debates over appropriate rates of economic growth, content of economic growth, and the efficient and equitable spatial distribution of externality-generating activities. Even if emissions charges are not accepted as an instrument of national policy, the potentially great incentive and efficiency advantages of this approach argue strongly for a selective experimentation with emission charges at the state and local level.

In second-best situations where treatment cost and damage function data are not available, or if possibly serious nonconvexities are present in the production possibility set (i.e., where optimization is not feasible), the Baumol and Oates strategy of establishing reasonable environmental standards to be achieved through emission charges is a least-cost, second-best solution. Also, in this case, the supplementation of federal with local premium standards and charges where locally desired is a promising option for achievement of efficient and equitable allocation of economic growth and environmental quality across regions.

REFERENCES

Anderson, Frederick R., Allen V. Kneese, Philip D. Reed, Serge Taylor, and Russell B. Stevenson. *Environmental Improvement Through Economic Incentives.* Baltimore: The Johns Hopkins University Press for Resources for the Future, 1977.

Bailey, Martin J. "Costs and Benefits of CFM Control." Bureau of Business and Economic Research and Environmental Protection Agency Conference on Ozone Damage and Regulation. Port Deposit, Maryland (July 1978a).

---

9. This interregional hierarchical concept is also applicable to the international set of nations, under some international environmental authority, subject to necessary adjustments appropriate to relationships between sovereign nations. See proposal of John H. Cumberland (1978, pp. 1–10). The importance of establishing international standards for environmental protection is especially important in the expanding set of emissions, which have global effects, possibly of an irreversible nature, on such phenomena as background radioactivity, stratospheric ozone, and atmospheric carbon dioxide.

———. *Measuring All the Benefits of Life-Saving*. Bureau of Business Economic Research, University of Maryland (1978b).

Baumol, William J., and Wallace E. Oates. *The Theory of Environmental Policy*. Englewood Cliffs, N.J.: Prentice Hall, 1975. Chap 8.

Behr, Peter. "Controlling Chemical Hazards." *Environment* 20, no. 6 (July/ August 1978).

Buehring, W. A., R. L. Dennis, and A. Holzl. *Evaluation of Health Effects from Sulfur Dioxide Emissions for a Reference Coal-Fired Power Plant*. Research Memorandum RM-76-3. International Institute for Applied Systems Analysis. Laxenburg, Austria (September 1976).

Coase, R. H. "The Problem of Social Cost." *Journal of Law and Economics* 3 (October 1960).

Cumberland, John H. "Economic Analysis in the Evaluation and Management of Estuaries." *Estuarine Pollution Control and Assessment*. U.S. Environmental Protection Agency. Report on a conference held at Washington, D.C. (February 1975).

———. "Boundary Conditions and Influence on the Planning of Power Generating Industries." In *Energie and Umwalt* (Energy and Environment). Essen: Vulcan, June 1977.

———. "Planning Future Industrial Development in Response to Energy and Environmental Constraints." In F.E.I. Hamilton, ed., *Industrial Change*. London: Longman, 1978.

———. "The Impacts of a Nuclear Power Plant on a Local Community: Problems in Energy Facility Development." Chap. 11 in *Energy and the Community*. Cambridge, Mass.: Ballinger, forthcoming. Proceedings of a Colloquium on Energy and Patterns of Human Settlement, University of North Carolina at Chapel Hill.

——— and Kwang Choi. "Economic Analysis of Chloroform Removal from Drinking Water." Water Resources Research Center Technical Report no. 49. University of Maryland. College Park, Md., October 9, 1978.

——— and Bruce N. Stram. "Empirical Applications of Input-Output Models to Environmental Problems." In Karen R. Polenske and Jiri V. Skolka, eds., *Advances in Input-Output Analysis*. Cambridge, Mass.: Ballinger, 1976.

——— and Bruce N. Stram. "Waste Treatment, Mass Balance, Entropy and Constraints on Growth." Working Paper no. 77-16. Department of Economics and Bureau of Business and Economic Research, University of Maryland. College Park, Md., 1977.

Dales, J. H. "Land, Water and Ownership." *Canadian Journal of Economics* 1, no. 4 (November 1968).

Denison, Edward F. "Effects of Selected Changes in the Institutional and and Human Environment upon Output Per Unit of Input." *Survey of Current Business* 58 (May 1978).

Dennis, R. L. *The Smeared Concentration Approximation Method: A Simplified Air Pollution Dispersion Methodology for Regional Analysis*.

Research Memorandum RR-78-9. International Institute for Applied Systems Analysis. Laxenburg, Austria (July 1978).

Freeman, A. M., III, R. H. Haveman, and A. V. Kneese. *The Economics of Environmental Policy*. New York: Wiley, 1973.

Georgescu-Roegen, Nicholas. *The Entropy Law and the Economic Process*. Cambridge, Mass.: Harvard University Press, 1971.

Johnson, Warren B., Ralph C. Sklarew, and Bruce Turner. "Urban Air Quality Simulation Modeling." *Air Pollution*. Vol. 1, 3d ed. In Arthur C. Stern, ed., *Air Pollutants, Their Transformation and Transport*. New York: Academic Press, 1976.

Kneese, Allen V., and Blair T. Bower. *Managing Water Quality: Economics, Technology and Institutions*. Baltimore: The Johns Hopkins University Press for Resources for the Future, 1968.

_____, Robert U. Ayres, and Ralph C. d'Arge. *Economics and the Environment: A Materials Balance Approach*. Washington D.C.: Resources for the Future, 1970.

Mishan, Ezra, and Talbot Page. "The Methodology of Cost Benefit Analysis with Particular Reference to the Ozone Problem." Bureau of Business and Economic Research and Environmental Protection Agency Conference on Ozone Damage and Regulation. Port Deposit, Maryland (July 1978).

M.I.T. *User's Manual for the M.I.T. Transient Water Quality Network Model —Including Nitrogen-Cycle Dynamics for Rivers and Estuaries*. National Technical Information Service PB-264 925 (January 1977).

Mough, H. Thomas, III. "Chemical Carcinogens: How Dangerous Are Low Doses?" *Science* 202, no. 4363 (October 1978).

National Academy of Sciences. *Chloroform, Carbontetrachloride, and Other Halomethanes: An Environmental Assessment*. Washington, D.C. 1978a. Chap. 8.

_____. *Kepone/Mirex/Hexachlorocyclopetadiene: An Environmental Assessment*. Washington, D.C. 1978b.

Olson, Mancur, Jr. "The Principle of 'Fiscal Equivalence': The Division of Responsibilities among Different Levels of Government." *American Economic Review, Papers and Proceedings* 59 (May 1969).

Stram, Gordon H. "Transport and Diffusion of Stack Effluents." *Air Pollution* Vol. 1, 3d ed. In Arthur C. Stern, ed., *Air Pollutants, Their Transformation and Transport*. New York: Academic Press, 1976.

Thoss, Rainer. "A Generalized Input-Output Model for Residuals." In Karen R. Polenske and Jiri V. Skolka, eds., *Advances in Input-Output Analysis*. Cambridge, Mass.: Ballinger, 1976.

Tietenberg, T. H. "Specific Taxes and Pollution Control: A General Equilibrium Analysis." *Journal of Economics* 84, no. 4 (November 1973).

_____. "On Taxation and the Control of Externalities: Comment." *American Economic Review* 64, no. 3 (June 1974).

_____. "Spatially Differentiated Air Pollutant Emission Charges: An Economic and Legal Analysis." *Land Economics* 54 no. 3 (August 1978).

DISCUSSION

Optimizing and Satisficing in Environmental Policy

MANFRED E. STREIT

From the multiplicity of issues raised in Professor Cumberland's thorough and lucid analysis, I found a methodological problem particularly stimulating. It emerges from his proposition to use the results of an optimizing approach as a reference system for any efforts to solve the policy problems to which he addresses himself. Optimization along Pigouvian lines is set against a merely satisficing approach. Admittedly, the former approach leads to clear-cut conditions for an optimal and consistent allocation of public funds for policy purposes: it is necessary to equate marginal benefits per monetary unit spent between environmental and other policy programs; as to environmental policy, efficiency requires once more equating the marginal benefits per monetary unit spent for abatement of each pollutant discharged into each environmental medium at each location.

Against this decision rule, a first general objection can be made on the grounds that Pigou's allocative rule and the marginal conditions for a Paretian optimum amount to the same thing; hence it is subject to the same well-known and severe criticisms, including the problem that the Pareto criterion is only one of many equally acceptable value judgments. Although this is duly acknowledged in Cumberland's paper, optimization efforts are still favored at least in principle. It is argued that abandonment of optimization efforts in favor of satisficing procedures would perpetuate the risk of significant losses in welfare; thereby it must be assumed that the black box, called welfare, can be reasonably filled, a point which will be taken up later. With respect to the information problem that is linked with the allocation rule, fragmentary evidence, suggesting that the conceptual and data barriers to damage-function analysis are beginning to yield, is considered a sufficient reason to discard decisions to abandon an optimizing approach as premature.

Even if one accepts for a moment the very popular procedure, from which I would not completely exclude myself, to acknowledge the shortcomings of an approach based on Paretian welfare economics and forget about it when coming to policy recommendations, optimization still remains a dubious procedure. At least one further condition has to be met when trying to optimize as an expression of global rationality, compared with satisficing, which follows from limited rationality: the decision situation must be one equivalent to certainty. This requires, first, that for the necessarily uncertain outcomes of the environmental and nonenvironmental policy programs, out of which the optimum course of action has to be chosen, the mean values of the corresponding joint probability distributions are known. Second, the decision situation must be such that it appears rational to consider only the expected values and not additional properties of the probability distributions; this implies a situation comparable to an insurance problem and, for the decision maker, a neutral attitude toward risk. That these requirements can be considered as fulfilled in the case of decisions on economic and environmental policy can be strongly questioned.

Furthermore and as also indicated in Professor Cumberland's paper, the decision problems in this field are sequential ones due, for example, to changing technical, economic, environmental, and last not but not least, to political conditions. And there, to my knowledge, practicable solutions for optimization have still to be developed; on the other hand, the difficulties to be tackled when applying a satisficing approach to sequential decisions, although serious enough, appear to be considerably smaller. Even if these technical problems could be set aside, all the material problems concerning intertemporal choice remain; this aspect has been explicitly excluded from the considerations in the paper but must nevertheless be born in mind when evaluating the policy recommendations.

Turning next to the black box, called welfare, advances in the understanding of damage functions are mentioned. They are expected on the biological side from an expanded knowledge of dose-response relationships and, on the economic side, from work on the value of life. As far as it would be possible to use such results at least for partial sensitivity analyses on the damage involved, the outcomes may provide valuable information for those making policy decisions. However, as long as decisions are not to be delegated to the experts, the privilege and the burden of evaluating and deciding on trade-offs must remain with those entitled in a democracy to be concerned with public goods, including environmental policy, that is, the political entrepreneurs. This means that welfare judgments are subjected to political processes that cannot be overrun by more or less sophisticated normative statements originating from welfare economics. As a consequence, it may be advisable to extend the interdisciplinary approach that is favored in the paper on the theory of politics, as stressed in Professor Frey's contribution. One of the implications for policy recommendations would be that they have also to be judged with respect to their efficiency in view of the political process involved. Taking this into account, the alleged strength of the argument in favor of centralizing the administration of all environmental services within a single agency must at least be reconsidered in the light of what is known about how administrations and political institutions work on the national, regional, and local levels.

In view of possible disparities in environmental preferences across regions, the actual recommendation in the paper implies a two-stage procedure. National environmental quality standards enforceable via charges or regulations by a supraregional authority are combined with local surcharges. The reasons given for national standards appear to carry different weights. There is, first, reference to a paternalistic value judgment in the sense that local residence ought to be protected from lack of information; this argument could perhaps be substantiated by pointing at the alleged danger of a shortsighted, environmentally ruinous competition between regions to improve their material wealth. Second, the national interest is mentioned as standing on dubious federal constitutional and economic grounds. Indeed, if one does not believe in a mythical entity called the nation that has special interests, the argument must have something to do with the doubts one can have as to the provision of some public goods if the corresponding decisions were to be made via a bargaining process between sovereign regions and with what can be called fiscal equivalence or, more conventionally, institutional internalization of externalities. The latter leads to the problem of spillovers, positive as well as negative, and to the third reason, namely federal minimum standards as starting points for interregional negotiations and arbitration in case of spillovers. A final, very valid and related argument refers to federal standards as means to protect politically and economically weak regions against environmental aggression.

As to regional surcharges, a possibly important question remains undiscussed. Surcharges are conceived to allow for regional environmental preferences that imply opportunity costs in terms of regional product. If political decisions on regional environmental standards are to be properly made, it is necessary to develop technical and institutional arrangements through which these opportunity costs are at least clearly signaled to the decision makers. Otherwise it may well happen that after having decided in favor of a comparatively high environmental standard, a region comes in for federal or interregional grants-in-aid although it is falling behind owing to self-inflicted environmental brakes to economic development. But to be able to discriminate between economic and environmental factors affecting regional-development-secured empirical knowledge on the factors affecting spatial development in a concrete economy is required. Looking at the findings of regional economics, the situation does not appear very promising. Once again, environmental policy in general and optimizing strategies in particular are up against the information problem.

Taking into account the information problem, it may be finally worthwhile to compare the policy recommendations based on optimizing with those most likely leading merely to satisficing results. According to the first approach, basically favored in the paper, an appropriate set of federal emission charges combined with optimal local surcharges is recommended. Thereby "appropriate" must presumably be interpreted as providing via charges or regulations a minimum environmental standard for all regions, and "optimal" as matching the requirement of efficiency and consistency across pollutants, media, and locations when being added to the federal charge. From an analytical point of view, this approach is undoubtedly attractive and presents a valuable starting point. But to be put into practice, it would require telescopic faculties to achieve the implied global rationality. And it would not be sufficient, to be able to comply at least partially with the optimization requirement by equating marginal social costs and benefits whereever possible. In this case, arguments analogous to those put forward in the theory of second best would apply, that is, an unavoidable violation of the requirement for optimization with respect to one of the problems to be simultaneously solved can justify, on efficiency grounds, violation of this requirement even in those cases where it could be principally met.

On the other hand, a satisficing program could consist, among others, of the following elements: (1) a national minimum standard and possibly additional requirements as to regional environmental quality, to be achieved by minimizing costs of control; (2) procedures to revise standards as well as charges and regulations in appropriate time intervals in the light of experience with environmental controls, identifiable trade-offs between environmental and other policy achievements, observed inconsistencies, and changing political weights attached to the conflicting goals concerning environment, economic performance, and equity; (3) budget decisions on the collection of information and on investment into applied scientific research to be made according to identifiable gaps in our knowledge on efficient means of environmental control, and not according to potential contributions to a welfare total that is and will be unknown.

Such an approach, it appears, would have much in common with the procedures discussed in other contributions to this volume, for example, by Professor Potier. And in view of the tremendous problems to be solved there, the approach should still be challenging enough, although representing a "second-best" solution.

DISCUSSION

On Transfrontier Pollution in an Interregional Setting

RALPH C. d'ARGE

Professor Cumberland's paper attempts through an examination of selected current U.S. environmental studies and policies to consider and evaluate the concept of consistency in environmental regulation and evaluation. After clearly delineating that consistency has a very special and precise meaning in normative economics,[1] Cumberland analyzes in depth the problem of consistency when "disparities" exist in space, time, environmental preferences, and governmental goals and objectives. This is a monumental task, and I believe that Cumberland more than anyone has clearly and concisely identified the major issues now present between actual policies and "consistent" environmental policies. Perhaps the major implicit point arising from his examples is that we should continue to strive for even approximate estimates of environmental damages such that a large-scale over- or underestimate of the optimal degree of control does not occur.

I have three major concepual problems with the paper. First, the definition of "consistency" is too narrow to adequately bridge the gap between specialized arguments on the conceptual underpinnings of efficiency and actual policy actions. U.S. environmental policy is enacted and administered within a milieu of noneconomic considerations and objectives. Thus, a broader set of models may need to be examined to discuss "consistency." Second, Cumberland's definition of consistency is really a measure of efficiency. It reminds me of the consistently lazy worker who clearly is not efficient. The two concepts are sometimes treated identically in the Cumberland paper. A perhaps more illuminating set of definitions would be to define efficiency as a state achieved by a set of controls such that the Pareto criterion is fulfilled. We can then define equity according to some principle of fairness; that is, all polluters are treated equally. Finally, "consistency" can be defined as a state

---

1. Consistency is defined as one typically necessary condition for efficiency across time, space, etc., mainly where marginal control cost is equated with marginal damages for each pollutant at each point in time and at each location.

where the same policy will be applied through time or space, given replication of similar types of environmental problems. I am not fully satisfied with these definitions, but in my mind they highlight the major differences between the concepts. A policy could be efficient and equitable but not consistent. For example, if differential effluent charges by region with lump-sum transfers to maintain equal regional incomes were applied but their level changed drastically and unexpectedly through time, equity and efficiency objectives could be achieved but a consistent policy through time would not. Alternatively, the policy could be one of a single effluent charge levied on all regions that would neither be efficient except under extreme conditions nor equitable but would be consistent.

A third underlying problem of the paper is that while it contains a very useful state-of-the-art examination of regional air quality dispersion models, it does not examine the economic implications of reliability and accuracy of these models. For example, most atmospheric diffusion models are reasonably accurate for normal conditions; that is, wind speed and direction, temperature, and nonextreme vertical temperature differences. Where they tend not to be accurate is when atmospheric conditions are extreme and/or the landscape is not a flat plain. The first question that arises is what kind of tax should be applied to pollution when extreme conditions occur as compared with normal conditions. There are many examples of partial solutions to this problem in economics, for example, two-part tariff and peak pricing, but they have as yet not been intensively examined within the specialization of environmental economics.

Another issue is why the business community almost unanimously rejects the application of an effluent charge under normal conditions and tends to embrace an emission standard. Cumberland briefly analyzes this question and concludes that "arbitrary central decision-making" may stall acceptance of national effluent charges. I believe there is more to it than that. The reasons for nonacceptance of national effluent charges as opposed to standards may include:

1. Most important, the firm *does not* have to pay for residual pollution loadings. It, by law or regulation, receives a partial entitlement to the use of the airshed or watercourse.

2. Financial flows because of various tax structures allow firms to achieve standards more easily than outright taxation. The firm can also argue that if it complies most of the time, then it is meeting the standard. Alternatively, the firm might be charged for the time it does not meet the standard.

3. Tax rates appear to be more volatile and changing than a standard based on engineering technologies and accepted principles of control on emissions. The firm can also base its arguments on emissions in comparison with other firms rather than on *implied* damages it may be causing.

4. Emissions standards are generally based on the amount emitted per unit

of output or some input, that is, parts per million of pollutant per million Btu's which allows the firm more flexibility than basing a tax on pounds of emissions. For example, for coal-fired plants given a standard based on parts per million emissions of sulfur oxide per million Btu's of heat energy produced, the firm has the following internal options: (a) change the amount of sulfur emitted by use of stack scrubbers or other add-ons; (b) increase heat efficiency conversion such that the ratio of SO_x to Btu's is reduced; with a tax, there might be no incentive for the firm to do this; (c) convert to low sulfur coal and reduce parts per million emissions. Under standards, in many circumstances, the firm would not have to consider reduction in production as a viable economic alternative, which it might under a tax.

5. Tax collectors tend to be more persistent and aggressive in monitoring than engineers checking compliance. If the tax collector discovers higher emissions, his agency is rewarded, whereas not meeting a standard generally provides little incentive for the agency or personnel involved. Compare the business reaction to an audit by the U.S. Internal Revenue Service with an inspection for product quality control. Taxes appear to have been applied only where the business community is not a significant political power within the community.

6. Some firms may object to the relative loss to their comparative area advantage with nationally consistent effluent charges. They may have already selected an area of low potential damages to secure their long-term development.

This is only a partial list, but it is suggestive of some of the reasons firms may dislike charges even if they do not object to the principle of their application in time or space.

What we are witnessing both in the United States and elsewhere in regional environmental management is a movement, albeit a trajectory, toward more balanced individual negotiation between polluters and agencies. In addition, the more extreme environmental voices are *not* being listened to. I predict the major issue will be one of resolving competing interests in both Western Europe and the Americas. How will these issues be solved? I submit that (1) benefit-cost analysis in both market and nonmarket terms will have a predominant influence, and (2) it will not depend on who is willing to pay but on who actually pays. That is, if the natural environment is to be preserved, environmentalists must be willing to pay, not assert that they will, through political support or actual purchase of environmental rights in the courts and marketplace.

Cumberland has done our profession a distinct service to analyze so carefully current technical issues. But, as he has experienced in his own state, economists are long on advice but short on ability in terms of their efficiency-related methodologies.